"If you're new to sheet pan cooking, start here—there's no better place to begin your adventure. And if you're a long-time fan, I think you'll be as excited as I am to cook from *Hot Sheet*. The recipes are seductive, smart, and wildly imaginative—also practical and everyday doable. Olga and Sanaë have stretched what we can do with this simple kitchen staple and given us a book that sparkles with great ideas."

—DORIE GREENSPAN, *New York Times* bestselling author of *Baking with Dorie* and *Everyday Dorie*

hᵒt sheet

Sweet and Savory Sheet Pan Recipes for Every Day and Celebrations

OLGA MASSOV AND SANAË LEMOINE

PHOTOGRAPHS BY JOHNNY MILLER

HARVEST
An Imprint of WILLIAM MORROW

hot sheet

HarperCollins books may be purchased for educational, business, or sales promotional use. For information, please email the Special Markets Department at SPsales@harpercollins.com.

FIRST EDITION

Designed by Renata DiBiase

Photography © 2024 by Johnny Miller

Library of Congress Cataloging-in-Publication Data has been applied for.

ISBN 978-0-06-324387-3

24 25 26 27 28 IMG 10 9 8 7 6 5 4 3 2 1

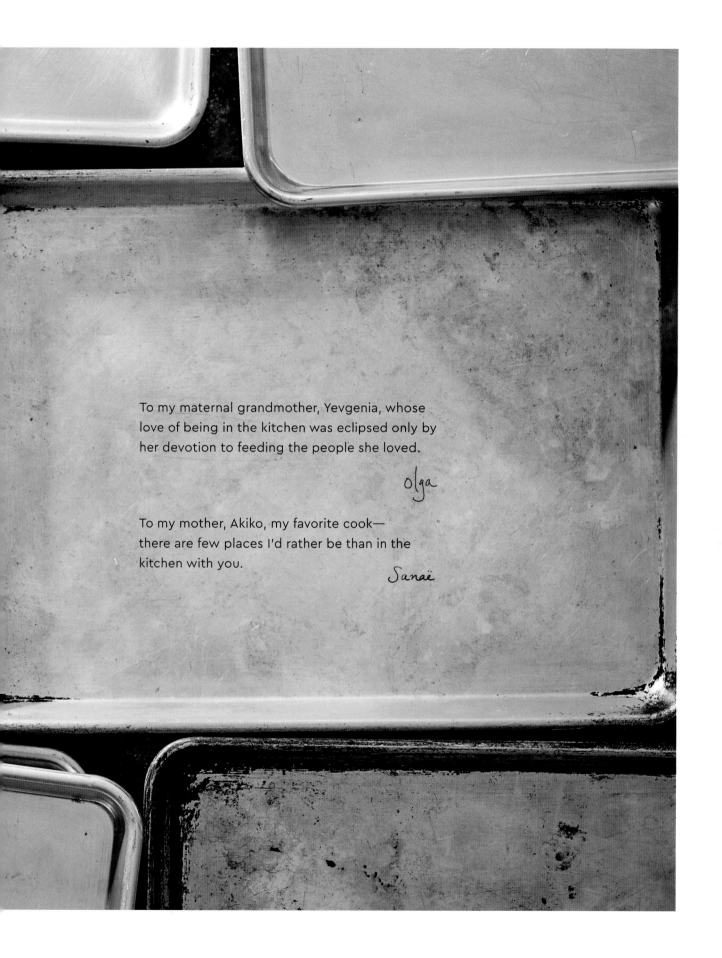

To my maternal grandmother, Yevgenia, whose
love of being in the kitchen was eclipsed only by
her devotion to feeding the people she loved.

Olga

To my mother, Akiko, my favorite cook—
there are few places I'd rather be than in the
kitchen with you.

Sanaë

Contents

Chapter 8 268
Simple Pantry Recipes

Introduction

How This Book Came to Be and Why (We Believe) You Need It

We suppose that the goal of every cookbook author is to tell you: This is the cookbook you need above and beyond all others.

We can't tell you that. We'd be lying.

Cookbooks are, by and large, an elective expense, and we want ours to earn a permanent spot in your kitchen by making your life easier and more delicious and leaving you with fewer dishes to clean.

Which is why we think that if you cook at home—whether you're a novice just getting your sea (kitchen?) legs or a seasoned, experienced home cook—this book is for you, intended to minimize active cooking and cleanup time. (If there's one thing food writers and recipe developers truly loathe, it's washing dishes, and because we have to do so much of it, we're always devising ways of doing that as little as possible.) How? By using a simple, inexpensive, and durable piece of kitchen equipment you likely already have in your kitchen—the sheet pan.

A sheet pan, usually aluminum or stainless steel, with a low rim and rolled lip, is the underappreciated workhorse of the kitchen (we expand on what to look for when shopping for sheet pans on page 5). And just like any reliable, functional item, the sheet pan has probably never been rated as the sexiest kitchen tool in your arsenal. It doesn't have the glossy appeal of a Dutch oven or the storied craftsmanship of a Japanese santoku knife. It gets the job done, it acquires patina through years of use, and it just keeps living on. The sheet pan is so unremarkable that we often forget just how extraordinary it is—how much mileage we can get out of it for a modest price, how little upkeep it requires, and how it serves up meal after meal for years on end. While it's easy to write sheet pans off as boring and unimaginative, nothing can be further from the truth.

We like to think of a sheet pan as a kitchen superhero: With the exception of soups and certain stews, you can use it to cook just about anything, including appetizers and desserts. It's light, stackable, and easy to care for. In other words, a sheet pan has a utilitarian sensibility and is at once contemporary and timeless.

We wrote this cookbook to make it truly work for you, to be practical and reliable enough to return to for many occasions, whether you're baking a birthday cake for someone special, hosting a weekend brunch, making supper at the end of an exhausting workday, or throwing a dinner party. The recipes that made the cut—and there are plenty that didn't—draw on our diverse cultural and culinary backgrounds, and are meant to be accessible and inspiring to home cooks of varying skill levels.

One of the greatest discoveries along the way is how often we've come to rely on these recipes for our everyday cooking, how seamlessly we've folded them into our repertoire. Of course, some of these dishes we've been making for years and were already on regular rotation, but others are new additions, and yet already feel like "classics" in our kitchens.

As you read and cook from this book, you'll notice that some of the recipes come from Olga, some come from Sanaë, and some come from both of us. But even when just one of our names is attached to a recipe, most likely there are hours of conversations and collaboration behind it—from our many phone calls, Zooms, and texts in the time we spent writing this book together.

Olga + Sanaë

Olga

The idea for this cookbook came out of a pitch I proposed to the Food team at the *Washington Post*, where I'm an editor. We were in the first year of the pandemic, and everyone was hunkered down and working remotely. In early fall, with Thanksgiving not too far off, we kept wondering: How do we mark a holiday that holds so much meaning for so many but also acknowledge that almost no one would be hosting a sizeable feast? The large, plentiful table surrounded by family and friends was suddenly looking a lot smaller. My general approach to life is to let myself feel what I need to feel, and then move on. Sometimes you're dealt a less-than-ideal hand, and that's the hand you play. Thanksgiving is my favorite holiday, and I've hosted it just about every year since I was a teenager. Few things bring me greater joy than peering into the dining room from the kitchen and seeing a table surrounded by my

people, talking and eating. That wasn't happening, but no one was taking Thanksgiving away from me.

I suggested that we create a Thanksgiving issue focused on smaller spreads and made entirely on a sheet pan. In my case I would roast a duck—something delicious, easy to do—along with a side or two, for a one-pan celebratory meal that would feed a few mouths but still feel special and elevated. The team universally loved this idea, and before the meeting was over, my colleague Ann Maloney volunteered to develop a recipe for roasted chicken with Hasselback potatoes; and another using turkey legs; our section head, Joe Yonan, who writes a weekly vegetarian recipe column, produced a stuffed delicata squash meatless centerpiece we all fought over. And this is how we did Thanksgiving 2020 at the *Post*.

Thanksgiving came and went that year—and, yes, I used a sheet pan to make a small dinner for our family of three—but I couldn't stop thinking about sheet pans writ large. What else could I make on them? Eggs and bacon for a family breakfast? Yep. Large frittatas or pancakes that allowed everyone to eat at the same time? Certainly. Layer cakes or "fried" rice? No doubt. What would the limit be?

I confided to Sanaë my sheet pan obsession and how I thought it'd make a great book. Sanaë, who has a keen eye for good ideas as well as impeccable taste, in addition to being an incredible cook, started texting me ideas right and left. All amazing. All inspiring. And as I gathered these ideas into a list, it felt wrong to not include her on this journey as a full-fledged coauthor. I looked to her as a partner. Sheepishly, I asked her if she was interested in coauthoring a book, and to my great delight, she said yes! So, here we are.

Sanaë

I discovered the sheet pan somewhat recently. I was raised on my mother's Japanese cooking, which requires multiple pots and pans. In our household,

we had one or two baking sheets for the occasional batch of cookies, but mostly they languished above the oven. When I first cooked on a sheet pan in my midtwenties, I was blown away. I had no idea you could bake entire savory meals on its surface and that it had such an extraordinary range. In fact, I fell so hard and fast that I went through a year of cooking almost exclusively on the sheet pan—fiercely loyal and devoted to this new utensil.

I came across the half-sheet pan in the test kitchen of the meal kit delivery service Marley Spoon (now called Martha Stewart & Marley Spoon) when I was hired as a recipe editor. I had just finished a teaching fellowship, was toiling away on my first novel, and desperate for a full-time job—ideally with a connection to food, my other passion alongside writing fiction. Although I was raised in a family of talented home cooks, I hadn't gone to culinary school, so I spent those early weeks in the test kitchen observing, learning, washing every pot and pan that came my way, and hunting down ingredients for photo shoots. I was fortunate to be taken under the wing of two incredible mentors—Jennifer Aaronson and Dawn Perry—who taught me almost everything I know about recipe writing and developing. And most important, they introduced me to the rimmed baking sheet, aka the sheet pan. Their recipes were exceedingly simple but always surprising and often more elegant than an elaborate stovetop meal.

Alongside Jennifer and Dawn, I started to cook on the sheet pan until it became the vessel I turned to most often for its convenience and ease. I became bolder, experimenting with different flavors, ingredients, and techniques. I learned how to cook several components of a meal on the same sheet pan and how to wilt tender greens using the residual heat from its generous surface. I was delighted at how perfectly it accommodated one of my favorite baked goods—the sweet or savory galette. (Plus, the rimmed lip caught any leakage from fruit tarts.) I loved its opaque silver surface, a blank canvas for colors and textures. During the photo shoots we showed off how gorgeous the food looked strewn over the sheet pan—along the edges, burnished and crisp; the spacious center, always abundant and inviting.

My appreciation for the sheet pan deepened over the years, until it became a necessity after I moved into an apartment that came with a windowless kitchen and no ventilation. The gas range was wedged against a wall, making half of the burners a pain to access. So, I started using the oven and my sheet pans more than ever, roasting at different temperatures and broiling to achieve a beautiful crust or "sear" without having to smoke up my home.

Olga and I met in 2018 when I was working at Phaidon as a cookbook editor. I started a month after she left, so we had never crossed paths, but I sat at her desk and studied her old files, hoping they might teach me how to be successful in this demanding and often mysterious job. One morning, on a whim, I emailed Olga, introducing myself and asking if she would like to meet. It's rare for me to contact a stranger out of the blue, and I held my breath, waiting for a response that arrived within the hour. A few days later, we met over pastries at Bien Cuit in Brooklyn, and quickly became the closest of friends.

Our friendship grew through our mutual love of food, for both cooking and eating. While our styles of cooking are different, as are our backgrounds, we noticed a rare chemistry in our conversations about food. We could talk about recipes on end, exchanging ideas, building off each other's questions, expanding our understanding of an ingredient or dish. It was always exhilarating, the hours going by in the blink of an eye. So often, midconversation, we'd experience that aha moment of "This is exactly what the recipe needs, I *must* try this now, why didn't I think of it myself?!" We cooked each other's recipes from a distance (I live in Brooklyn, Olga in Silver Spring, just outside of DC), and over the years, our appreciation for each other only deepened. When Olga asked me if I'd like to write a cookbook together, I couldn't believe my luck. The answer was obvious—*bien sûr* (of course)!

Let's Talk About Ovens

Ovens are . . . unpredictable. They're finicky, unreliable, all different, all temperamental (some more than others). Some ovens run hot; others run cooler; some wildly fluctuate in temperature from one minute to the next; others might not circulate their heat very well. There are convection ovens and regular ovens; gas ovens and electric ovens; large ovens and teeny-tiny apartment ovens. Some have broilers inside the oven, others have a broiler drawer. Some are extremely hot on top but not on the bottom; and others are the opposite.

There is always a period of acclimatization when you're getting to know your oven's personality and are tearing out your hair at the fourth burnt cake. But once you and your oven are in sync, it can become the most rewarding, symbiotic, and intuitive relationship. The secret to getting there is trial and error, a lot of patience, *and* an oven thermometer (read more about the oven thermometer on page 7). Most of the recipes in this book rely on an oven rack set in the middle of the oven, which is best suited for allowing the hot air to circulate evenly around the food and results in more even cooking. However, some use two racks in various permutations, so please read that part carefully—and frankly, the rest of the recipe, too—before starting to cook. Different ovens have different heating units, so it might also be helpful to consult your appliance manual or check online.

Sheet Pan 101, Plus How to Care for Them

A sheet pan is a wide, shallow baking sheet made of metal, usually aluminum or stainless steel, with a rim 1 inch (2.5 cm) tall around its edges. Its low sides and generous surface area encourage airflow and browning. It is inexpensive, durable, easy to store, and will last a very long time. Full-sheet pans are popular in commercial, restaurant, and professional kitchens, where ovens are a lot wider than what home cooks have.

In this book, when we talk about sheet pans, we will mostly refer to **half-sheet** (18 × 13-inch/46 × 33 cm) and **quarter-sheet** (9 × 13-inch/23 × 33 cm) pans. The latter work especially well for smaller ovens or households, as well as cooking several things at the same time. There are also eighth-sheet pans that we like to have on hand but are not necessary for this book (see more on page 7). We always specify the size of the sheet pan—half or quarter—in our recipe directions. (And if your pan size is slightly bigger or smaller, it should be okay; sheet pan recipes are fairly forgiving. You may need to slightly adjust cooking times or ingredient amounts—or both.)

When shopping for sheet pans, look for thick, heavy-gauge (13- to 18-gauge) metal, either stainless steel or aluminum. It's counterintuitive, but the higher the gauge, the thinner the sheet pan. Our current favorite half-sheet pan is from Nordic Ware—you can buy two for about $25—but we also love a sturdy one made by Chicago Metallic. We don't like to use coated, nonstick, or dark metal sheet pans for a variety of reasons: The coating may scratch off and the dark metal might skew your baking/roasting time and overbrown your ingredients before they're cooked through.

Sheet pans, like people, contain multitudes: They are stellar cooking vessels (we wrote a whole book here as an ode to them!) and do double-duty as trays—when you're grilling outside, they are helpful in hauling ingredients and equipment back and forth—and as sections when organizing your fridge or pantry. (Sanaë has even used one as a makeshift umbrella during a summer rainstorm in New York City.)

Yes, you can even put them in the dishwasher, but don't be alarmed at the dull patina after a cycle: They'll still be serviceable but may be more muted in appearance. And if over time your sheet pans are completely covered in splotches and spots, that's no reason to discard them! In fact, they become heirlooms, the wear and tear doubling as timelines of all the cooking adventures you've had through the years.

If you don't own any sheet pans yet, we recommend acquiring at least two half-sheet pans and one quarter-sheet pan. We like to keep a few extra sheet pans on hand because they easily nest and have a relatively small footprint in your kitchen. Despite her small Brooklyn home and lack of storage space, Sanaë has five half-sheet pans. Stacked, they're barely 2½ inches (6.5 cm) tall.

If this is the first you're hearing of **eighth-sheet pans**, don't fret—they're not as famous as their half and quarter cousins—but these tiny pans are ideal for toasting a small quantity of nuts, baking single-serving cookies, and even organizing your mise en place. Sanaë and Olga use them for reheating food in their toaster ovens.

Caring for sheet pans is extremely simple: Our preferred method is to hand-wash them with warm, soapy water and dry them with a kitchen towel. Most of the time, this simple job takes a few minutes. However, there are times when food gets really stuck on there—or the sheet pan gets super greasy. A 30-minute soak (or sometimes overnight) with baking soda, Barkeeper's Friend, or Bon Ami, will loosen most of the gunk and help break up the grease. Once in a while, you may need something very heavy-duty to scrape extremely persistent bits of food off. For situations that seem beyond repair, we turn to a trusty steel wool pad like S.O.S. or Brillo. That said, when we're cooking ingredients that are likely to really stick, such as fish or certain cheeses, we line our sheet pans with parchment paper or aluminum foil, so make sure to always follow our directions there.

Our Favorite Kitchen Tools Besides (Obviously) Sheet Pans

Yes, every cookbook has one of these sections, so much so that you might roll your eyes and think, "Seriously, not another section on what I need in my kitchen." But hear us out. As those living in kitchens with small ovens and no ventilation (Sanaë) and those who test and develop recipes daily (Olga), every inch of space must be earned—and kept. So, this compilation is a list of items that we are especially fond of and rely on regularly. Some are a bit of an investment, while others will be so inexpensive you might wonder what's the catch. (Spoiler alert: There isn't one.)

KITCHEN SCALE: At the risk of sounding like a broken record AND repetitive with other must-have tools in cookbooks, let us repeat what others have said so much better than we could: A digital kitchen scale is your (super-cheap) insurance policy for recipe success, especially when it comes to baking. This is why including weight measurements in grams throughout our book was nonnegotiable for us. Volume (i.e., cup) measuring for dry ingredients is unreliable at best (if you want a dissertation on just how unreliable it is, pick up a copy of Claudia Fleming's most excellent *Delectable* and read all about it), but a gram is a gram is a gram. Sanaë relies on her trusty Escali digital scale, while Olga loves her OXO one.

OVEN THERMOMETER: This might be the second most important tool after the kitchen scale, especially for this book. All ovens are different; some run a little hot, some run a little cold. We like to keep two thermometers in our ovens to make sure the temperature is correct and to account for hot spots. The temperature of gas ovens will fluctuate slightly throughout baking—don't worry, this is normal (see Let's Talk

About Ovens on page 5). The recipes in this book were tested in both an electric and a gas oven, and we've always provided a visual indicator and approximate time or range to account for discrepancies in oven temperatures. That said, we recommend owning one or two oven thermometers that you can hang on the racks. You can find them at well-stocked supermarkets, hardware stores, department stores such as Target, or online. They're about $5 and will save you loads of heartache and guessing of that eternal question, "What is the actual temperature of my oven?"

MIXING BOWLS: Large, medium, small (in multiples) mixing bowls are indispensable. We love stainless steel, which is indestructible, can be bought for a song at restaurant supply stores, and stacks for more compact storage.

OFFSET SPATULAS: Especially the small ones! These are so useful in smoothing out batters, getting into smaller spaces for frosting application and decoration, transferring ingredients or cooked food from one place to another, as tiny spatulas for flipping, and so on. They are about $5 apiece, so grab a couple and you'll be glad to own them. Keep in mind the ones with wooden handles cannot be washed in a dishwasher.

WIRE RACKS: We recommend having at least two on hand. They are important for cooling cakes and cookies, as they allow the air to circulate on the bottom.

MICROPLANE RASP GRATER: It might go down as the cliché of all cookbooks, but we bet this (along with a kitchen scale) is the most recommended tool for the kitchen. Don't tell us you already have a zester; if it's not a Microplane brand, please get one, and then we can have a compare-and-contrast conversation. It'll do far more than zest your citrus (though it does that task with unmatched excellence). Use it to grate chocolate, hard cheeses such as Parmigiano-Reggiano, nutmeg, ginger, and garlic, just to name a

few tasks. It will become an indispensable workhorse of your kitchen cabinet.

Y VEGETABLE PEELER: Our favorite is the Kuhn Rikon Original Swiss Peeler, which seems to stay sharp forever. It's light and powerful—not just for peeling fruits and vegetables, but also for shaving hard cheeses such as Parmigiano-Reggiano, and for removing strips of citrus zest.

PAINTER'S TAPE AND A SHARPIE MARKER: It doesn't matter if you cook a lot or a little, it's always helpful to open your fridge and at a glance know (a) what's in it and (b) how long it's been there. Even if we put leftovers in a clear glass container, we make sure to label what's inside. (FYI, this is how restaurant and test kitchens are run.) Olga likes to take it up a notch; If she ever decants leftover broth into a container, she writes on the label just how much is in there.

CERAMIC GINGER GRATER: While Olga is normally allergic to a tool that does just one thing (who has the space for that in their kitchen?), she makes an exception for the Kyocera ceramic ginger grater, which does such a stupendous job grating ginger that it's worth letting it into one of your drawers. And, because it's tiny, it doesn't feel like such a huge sacrifice of space.

TINY WHISK: We love these for how effectively they blend sauces, whisk eggs, and mix up spices. They are also visually adorable. Cute, small, and functional, what else do you need?

CANNING FUNNEL: Do yourself a favor and get one of these. It makes decanting food into jars so much easier and neater. Less time to clean means more time to do whatever else you want to do.

PARCHMENT PAPER AND ALUMINUM FOIL: The day we discovered premeasured parchment sheets for half-sheet pans was a complete game changer. They save time, and because these sheets lie flat, there's no unfurling them and trying to get them to fit perfectly—they already do! Depending on what you cook—granola or a tart that doesn't leak, for instance—you can reuse parchment paper, which is better for your wallet and the environment. Sometimes we call for aluminum foil to tightly cover and seal the contents of the sheet pan, or to line the sheet pan for easier cleanup.

RULER: We rely on metal rulers whenever we have to measure and trim cake layers, roll out pie crusts, and figure out yields. We like rulers that have inches on one side and centimeters on the other.

SIEVES: Look for sieves of a few sizes—small and large should do it—that are fine-mesh but not so fine that fine sea salt or table salt gets stuck in them. They are great for straining and sifting, easy to find, and inexpensive.

THIN METAL SPATULA, ALSO KNOWN AS A "FISH SPATULA": We use this spatula almost daily to flip ingredients on the sheet pan or transfer them to a plate. These spatulas are made of stainless steel and are just flexible enough to slide underneath the most delicate items. They're also terrific for lifting warm cookies from the sheet pan and onto a wire rack to cool. OXO makes one with a rubbery handle, which you can clean in the dishwasher.

CHOPSTICKS: One of Sanaë's most beloved kitchen tools is a set of long cooking chopsticks—called *saibashi* in Japanese—that she uses for just about everything: To stir noodles, pick up small items on a sheet pan and flip them or transfer them to a plate, and whisk eggs. They often replace a spatula, whisk, or fork. You can buy them online or at Asian grocery stores.

BENCH SCRAPER: Cheap and virtually indestructible, it can be used not just to shape or manipulate baked goods, but also to transfer chopped ingredients to a sheet pan or bowl, scrape the counter down to clean it, and cut butter into cubes (much better than a knife!).

ELECTRIC RICE COOKER: This might seem like an unusual one given the topic of our cookbook, but we both adore our electric rice cookers and can't imagine our lives without one. In fact, when Olga's movers lost her rice cooker a few years ago, she immediately purchased a new one. Our favorite brand is Zojirushi, and we prefer the 5½-cup (1.3-liter) capacity. It's an investment, for sure, but one that will last years and save you hours of work. One of its brilliant features is keeping rice warm and moist for several hours. It also allows you to perfectly and easily cook big portions without any additional effort beyond rinsing the rice.

Our Must-Have Pantry Items

As someone who writes about and edits recipes for a living, Olga's pantry is overflowing, and Sanaë's is extensive as well, with a focus on Japanese and French ingredients. We don't expect everyone to go out and procure all these items at once, but we want to make a case that a well-stocked pantry will infuse your meals with a lot more flavor and, with very little effort on your part, take them from good to great.

We won't go into the basics of canned goods, such as beans and tomatoes; having a few boxes of your preferred brand of pasta (in several shapes) or cans of coconut milk and dried herbs and spices you like—because those are obvious to most home cooks, even beginners. We're mentioning ingredients that might not sound as intuitive but ones we really like to have on hand and that appear over and over in this book.

FURIKAKE: Has Olga ever topped a bowl of cacio e pepe with furikake? Guilty. Was it traditional? No, but it sure was delicious. Furikake is a Japanese condiment often made from a blend of sesame seeds, seaweed, bonito flakes (there are vegan furikake blends out there, too), salt, and possibly other seasonings, that's usually sprinkled over rice to add texture and umami. It also looks delightfully festive and we're at a loss when our pantry is without it. Olga has passed on her furikake obsession to her husband and kid—so suffice it to say that they go through a lot of this stuff. And Sanaë rarely eats rice without furikake (her favorite kind is a simple blend of bonito flakes, toasted sesame seeds, and nori). Sometimes she'll even bring a jar in her bag in case she comes across a bowl of white rice that needs a little pizzazz.

MAPLE SYRUP: This just might be our favorite way to add sweetness. We prefer the Dark Amber kind, with its deep molasses notes and earthy finish. We use it in granola (pages 33 and 35), to sweeten frostings (page 217), to make simple syrup for cocktails, and even to sweeten a salad dressing (start with ½ teaspoon and add more to taste).

MISO: We love shiro miso (white miso), which is available at most American grocery stores. It adds a punch of umami to everything it touches including Twice-Baked Potatoes with Shiitakes and Miso (page 192) and Roasted Shallots with Maple-Miso Butter (page 63). Because it's a fermented product, it keeps for a long time in the fridge. Make sure to use a clean spoon when you're scooping it out.

SALT: We both love salt. Seasoning is a balance between exercising restraint and being aware that an appropriate amount of salt will bring out the very best flavors of a dish or ingredient. For instance, what makes our brownies so sublime is a generous amount of salt to enhance the sweetness and rich chocolate notes. Our preferred salt—unless we say otherwise in the recipe—is **Diamond Crystal kosher salt**. We developed and tested all the recipes in this book with Diamond Crystal, and the listed amounts of kosher salt are specifically for that brand. It's easy to grab a generous pinch, sprinkles nicely, and is less salty per unit of measure than other kinds such as Morton or fine table salt, so you are less likely to overseason your food. Remember, you can always use more salt, but it's just about impossible to go in reverse. If you need to write out a quick conversion (to keep using your preferred salt), here's one: 1 tablespoon Diamond Crystal kosher salt = 2¼ teaspoons Morton kosher salt = 1½ teaspoons fine sea salt or table salt. Flaky salt, such as Maldon, is our go-to for finishing dishes, such as salads or desserts. For a final sprinkle before serving, Sanaë always keeps a jar of fleur de sel, a French sea salt that she brings back from Brittany when she visits family.

ALUMINUM-FREE BAKING POWDER: We dislike the "tinny" taste regular baking powders have and buy ones that have "aluminum-free" on the label. Luckily, they're widely available.

PARMIGIANO-REGGIANO CHEESE: We use so much of it that we buy it both in hunks and pregrated at our supermarket cheese aisle, and while it's not cheap, we find that the real deal packs so much more flavor than generic cousins.

LEMONS: We both buy bags of lemons because we use them so often and are terrified of running out. From dressings for the Simplest Arugula Salad (page 274) to adding them to water, roasting them with poultry, and Lemon Bars for Winter Blues (page 238). If a recipe calls for just lemon zest and no juice, save the zested lemon for squeezing over a salad or slicing into a glass or pitcher of water. You can also tightly wrap the zested lemon and keep it in the refrigerator for up to 3 days. Or throw it in the freezer for up to 1 month; as we learned from our copyeditor, Kate Slate, freezing breaks down the cell walls of the lemon and allows you to get more juice out of it!

FROZEN FRUIT AND VEGETABLES: Harvested at peak ripeness, chopped and frozen, these are a must for your freezer. You're that much closer to having a balanced (read: with vegetables) meal on the table without having to do any of the washing, rinsing, trimming, or chopping. We rely on frozen vegetables and fruits for several recipes, such as Sausages with Fennel, Peaches, and Spinach (page 105) and Sheet Pan "Fried" Rice (page 200).

HEAVY CREAM: We always have a small carton in our fridges. Add a splash of it to desserts such as our Granola-Topped Apple and Pear Crisp (page 244) to balance the sweetness. Stir it into arrabbiata or marinara for a creamy, silky, luxurious sauce (page 173). And should you have guests over that take their coffee with half-and-half, just mix equal parts of heavy cream and milk, et voilà!

RICE: Both of our pantries are fully stocked with rice—we cook and eat rice several times a week. Olga buys it in twenty-pound bags because her family eats so much of it. If we had to pick just one rice to have on hand, short-grain white rice is the one we'd choose. However, our love of rice runs deep, and we often have jasmine, basmati, sushi, black, and many others on hand. The only rice we rarely stock (because we don't love the taste, it takes longer to cook, and has a shorter shelf life) is brown rice—Sanaë ate too much of it as a child, since she had it three times a day—but you do you.

HOT HONEY: Hot honey is a bit like an artfully tied neck scarf—elegant and simple, it instantly transforms the outfit, or in this case, dish. You only need a drizzle to zhuzh up a dish, such as Roasted Dates with Blue Cheese and Hot Honey (page 58), Slab "Bee Sting" Pizza (page 205), or Hot Maple-Coconut Shrimp with Mango and Broccoli (page 138).

DATES: Nature's candy, or so we like to think! We like unpitted Medjool dates the best, as they keep longer than the pitted kind and are likely to possess lush, velvety interiors. The pitted ones often taste dry and rubbery, and pitting a date isn't complicated or time-consuming. Besides starring in one of our favorite starters (Roasted Dates with Blue Cheese and Hot Honey, page 58), it's magical in a savory main such as Chicken Faux-gine with Olives, Dates, and Preserved Lemon (page 93). And aside from being a stellar addition to cheese plates, tossing a date into your smoothie will add gentle sweetness without refined sugar.

CULTURED SALTED BUTTER: This is one of our favorite ingredients, and although it's expensive in the States—devastating given how affordable it is in France!—we can't live without it. Sanaë always has some in the fridge—either Beurre D'Isigny or Rodolphe Le Meunier's Beurre de Baratte—for spreading on toast or making brownies. She recommends cutting thin slices, almost like cheese, and placing them on the bread for the perfect butter to bread ratio. (Once you've tasted a piece of bread with cultured salted butter, it's hard to go back.) Olga, too, keeps it in her fridge, for toast or biscuits. Her favorite butter is Les Prés Salés, made with coarse Camargue salt, which can be tricky—and pricey—to find in the States, but is absolutely worth the splurge.

CRÈME FRAÎCHE: This thick, cultured French cream is ubiquitous and affordable in France, and has become increasingly available in the United States. It's much thicker and tangier than heavy cream, but less sour and richer in flavor than sour cream. We always keep a container in our respective fridges and will often top desserts with a spoonful. Olga loves to put a small dollop of it alongside her Sour Cherry Slab Pie (page 222), whisk it into frosting for her "Make Someone Happy" Cake (page 217), or just eat it off a spoon. Sanaë loves to cut her whipped cream with crème fraîche for its tangy flavor, plus it helps stabilize the cream, so it holds its shape longer. She recommends a 1:1 ratio (half heavy cream, half crème fraîche) and then whipping them together until soft peaks form.

DIJON MUSTARD: As you cook through this book, you'll quickly notice that we both love Dijon mustard and use it a lot. We prefer the French kind, such as Maille Extra-Forte or Amora (Sanaë sometimes brings back a gigantic jar of Amora from France), as they provide the strongest nose-clearing heat. Try stirring a teaspoon into your salad dressing. Stateside, Olga swears by Dijon mustard from Trader Joe's, which is punchy and strong and is a great dupe for Amora.

ALL-BUTTER FROZEN PUFF PASTRY: Several of our recipes call for puff pastry sheets. We highly recommend an all-butter puff pastry, which you'll usually find in the frozen aisle and requires thawing for a few hours or overnight in the refrigerator. Our favorite brand for its unparalleled quality, texture, and butter flavor is Dufour, which we used for developing all recipes that use puff in this book. One 14-ounce (397 g) sheet is $12 to $14 dollars, so we try to restrain ourselves to using just one sheet per recipe, unless we absolutely need two, such as in the XL Galette des Rois (page 258). Sometimes we can find it on sale, in which case we purchase two or three boxes to keep in the freezer. If you want your puff pastry baked goods to truly sing, it's really worth splurging on Dufour.

While testing recipes for this book, we also tried Trader Joe's, another all-butter puff pastry that's a decent, less pricey option, but available only seasonally and not as delicious as Dufour; and Pepperidge Farm, which is widely available and inexpensive but lacks any butter whatsoever, yielded results that were fine but nothing to write home about. Keep in mind that brands of puff pastry come in wildly different sizes and dimensions—for example, Pepperidge Farm comes in two 8.5-ounce (240 g) sheets—so the guide we provide with the 4-inch (10 cm) pastries in Puff Pastry Danishes (page 39) is really just a suggestion. You may have pastries closer to 3.5 inches or 5 inches. What's important, as we say in the recipe, is that they be square.

PANKO: These Japanese bread crumbs are lighter and crunchier than regular bread crumbs, and we love the crust they create around an ingredient as they crisp up in the oven. Since none of our recipes call for deep-frying, we sometimes ask that you stir the panko bread crumbs with olive oil or melted butter to achieve that deeply golden color, but you'll still use significantly less fat than if you were deep-frying.

Our Favorite Kitchen Tricks

Here are a few of our favorite culinary hacks that will make using this cookbook and cooking in general a bit easier.

GREASING/SEASONING SHEET PANS BEFORE ADDING FOOD: A trick Olga learned from Ina Garten is to grease the sheet pan with a little oil and sprinkle it lightly with salt, so whatever you put on the sheet pan gets a little seasoning on the bottom.

FREEZING GINGER: Not only will it keep longer, but you can also grate it without those annoying stringy bits getting stuck in your grater.

FREEZING LEFTOVER CHIPOTLES IN ADOBO AND/OR CANNED TOMATO PASTE: Ever opened a can of chipotles in adobo to use just one chile and then scratched your head wondering what do to with the rest? Hint: It's not relegating it to the back of the fridge only to forget about it and then rediscover it covered with all shades of mold. Instead, cut up several pieces of wax paper, roughly 4-inch (10 cm) squares, and plop a chile or two with some sauce (or 1 to 3 tablespoons of paste), on each of the pieces. Gently wrap the pieces, place in a lidded container, label that puppy with painter's tape and a Sharpie (see page 8), and freeze it. When you need a chipotle or tomato paste, just grab and thaw as much as you need. If you need these quickly, pop them in the microwave for 10 to 15 seconds to soften.

FREEZING RICE: If you have leftover rice, cool it completely and refrigerate it overnight in an airtight container to make fried rice the next day. If you are keeping the rice for more than three days, we highly recommend freezing it. (Sanaë's mother is a stickler when it comes to storing rice—she rarely keeps it in the fridge for more than a day—so unless Sanaë is making fried rice, she will freeze leftover rice even for the next day, as it best preserves its flavor and texture.) To freeze leftover rice, divide it into individual portions of about 1 cup (160 g) each, tightly wrap in plastic to trap the moisture, and let cool to room temperature. (Don't leave it out for too long at room temperature—at the most 1 to 2 hours.) Place the wrapped rice in a resealable bag and freeze for up to 1 month. Alternatively, you can store the rice in small, airtight containers. To thaw, take an individual portion of rice and remove the plastic wrap (if it is wrapped). You may need to thaw the packet in the fridge or at room temperature to remove the wrap; otherwise, you can microwave it for 30 seconds, so the plastic can be easily removed. Place the rice in a microwave-safe bowl and loosely cover the bowl with a paper towel. Microwave in 1-minute increments, stirring once, until hot. Alternatively, you can steam the frozen rice (plastic wrap removed, if using) in a bowl placed inside a steamer basket.

ADDING SALT TO ACIDIC INGREDIENTS: Making a vinaigrette? Add salt to lemon juice or vinegar (whatever the acid of your choice is) to dissolve it first, then proceed with the rest of the dressing.

Chapter 1

Breakfast
and Brunch

Oven Ratatouille with Eggs

SERVES 4 TO 6

1 red bell pepper (8 oz/227 g), cut into 1-inch (2.5 cm) pieces

1 large zucchini (10 oz/283 g), cut into 1-inch (2.5 cm) cubes

1 large eggplant (1 lb/454 g), cut into 1-inch (2.5 cm) pieces

1 medium red onion (7 oz/ 198 g), cut into 1-inch (2.5 cm) pieces

1 tablespoon herbes de Provence

⅓ cup (80 ml) plus 2 tablespoons extra-virgin olive oil, plus more for drizzling

1½ teaspoons kosher salt, plus more to taste

Freshly ground black pepper

1 pound (454 g) tomatoes (see Hot Tip!), cut into 1-inch (2.5 cm) pieces

4 to 6 large eggs

½ cup (25 g) fresh flat-leaf parsley leaves

½ cup (25 g) fresh basil leaves

Toasted sourdough bread slices, for serving

Ever since I discovered roasted ratatouille, it's become my preferred way of making the classic Provençal dish. Ratatouille is usually prepared on the stove: The vegetables cook in their juices, resulting in a soft, aromatic stew that can be eaten with a spoon. In the oven, however, the very same ingredients transform into an exquisite, concentrated version—what I call "essence of ratatouille." The secret to all this softness and caramelization is a generous pour of olive oil. Don't be daunted by the amount of oil. It infuses with the sweet vegetables, and you'll want to soak it up with thick slices of toasted bread.

To make this a substantial breakfast or brunch meal, I've cracked eggs directly onto the sheet pan—the oven heat gently sets the whites while keeping the yolks runny. But you could easily omit the eggs (or replace them with large pieces of feta) and serve the ratatouille for dinner alongside a green salad. Like with a traditional ratatouille, leftovers (minus the eggs, which should be eaten immediately) are even more delicious the following day. They can be reheated or eaten at room temperature.

Sanaë

Position a rack in the middle of the oven and preheat to 425°F (220°C).

In a large bowl, combine the bell pepper, zucchini, eggplant, onion, herbes de Provence, ⅓ cup (80 ml) of the olive oil, and the salt. Generously season with pepper and toss to combine.

Transfer the vegetables to a half-sheet pan and spread in an even layer. Roast for about 20 minutes, or until starting to soften and turn golden at the edges.

Remove the sheet pan from the oven. Stir the vegetables and redistribute in an even layer. Scatter the tomatoes over the vegetables. Season the tomatoes with salt and pepper and drizzle everything with the remaining 2 tablespoons oil. (Do not stir the tomatoes.)

continued

Return to the oven and roast for 20 to 30 minutes, or until everything is softened and golden brown at the edges.

Stir everything together. Using a spoon, push aside the vegetables to make 4 to 6 small spaces for the eggs. Carefully crack 1 egg into each space.

Return to the oven and bake for 6 to 7 minutes, or until the eggs are just set (the yolk will be runny; bake for an extra few minutes if you prefer the yolk to be cooked through).

Season the eggs with salt and pepper. Drizzle with a little oil, if desired, and scatter the parsley and basil over everything. Serve with the toasted bread.

HOT TIP! You can use any variety of tomatoes here, such as on the vine, cocktail, cherry, heirloom . . . as long as they are ripe and sweet. If using smaller tomatoes, such as cherry or grape, halve them or leave them whole.

Roasted Strawberries with Yogurt and Sumac

SERVES 4

1 pound (454 g) strawberries, hulled and halved through the stem

1 tablespoon sugar (dark brown, light brown, or granulated)

1 tablespoon extra-virgin olive oil, plus more for drizzling

1 cup (255 g) whole-milk Greek yogurt or labneh

Ground sumac, for sprinkling

Flaky sea salt, such as Maldon, for serving

Fresh tarragon, Thai basil, or thyme leaves, for serving

Roasting strawberries is an easy way to revive and sweeten even the saddest out-of-season fruit. (Though using juicy, sweet peak-season berries will result in the most gorgeous expression of this recipe.) I love pairing them with a sprinkle of sumac—it's a little tangy and sour—and fresh herbs, such as tarragon, Thai basil, or thyme. If you are using thyme, make sure to crush the leaves between your fingers to release their oils and aroma. You could serve this dish in individual bowls or family-style in a large shallow bowl as part of a brunch spread. For a heartier breakfast, top with granola (see pages 33 and 36 for our granola recipes). One of my favorite variations is to make a dessert by replacing the yogurt with vanilla ice cream or whipped cream, in which case serve the strawberries with a scoop or dollop on the side.

Sanaë

Position a rack in the middle of the oven and preheat to 425°F (220°C). Line a quarter-sheet pan with parchment paper.

In a large bowl, gently toss the strawberries with the sugar and oil. Arrange in a single layer on the prepared sheet.

Roast for 20 to 25 minutes, rotating the pan front to back halfway through, or until the strawberries are softened and starting to caramelize at the edges.

Divide the yogurt among four shallow bowls and spread in a circular motion using the back of a spoon. Top with the strawberries and drizzle with a little oil. Sprinkle with some sumac and flaky sea salt. Top with the fresh herbs and serve immediately.

All-the-Herbs Frittata

SERVES 4 TO 6

¼ cup (60 ml) plus
1 tablespoon extra-virgin olive
oil, plus more for the pan

8 large eggs

½ cup (120 ml) whole milk

1 teaspoon kosher salt, plus
more as needed

½ teaspoon freshly ground
black pepper, plus more as
needed

1 heaping cup (50 g) chopped
fresh tender herbs, such as
dill, flat-leaf parsley, cilantro,
mint, and/or chives, divided

Finely grated zest and juice
of ½ lemon

3 cups (60 g) baby arugula,
for serving

Flaky sea salt, for sprinkling

This frittata is inspired by Persian *kuku*, an egg dish that is rich in fresh herbs. Though I grew up in Russia, using fistfuls of fresh herbs in many dishes was common, and when I tasted my first kuku, it felt familiar, like home. But it wasn't until I got to work on the cookbook from the now-shuttered beloved Brooklyn restaurant Franny's that I learned a new-to-me technique that forever changed how I make this dish. While most frittata recipes will have you place a skillet—or a sheet pan, if you will—in a very hot oven, which will cause the frittata to puff and come out generously burnished, Franny's chef-owner, Andrew Feinberg, cooked the frittata at a low temperature for the most delicate, silky texture. Served with our Simplest Arugula Salad (page 274), this makes a fantastic weekend breakfast or brunch, or a comforting weeknight meal when whisking a few eggs and placing them in the oven is about as much as you can muster.

Olga

Position a rack in the middle of the oven and preheat to 300°F (150°C). Generously grease a quarter-sheet pan with oil and place it in the oven while it's preheating.

Meanwhile, in a large bowl, whisk together the eggs, milk, ¼ cup (60 ml) of the oil, the kosher salt, and pepper until combined. Add all but 1 tablespoon of the fresh herbs and whisk to combine.

Remove the hot sheet from the oven and place it on a heatproof surface. Carefully pour the egg mixture into the pan and return to the oven. Bake for 15 to 20 minutes, or until the eggs are just set but remain barely jiggly in the center.

Remove from the oven and let cool for 5 minutes.

Meanwhile, in a small bowl, whisk together the lemon zest, lemon juice, the remaining 1 tablespoon oil and 1 tablespoon herbs, and a pinch each of kosher salt and pepper.

Slice the frittata and divide among four to six plates. Add a mound of arugula and drizzle with the lemon-herb dressing. Sprinkle with flaky sea salt and a pinch of pepper, if you like.

Savory Bread Pudding with Leeks and Pancetta

2 large eggs

2 cups (480 ml) whole milk

½ teaspoon kosher salt, plus more to taste

Freshly ground black pepper

8 ounces (227 g) baguette, torn into bite-size pieces (5 heaping cups)

2 medium or large leeks, white and pale-green parts only, sliced ¼ inch (6 mm) thick

4 ounces (113 g) pancetta cubetti, or bacon, cut into ¼-inch (6 mm) strips

6 sprigs fresh thyme, leaves picked

3 tablespoons extra-virgin olive oil, plus more as needed

½ bunch fresh flat-leaf parsley, coarsely chopped (⅔ cup)

1 cup (113 g) grated Gruyère cheese, divided

One of the pleasures of cooking at home is taking a dish you love—for instance, a breakfast-style savory bread pudding—and making it taste exactly how you want. This one features some of my favorite ingredients (leeks, Gruyère, parsley) and achieves my ideal ratio of custardy bread to crisp topping. I prefer the mild flavor and plentiful crust of a baguette, though a loaf of sourdough would be lovely, too. If you have a scale, I highly recommend weighing the bread, as baguettes come in varying sizes in America. Too little bread will make the pudding soggy, and too much will make it dry.

You can double the ingredients and bake the bread pudding in a half-sheet pan to feed a crowd: Roast the leeks an extra 10 minutes and bake the assembled bread pudding 5 to 10 minutes longer for the center to fully cook through. And make sure to build the bread pudding in the same half-sheet pan that you used for roasting the leeks and pancetta (no need to wipe it clean!).

Sanaë

Position a rack in the middle of the oven and preheat to 375°F (190°C).

In a large bowl, whisk together the eggs, milk, salt, and several grinds of black pepper. Add the bread and toss to coat. Set aside to soak, stirring from time to time.

Meanwhile, on a half-sheet pan, toss together the leeks, pancetta, thyme, and oil. Season with salt and pepper and stir to combine. Roast for about 20 minutes, stirring halfway through, or until the leeks are softened and golden and the pancetta is crispy.

Drizzle a little oil into a quarter-sheet pan and coat the bottom and sides with the oil.

To the bowl with the soaked bread mixture, add the parsley and half of the Gruyère. Add the cooked leeks and pancetta and stir to combine. Transfer the bread mixture to the prepared quarter-sheet pan, along with any remaining liquid, and spread in an even layer. Sprinkle with the remaining Gruyère and drizzle with a little oil.

Bake for 40 to 45 minutes, or until golden, puffed, and cooked through. Let rest for 5 minutes before serving.

Sweet Coconut Bread Pudding with Lime

SERVES 6

2 tablespoons (1 oz/28 g) unsalted butter, cut into small pieces, plus more for the pan

12 ounces (340 g) brioche (10 slices), cut into 1-inch (2.5 cm) cubes

One 13.5-ounce (400 ml) can unsweetened full-fat coconut milk, divided

¼ teaspoon kosher salt, plus more as needed

5 large eggs

⅔ cup (160 ml) heavy cream

5 tablespoons coconut sugar, divided

Maple syrup, for drizzling

1 lime

Sweet-Salty Coconut Flakes (optional; recipe follows)

This soft, decadent bread pudding is the perfect star of, or addition to, a brunch spread. You could serve it for dessert, too, in which case I might add a scoop of coconut or vanilla ice cream. You can swap in challah or milk bread for the brioche. Just make sure to toast it first, as it prevents the bread from disintegrating when it soaks in the coconut-cream-egg mixture.

I love coconut sugar because its fine granules dissolve easily and quickly in the coconut milk mixture, and it lends a deep, caramel flavor, though you can also use dark brown sugar if you prefer or can't find coconut sugar. The result will be equally delicious. The coconut flakes are optional, but they offer such a welcome crunch that I urge you to make them if you have time. (Plus, any leftover flakes make for a terrific snack!)

Sanaë

Position racks in the lower and upper thirds of the oven and preheat to 350°F (180°C). Butter a quarter-sheet pan.

Arrange the brioche in a single layer on two half-sheet pans. Toast, flipping halfway through and switching the sheet pans from top to bottom, for 5 to 10 minutes, or until the bread is pale golden and dry to the touch. Set aside to cool.

Shake the can of coconut milk to mix it well before opening (see Hot Tip!). Measure ⅓ cup (80 ml) coconut milk into a small bowl, add a pinch of salt, and stir to dissolve. Set aside for serving.

In a large bowl, whisk the eggs until combined. Add the remaining coconut milk, the cream, 3 tablespoons of the coconut sugar, and the salt. Whisk well until combined and smooth. Add the bread and, using a large spoon, gently stir to evenly soak and coat the bread in the liquid. Transfer to the prepared quarter-sheet pan, along with the liquid, and set aside for 5 minutes.

Dot the surface with the butter pieces and sprinkle with the remaining 2 tablespoons coconut sugar. Place the quarter-sheet pan in a half-sheet pan to catch any overflow.

continued

Bake for 30 to 35 minutes, or until puffed and golden.

Serve hot or warm in individual bowls. Drizzle the maple syrup and reserved coconut milk over the pudding. Using a Microplane rasp grater, grate the lime zest over the pudding. If desired, top with the sweet-salty coconut flakes.

HOT TIP! If the coconut milk is completely separated, pour into a microwave-safe bowl. Microwave in 10-second increments, whisking after each increment, until smooth and combined. (Alternatively, gently heat the coconut milk in a pot over low heat, whisking, until smooth and combined.)

Sweet-Salty Coconut Flakes

1 cup (80 g) unsweetened coconut flakes

1 tablespoon maple syrup

¼ teaspoon kosher salt

Position a rack in the middle of the oven and preheat to 300°F (150°C). Line a quarter-sheet pan with parchment paper.

In a medium bowl, combine the coconut flakes, maple syrup, and salt. Mix well with your fingers to coat the coconut. Transfer the coconut flakes to the prepared sheet pan and spread in a single layer.

Bake the coconut flakes for 8 to 12 minutes, stirring halfway through, or until deeply golden and fragrant. Cool to room temperature. (The toasted coconut flakes will keep in an airtight container at room temperature for up to 1 week.)

Giant Buttermilk-Cornmeal Pancake with Blueberries

SERVES 6 TO 8

2 cups (250 g) all-purpose flour

½ cup (83 g) fine or medium-grind cornmeal

Finely grated zest of 1 lemon (1½ teaspoons)

1 teaspoon baking powder

1 teaspoon baking soda

¾ teaspoon kosher salt

4 tablespoons (2 oz/56 g) unsalted butter, plus more for serving

3 large eggs

3 tablespoons (36 g) granulated sugar or honey (63 g)

2½ cups (600 g) well-shaken buttermilk

1½ teaspoons vanilla extract

1 cup (145 g) blueberries, plus more for serving

Maple syrup (optional), for serving

Chopped strawberries (optional), for serving

Sliced bananas (optional), for serving

Just about everyone I know loves pancakes, which to me is a hallmark of a leisurely weekend morning. However, there's a catch: It's a leisurely morning for everyone except the designated pancake maker, who is turning out batch after batch until they run out of batter, and then are often left with cold pancakes for themselves. Especially if you're having people over for brunch, this seems like not so much fun. You want to be hanging out with your guests—over coffee or mimosas—and not be stuck in the kitchen.

Enter the mighty oven pancake. Instead of frying individual pancakes, you dump the batter into the sheet pan and bake it. The resulting big pancake is fluffy, tender, and crispy on the edges. And the best part is everyone gets their breakfast at the same time.

Olga

Position a rack in the middle of the oven and preheat to 400°F (200°C).

While the oven preheats, in a medium bowl, whisk together the flour, cornmeal, lemon zest, baking powder, baking soda, and salt until combined.

Add the butter to a half-sheet pan and place in the oven for 5 to 6 minutes, or until it melts, smells nutty, and the solids brown. Gently tilt the pan around to ensure the butter is coating the bottom and sides of the pan and set aside on a heatproof surface.

In a large bowl, whisk together the eggs and sugar until light and airy, about 1 minute. Whisk in the buttermilk and vanilla until combined. Carefully pour the melted browned butter in the sheet pan into the buttermilk mixture. Set the sheet pan aside and wipe the corner you used for pouring. Whisk the buttermilk mixture to incorporate the butter.

Add the flour mixture to the wet ingredients, whisking gently just to combine; some lumps are fine. Place the empty sheet pan in the oven for 1 minute to heat, then remove and set on a heatproof surface. Transfer the batter to the hot sheet and use an offset spatula to evenly

continued

spread the batter. Evenly sprinkle the blueberries over the top of the pancake.

Bake for 17 to 20 minutes, or until cooked through and light golden brown. Remove from the oven, cut into individual pieces, and serve warm. If desired, serve with maple syrup, strawberries, and/or bananas.

HOT TIP! I love a blueberry pancake, but you may be a chocolate chip person, or maybe you like nuts—or perhaps you're a pancake purist and balk at the idea of anything contaminating that beautiful pancake texture. Feel free to experiment and find your favorite combination. Or, you can do like my *Washington Post* colleague Becky Krystal did: Make rows of preferred toppings in case you've got a house divided.

Pecan-Ginger Granola Bars

MAKES 12 BARS

1½ cups (153 g) old-fashioned rolled oats

4 tablespoons melted coconut oil, extra-virgin olive oil, or melted butter, divided, plus more for the pan

2 cups (200 g) pecan halves

1 cup (135 g) sunflower seeds

¼ cup (38 g) finely chopped crystallized ginger

2 tablespoons flaxseed meal

1½ teaspoons ground ginger

1½ teaspoons kosher salt

⅓ cup (80 ml) maple syrup

These are perfect for when you don't have time for breakfast, or need a midmorning or afternoon snack. I tried several iterations of granola bars to find the one I like best—crisp and toasted, without being hard or brittle. Grinding the pecans and using coconut oil resulted in a texture I love: A little crumbly when you bite into it, a little soft, and not too dry. I also wanted the right amount of sweetener. There should be enough to bind the ingredients together without resulting in a cloyingly sweet bar. You'll get a double hit of ginger with ground and crystallized, though if you don't like ginger, simply leave it out or replace it with dried fruit, such as dates or figs, or coarsely chopped dark chocolate.

This recipe requires a bit of work, as first you'll have to toast the ingredients, but doing so brings out the flavors of each one and creates a beautiful crisp-tender texture. It makes a big quantity of bars that you can keep for a while, so I think it's well worth the effort.

Sanaë

Position racks in the upper and lower thirds of the oven and preheat to 325°F (160°C). Line two half-sheet pans with parchment paper.

In a large bowl, combine the oats and 1 tablespoon of the oil and mix well to coat. Transfer to one of the prepared sheet pans. (Set aside the bowl without washing it, as you'll use it again later.)

On the second prepared sheet pan, spread the pecans on one side and the sunflower seeds on the other side. You want to keep them separate. Transfer both sheet pans to the oven (either rack is fine) and toast for 10 to 15 minutes, stirring halfway through but being careful to keep the pecans and sunflower seeds separate, or until the pecans and sunflower seeds are a shade darker and fragrant and the oats are pale golden. (The sunflower seeds and pecans will most likely be done before the oats.) Set aside for a few minutes until the pecans are cool to the touch.

In the large bowl you used earlier, stir together the oats, sunflower seeds, crystallized ginger, flaxseed meal, ground ginger, and salt.

continued

Add the cooled pecans to a food processor and pulse until finely ground. You should have a coarse meal that just begins to clump together. Don't overprocess, or you'll make pecan butter. Transfer the ground pecans to the bowl with the dry ingredients.

In a small bowl or measuring cup, whisk together the maple syrup and remaining 3 tablespoons oil. Pour over the dry ingredients and stir well to combine.

Oil a quarter-sheet pan and line with parchment paper, leaving a slight overhang over the long sides. Press the oat mixture into the sheet pan. Using a spatula or the back of a large spoon, press down into an even, compact layer.

Bake for 20 to 25 minutes, or until the edges look dry. If you want crispier bars, bake for 5 to 10 minutes more, or until pale golden. Allow to cool completely in the pan before lifting the parchment onto a cutting board. Cut in half lengthwise, parallel to the long side of the pan, then cut crosswise into 12 bars. Store in an airtight container at room temperature for up to 2 weeks.

Sanaë's Sweet and Salty Granola with Pistachios and Figs

MAKES ABOUT 12 CUPS

2½ cups (250 g) old-fashioned rolled oats

1½ cups (60 g) crispy brown rice cereal or Rice Krispies

1 cup (140 g) pistachios

1 cup (80 g) unsweetened coconut flakes

1 cup (110 g) walnut halves

1 cup (110 g) sliced almonds

1 cup (150 g) pumpkin seeds

¼ cup (53 g) dark brown sugar

¼ cup (35 g) white sesame seeds

1 teaspoon fine sea salt, preferably La Baleine brand, or 2 teaspoons Diamond Crystal kosher salt

½ cup (120 ml) extra-virgin olive oil

⅓ cup (80 ml) maple syrup

4 ounces (113 g) dried figs, coarsely chopped

Whole-milk yogurt (optional), for serving

Honey (optional), for serving

I can make granola in my sleep, without giving it much thought. I'll preheat the oven, put a large bowl on the scale, and weigh out the ingredients. I always bake it by feel, checking it every few minutes at the end of the cooking time, and taking it out of the oven when it's deeply golden brown and fragrant, just moments away from being burnt. (My dear friend Dawn Perry, the cookbook author of *Ready, Set, Cook*, calls this "taking it to the edge"! Her granola is always toasted to perfection.) I have a few secrets: (1) crispy brown rice cereal for texture and to cut through the chewy oats, (2) no stirring until the granola has cooled ensures some clumps, and (3) fine sea salt, as it dissolves and marries beautifully with the granola's subtle sweetness. I go heavy on the salt, so if you prefer a less salty granola, reduce the amount to your liking.

Sanaë

Position racks in the upper and lower thirds of the oven and preheat to 300°F (150°C). Line two half-sheet pans with parchment paper.

In a large bowl, stir together the oats, brown rice cereal, pistachios, coconut flakes, walnuts, almonds, pumpkin seeds, brown sugar, sesame seeds, and salt. Add the oil and maple syrup and stir well to combine. Divide the granola mixture between the prepared sheet pans and spread in an even layer.

Bake for 20 minutes. Switch racks, rotate the sheets from front to back, and bake for 15 minutes more. Switch and rotate the sheets again and bake for 5 to 15 minutes more, checking every 5 minutes, or until the nuts and coconut are deeply toasted and dark golden. Rely on your nose and eyes, as all ovens are different. (Careful, though, as the nuts will taste bitter if they burn).

Remove from the oven and immediately sprinkle the dried figs over the granola. Allow to cool completely on the sheet pans. Stir the figs into the granola, breaking it up into pieces, and store in an airtight container at room temperature for up to 4 weeks. If desired, serve the granola with yogurt and a drizzle of honey.

Sanaë's Sweet and Salty Granola with Pistachios and Figs; **Opposite** Olga's Birdseed Granola with Fennel and Dried Cherries

Olga's Birdseed Granola with Fennel and Dried Cherries

3 cups (300 g) old-fashioned rolled oats

1 cup (110 g) pecan pieces

1 cup (100 g) sliced almonds

1 cup (80 g) unsweetened coconut flakes

½ cup (70 g) sunflower seeds

½ cup (65 g) pumpkin seeds

¼ cup (50 g) quinoa

¼ cup (50 g) millet or amaranth seeds (optional)

¼ cup (40 g) sesame seeds (I do a mix of white and black)

3 tablespoons chia seeds

1½ teaspoons fennel seeds

1½ teaspoons kosher salt

1 teaspoon ground cinnamon

1 teaspoon ground ginger

¼ teaspoon freshly grated nutmeg

½ cup (100 g) coconut oil, melted (see Hot Tip!)

¼ cup (60 ml) maple syrup

¼ cup (55 g) packed dark brown sugar

½ cup (75 g) dried tart cherries, dried sweet cherries, or dried cranberries

I know the list of ingredients below is long, but what makes this granola so good is that it has varying textures and range of crunch. There are nuts, seeds, and grains, and the whole thing looks a bit like birdseed, but in the best possible way. It's also extremely forgiving: You can skip whatever you don't have and use more of what you do. Swap out, say, quinoa for raw buckwheat groats—or use both!—for your preferred crunch. I add a little fennel seed to take my granola just a hint over to the savory side, but what I love the most about it is that it's not too sweet, which is both better for your health and doesn't obfuscate whatever you sprinkle the granola over. I like to add dried tart cherries at the end—that bright tart note really makes the granola sing. Once you make it a few times, you may even stop measuring out the ingredients.

Olga

Position racks in the upper and lower thirds of the oven and preheat to 300°F (150°C). Line two half-sheet pans with parchment paper.

In a large bowl, toss together the oats, pecans, almonds, coconut flakes, sunflower seeds, pumpkin seeds, quinoa, millet (if using), sesame seeds, chia seeds, fennel seeds, salt, cinnamon, ginger, and nutmeg until combined. Add the oil, maple syrup, and brown sugar and stir well to coat. Divide the granola between the prepared half-sheet pans spread in an even layer.

Bake for about 45 minutes, stirring once and switching racks and rotating the pans front to back halfway through baking. The granola will be done when the nuts and coconut flakes are a rich golden brown and smell fragrant. You may need to bake the granola for another 5 to 10 minutes, depending on how golden brown the oats are looking, but keep an eye on it, because granola can burn quickly. Once it's done to your liking, turn the oven off and let the granola continue to crisp up in the oven until fully cooled off.

Add the dried cherries to the granola and briefly stir to combine. Transfer the granola to an airtight container and store at room temperature for up to 4 weeks.

HOT TIP! Use a liquid measuring cup with a spout for melting coconut oil in the microwave, then once it's added to the oat mixture, use the same cup to measure the maple syrup. Because the inside of the measuring cup will be oily, the syrup will slide right out—every drop!

Puff Pastry Danishes

MAKES 8 PASTRIES

1 large egg

4 ounces (115 g) brick cream cheese, at room temperature

2 tablespoons powdered sugar

¼ teaspoon vanilla extract

⅛ teaspoon kosher salt

1 tablespoon heavy cream

All-purpose flour, for dusting

One 14-ounce (397 g) sheet frozen all-butter puff pastry dough, preferably Dufour, thawed in the refrigerator

2½ tablespoons cherry preserves (or your favorite jam)

Demerara or granulated sugar, for sprinkling

We love a good Danish with a cup of coffee over breakfast or brunch. But unless you make them yourself—and they taste so much better freshly baked—you'll likely be eating Danishes that are just okay. We think you deserve better. These Danishes, made with store-bought puff pastry, though not traditional, are delicious and easy to throw together in the morning for a brunch dish that takes little effort. In minutes, you have the cream cheese filling; a few minutes later, your Danish squares are cut and shaped; add maybe 5 minutes to fill the Danishes, and another 30 minutes to bake them. Et voilà—Danishes in under an hour and mostly hands-off.

Depending on the brand of puff pastry dough you use—more on that on page 12—your puff may come in different dimensions and your Danishes may be bigger or smaller than 4 inches (10 cm), which is fine as long as your cut puff pieces are square.

Olga + Sanaë

Position a rack in the middle of the oven and preheat to 400°F (200°C). Line a half-sheet pan and a quarter-sheet pan with parchment paper.

Crack the egg into a small bowl. Spoon out roughly half of the yolk (don't worry if it's not exactly half) and transfer to a medium bowl; reserve the remaining egg white and half of the yolk. To the medium bowl with the half yolk, add the cream cheese, powdered sugar, vanilla, and salt. Using a hand mixer on medium-low speed, beat together the ingredients until smooth and a little fluffy, about 1 minute. (You can also just use a whisk and whisk the mixture vigorously until smooth and aerated.)

To the small bowl with the remaining egg white and half yolk, add the cream and whisk briefly to make an egg wash.

Lightly flour a work surface and roll the puff pastry dough out into a roughly 8 × 16-inch (20 × 40 cm) rectangle, then cut it into 8 roughly 4-inch (10 cm) squares (1). (It's okay if the squares are a little longer or shorter than 4 inches; what's important is that they are squares, or as close to squares as possible. A ruler is very helpful here.) Lightly flour the top of the dough squares as well.

Working with one square at a time, rotate it so a corner is facing you—like a diamond. Gently fold the right corner over to meet the left to

continued

form a triangle (1). (This might be the part where you discover that what you thought looked like a perfect square, in actuality, isn't one. If this happens, just use a sharp paring knife to trim the pastry accordingly and save the scraps to bake and eat as a cook's treat.)

Using a sharp knife, make a cut along one of the short sides, about ½ inch (1.3 cm) in from the edge, starting at the fold and stopping about ¾ inch (2 cm) short of the opposite corner (2). Repeat with a cut on the other short side.

Unfold the triangle to reveal a diamond shape with the attached corners at the top and bottom. Lift the separated corner on one side of the diamond and bring it across so its point is on top of the opposite corner (3). Repeat with the other separated edge. You should now have a diamond-shaped pastry with decorative twists, and a center exposed where the filling will go. Repeat with the remaining dough squares. If at any time the dough gets too warm and sticky, refrigerate it to refirm for about 10 minutes. If your shaped pastries are looking far from perfect, don't worry—they'll come out looking gorgeous once baked.

Transfer the shaped pastries to the prepared sheet pans, leaving at least 2 inches (5 cm) between them, as they will expand, and lightly brush with the egg wash (4). (You can fit six Danishes on the half-sheet pan, and two Danishes on the quarter-sheet pan.)

Dollop about 1½ tablespoons of the cream cheese mixture onto the center of each square (5). (You may need to use your finger to slide the filling off the spoon.) Fill a small bowl with cold water, then dip your finger in the water and make a small divot that will hold the cherry preserves, redipping your finger as necessary (you don't need to smooth out the filling all over—just the part that will get the preserves). Plop a scant teaspoon of cherry preserves into each divot (6).

Gently brush the sides of the dough with the egg wash a second time and sprinkle with the demerara sugar. Transfer the quarter-sheet pan to the refrigerator to chill while you bake the other pan.

Transfer the half-sheet pan to the oven. Bake for 22 to 25 minutes, rotating the pan front to back halfway through, or until the pastry is puffed up and golden. Transfer to a wire rack and let the pastries cool on the pan completely before serving.

Repeat with the quarter-sheet pan. Let cool completely before serving. The danishes are best the day they are made.

Chapter 2

Appetizers and Small Bites

Focaccia with Olive Oil and Soy Sauce Dip

MAKES ONE 18 × 13-INCH
(46 × 33 CM) FOCACCIA /
SERVES 8 TO 12

For the focaccia

6¼ cups (781 g) all-purpose flour

2 tablespoons (16 g) kosher salt

1 teaspoon active dry yeast

3½ cups (830 g) warm water

¼ cup (55 g) extra-virgin olive oil, plus more as needed

Flaky sea salt, such as Maldon, for sprinkling

For the soy sauce dip

¼ cup (60 ml) extra-virgin olive oil, or more to taste

2 teaspoons soy sauce, or more to taste

When I was working on a cookbook with the founders of Van Leeuwen ice cream, Ben Van Leeuwen introduced me to the wonder that were Saltie sandwiches. A tiny shop in Williamsburg, Brooklyn, Saltie turned out sandwiches that made you weep tears of joy. Served on their house-made focaccia, each bite was flavorful, surprising, and beguiling. To this day, I consider them the ne plus ultra sandwich maker. When they abruptly closed in 2017, I was devastated. To my delight, I found their focaccia recipe in their eponymously named cookbook, and it remains the best focaccia I've ever tasted. What I love even more about it is how unfussy and downright lazy the recipe is.

Olga

As we talked about focaccia and how much Olga loves the Saltie recipe, I mentioned dipping pizza crust in olive oil and soy sauce—a flavor combination that comes from my childhood, when my mother would serve steamed buns with olive oil and soy sauce for breakfast. Olga had the brilliant idea to try the focaccia with this sauce, almost as a play on the more traditional balsamic vinegar and olive oil. The result was delicious, and we immediately decided it belonged in the book. We recommend starting with the amounts we've suggested below, but be sure to taste the dipping sauce and adjust to your preference: You might want a little less or more soy sauce.

Sanaë

MAKE THE FOCACCIA: In a large bowl, whisk together the flour, kosher salt, and yeast until combined. Add the warm water and stir with a wooden spoon or bowl scraper until all the flour is incorporated and a dough forms—it will be very wet and sticky, and, if using a wooden spoon, you may want to use a scraper to help yourself. Add the oil to a 6-quart (6-liter) plastic food container with a tight-fitting lid (or a large, lidded pot of the same size or larger will do) and, using a pastry brush, distribute the oil all over the bottom and up the sides. Transfer the dough to this container, drizzle with more oil on top, and use your hand to coat the dough in the oil. Cover tightly and refrigerate for at least 8 hours and up to 2 days.

When ready to bake, generously oil a half-sheet pan. Transfer the dough to it and, using your hands, spread it out as much as possible, adding more oil as needed to keep it from sticking. Place the dough in a warm place and let rise, uncovered, until about doubled in bulk, 20 minutes to 1 hour. The rising time will vary depending on the season, humidity levels, and the temperature of your home. When the dough is ready, it should be fluffy and leisurely spread out on the sheet pan.

Position a rack in the middle of the oven and preheat to 450°F (230°C).

Pat down the focaccia to an even 1-inch (2.5 cm) thickness and use your fingertips to dimple the entire dough. If the dough is looking on the drier side, drizzle with more oil, then sprinkle with some flaky sea salt.

Bake for 25 to 30 minutes, rotating the pan front to back halfway through, or until the top is golden brown. Transfer to a wire rack and let cool completely on the pan. Slide out of the pan, then cut into slices.

MAKE THE SOY SAUCE DIP: In a small bowl, stir together the oil and soy sauce.

To eat the focaccia, tear a slice into pieces and dip into the soy sauce dip. Add more soy sauce and/or olive oil, if desired.

The focaccia is best on the day it is made, but is also delicious for the following 3 days, though it won't be as airy and billowy.

Chaat Masala "Nachos"

SERVES 6 TO 8

For the mint-cilantro chutney

1 big bunch fresh cilantro leaves (2 loosely packed cups)

1 cup (40 g) fresh mint leaves

1 serrano or jalapeño chile, seeded if you like less heat, coarsely chopped

1 garlic clove

3 tablespoons canola oil

½ teaspoon finely grated lime zest

3 tablespoons fresh lime juice, or more to taste

½ teaspoon kosher salt, plus more to taste

For the spiced chickpeas

One 15-ounce (425 g) can chickpeas, drained and rinsed, or 1½ cups cooked chickpeas

1 teaspoon kosher salt

1 teaspoon chaat masala, plus more to taste

1 teaspoon ground cumin

1 teaspoon ground coriander

1 teaspoon red chile powder, such as Kashmiri, or more to taste

1 teaspoon ground ginger

ingredients continued

Two of my favorite things to eat are nachos and *papri* (or *papdi*) *chaat*, a family of savory Indian snacks. And while Mexico and India are, geographically, far apart, they share many similar flavors. Ingredients such as cumin, coriander, chile, tamarind, cilantro, and lime, to name a few, are abundant in both cuisines. But combining the nachos and chaat didn't even occur to me until I made food writer Priya Krishna's nachos from her excellent cookbook, *Indian-ish*, and suddenly, merging my two favorite predinner snacks (who among us hasn't made a meal out of nachos or a favorite appetizer?) sounded like the best idea. I opt for a mild melting cheese such as queso Oaxaca (though you can easily sub in low-moisture mozzarella cheese) and top the nachos with tamarind and mint-cilantro chutneys, as well as dollops of yogurt.

Olga

MAKE THE MINT-CILANTRO CHUTNEY: In a blender or mini food processor, combine all but a few leaves of the cilantro, the mint, chile, garlic, oil, lime zest, lime juice, and salt and process until pourable and smooth, adding water 1 tablespoon at a time if needed, until the desired consistency is achieved. (If using a high-powered blender, such as a Vitamix, you may want to double the quantities of the chutney to get the blender to go. Any remaining chutney can be refrigerated in an airtight container for up to 5 days and is great to liven up anything from grain bowls to rice to your morning scrambled eggs.)

MAKE THE SPICED CHICKPEAS: Position a rack in the middle of the oven and preheat to 425°F (220°C). Line a half-sheet pan with parchment paper.

Spread the chickpeas on a kitchen towel and thoroughly pat them dry with another kitchen towel. Discard any loose skins.

In a medium bowl, whisk together the salt, chaat masala, cumin, coriander, chile powder, ginger, and turmeric. Add the chickpeas and oil and toss until coated. Transfer the spiced chickpeas to the prepared sheet pan and spread them out in an even layer (keep the bowl you used nearby).

continued

1 teaspoon ground turmeric

1½ tablespoons canola oil

For the nachos

6 ounces (half of a 12 oz/
340 g bag) good-quality
tortilla chips, such as Xochitl
brand

1 large tomato (12 oz/340 g),
diced

1 small red onion (4 oz/113 g),
halved and thinly sliced

12 ounces (340 g) queso
Oaxaca or low-moisture
mozzarella cheese, coarsely
shredded

⅓ cup (80 ml) whole-milk
yogurt (optional)

¼ cup (60 ml) tamarind
chutney, plus more for serving

Roast for 15 minutes, shaking the pan once halfway through.

Remove the hot sheet from the oven and spoon the chickpeas into the same bowl you used for seasoning them. Keep the oven on and hold onto the pan.

ASSEMBLE THE NACHOS: Add the tortilla chips to the sheet pan and top with the chickpeas, mixing them until evenly distributed. Scatter the tomato and onion on top, then follow with the grated cheese. Return to the oven for 8 to 10 minutes, or until the cheese is melted and starting to brown.

To serve, dollop with the yogurt (if using). Drizzle half each of the mint-cilantro and tamarind chutneys over the nachos. Garnish with the reserved cilantro leaves and serve with the remaining chutneys and yogurt on the side. This dish tastes best when served right away, so don't delay!

Sugar-and-Spice Candied Nuts

MAKES ABOUT 8 CUPS

¾ cup (165 g) packed dark brown sugar

¼ cup (50 g) granulated sugar

1 tablespoon minced fresh rosemary

2 teaspoons kosher salt

1 teaspoon ground cinnamon

1 teaspoon cayenne pepper, or more to taste

½ teaspoon smoked paprika

¼ teaspoon ground cumin

¼ teaspoon freshly grated nutmeg

1 large egg white, at room temperature

1 pound (454 g) whole raw nuts, such as walnuts, pecans, almonds, pistachios, and/or hazelnuts

Originally adapted from a recipe by pitmaster extraordinaire Elizabeth Karmel, these candied nuts make for a terrific addition to happy hour, party snack, or a thoughtful homemade gift. I've lost count of how many times I've gifted these only to get a text the next day from the recipient confessing to have eaten the whole lot and not shared them with anyone. In my version, I've upped the cayenne pepper, because I love a spicy-sweet combo, added rosemary for a piney green note, and snuck in a whisper of nutmeg to complement the nuts' earthy notes. If you're averse to spicy foods, start with less cayenne pepper and see if you prefer more heat. And, since nuts can be expensive, look to Costco for a deal.

Olga

Position a rack in the middle of the oven and preheat to 300°F (150°C). Line a half-sheet pan with parchment paper.

In a medium bowl, whisk together the brown sugar, granulated sugar, rosemary, salt, cinnamon, cayenne, smoked paprika, cumin, and nutmeg until combined; it's okay if a few lumps remain in the brown sugar. Pinch a tiny bit of the sugar-and-spice mixture and taste—if you prefer more heat, season with more cayenne pepper.

In a large bowl, using a hand mixer on high speed, beat the egg white with 1 tablespoon water until soft peaks form, about 2 minutes. Add the nuts and stir to coat evenly. Sprinkle with the sugar-and-spice mixture and toss until evenly coated.

Transfer the mixture to the prepared sheet pan and spread in a single layer. Toast for about 30 minutes, stirring every 10 minutes, or until fragrant and candylike.

Remove from the oven, transfer the pan to a wire rack, and let cool completely, separating the nuts with a spatula as they cool. When completely cool, transfer the nuts to a bowl or jar of your choice, breaking up any that are still stuck together. Store in an airtight container at room temperature for up to 4 weeks.

"Better than Chex" Party Cereal Snack Mix

MAKES ABOUT 5½ CUPS

¼ cup (60 ml) extra-virgin olive oil

¼ cup (60 ml) maple syrup

3 tablespoons coconut aminos

3 tablespoons nutritional yeast

1 teaspoon kosher salt

1 teaspoon ground cinnamon

½ teaspoon ground ginger

¼ teaspoon ground cumin

¼ teaspoon sweet or smoked paprika

¼ teaspoon cayenne pepper (optional), or more to taste

4 cups (4½ oz/125 g) Rice or Wheat Chex, or similar crunchy cereal

1 cup (3½ oz/95 g) sliced almonds

1 cup (1½ oz/43 g) broken pita chips

¼ cup (30 g) pumpkin seeds

¼ cup (35 g) sunflower seeds

Fewer things remind me of attempting to assimilate into American culture than the ubiquitous Chex snack mix served at every middle school party I attended. Learning how to make it was as indispensable as the realization that to even hope to fit in, I had to become fluent in *Beverly Hills 90210* to dissect the latest relationship woes between Brenda and Dylan (RIP, Luke Perry). These days I make my own version, using different spices and seasonings. I also throw in some crushed pita chips for unexpected texture and crunch. I know it's bold to riff on a beloved classic, but I am pretty confident you'll love it as much as we do at our house.

Olga

Position a rack in the middle of the oven and preheat to 300°F (150°C). Line a half-sheet pan with parchment paper.

In a small bowl, whisk together the oil, maple syrup, coconut aminos, nutritional yeast, salt, cinnamon, ginger, cumin, paprika, and cayenne (if using) until combined.

In a large bowl, combine the cereal, almonds, pita chips, pumpkin seeds, and sunflower seeds. Toss with the spice mixture until evenly coated and spread on the prepared sheet pan in an even layer.

Bake for about 45 minutes, stirring every 15 minutes, or until golden, toasted, and fragrant. Transfer the pan to a wire rack and let cool completely before serving.

Phyllo-Wrapped Feta with Tahini-Honey

SERVES 8 AS AN APPETIZER OR 4 AS A MAIN COURSE (WITH A SALAD)

Extra-virgin olive oil, as needed (see Hot Tips!)

1 pound (454 g) feta cheese, preferably sheep's or goat's milk or a blend, drained and patted dry

8 sheets phyllo dough (ideally 9 × 14-inches/23 × 36 cm), thawed overnight in the refrigerator if frozen

2 teaspoons fresh thyme leaves or 1 teaspoon dried, divided

Coarsely ground black pepper

¼ cup (56 g) well-stirred tahini

¼ cup (84 g) honey

2 tablespoons toasted sesame seeds (we love a mix of black and white), for sprinkling

Flaky sea salt, such as Maldon, for sprinkling

Crushed red pepper flakes (optional), for sprinkling

These phyllo-wrapped feta "presents," a riff on a Greek dish called *feta mi meli*, make a delicious, nearly effortless appetizer or a sweet-savory main (with a salad, see pages 274 or 277). When blasted with the oven heat, the feta, enclosed within golden, crisp layers of phyllo, softens into a creamy mess. We offer a twist on the traditional recipe with a tahini-honey spread on top, a pinch of thyme, and a shower of toasted sesame seeds. If you've been curious about phyllo—a thin dough popular in dishes of the Levant—but are intimidated to try it, this is a great starter recipe. Keep in mind that phyllo dries out quickly and needs to be covered with a damp—not wet—kitchen towel while you work with portions of it. But don't worry if your phyllo tears along the way—because of the layers, it's extremely forgiving, and you won't notice those tears once it's baked. Be sure to add the tahini-honey to the hot feta packets as soon as they come out of the oven, as the residual heat will melt the slurry and make it easier to spread.

Olga + Sanaë

Position a rack in the middle of the oven and preheat to 375°F (190°C). Lightly grease a half-sheet pan with a little oil.

Using a sharp knife, cut the feta into four 3- to 4-ounce (85 to 113 g) planks, about 3 × 4 inches (7.5 × 10 cm) and ¼ to ½ inch (0.6 to 1.3 cm) thick.

Working with 2 sheets of phyllo at a time—keep the remaining phyllo covered under a clean, damp towel—place a sheet of phyllo on a clean, dry work area, such as a large cutting board. Brush lightly with oil and place the second sheet on top. (If the phyllo tears in places, don't worry and keep going, as you will wrap the feta in it, and a few tears won't make a difference.) Place a piece of feta near one of the shorter sides of the phyllo stack, sprinkle with ½ teaspoon of the fresh thyme or ¼ teaspoon of the dried, and season with a few grinds of black pepper. Roll the phyllo to wrap the feta until you reach the other shorter side of the phyllo. Fold the longer sides underneath, and set the wrapped feta down, with the folded phyllo on the bottom, on

continued

the prepared sheet pan. Repeat three more times with the remaining phyllo, oil, feta, thyme, and pepper. Space the feta packages about 1 inch (2.5 cm) apart.

Gently brush the tops and sides of the phyllo with a little oil and transfer to the oven. Bake for 25 to 30 minutes (start checking at 20 minutes just to be sure), or until the phyllo is golden and crispy. (Don't worry if some of the feta has leaked through the sides.)

While the feta is baking, in a small bowl, whisk together the tahini and honey until thoroughly combined. If you want to pour, rather than spread, the mixture, whisk in 2 to 3 teaspoons cold water until you get a thick but pourable consistency. The mixture will be thick at first but will loosen when spread over the hot phyllo packet.

Remove the hot sheet from the oven and immediately spread or pour the tahini-honey over the top of the phyllo, spreading to the edges. Sprinkle with the sesame seeds, flaky sea salt, and pepper flakes (if using). Transfer to individual plates or a platter and serve hot.

HOT TIPS! Note that you'll need roughly ⅓ cup (80 ml) olive oil for brushing the phyllo.

Thaw phyllo in the refrigerator—not rushing this process will make the dough easier to work with, so plan ahead.

If your phyllo sheets are on the larger side, they will also work, but you will have more layers of phyllo—hardly a terrible thing.

Don't like thyme? Try another herb, such as dried mint, fresh or dried rosemary, or finely chopped fresh sage.

Roasted Cherry Tomatoes with Whipped Ricotta

SERVES 6 TO 8

4 garlic cloves, unpeeled

1½ pounds (680 g) cherry tomatoes

¼ cup (60 ml) extra-virgin olive oil

1 teaspoon granulated sugar

Kosher salt and freshly ground black pepper

2 tablespoons (1 oz/28 g) unsalted butter, cut into small pieces

1 cup (250 g) whole-milk ricotta cheese

Honey, for drizzling

2 sprigs fresh thyme, leaves picked

Flaky sea salt, such as Maldon

Fresh or toasted crusty bread, such as sourdough, for serving

Crackers (optional), for serving

Belgian endive spears (optional), for serving

Every once in a while, I'll host a fairly elaborate dinner for my friends, and this ricotta and tomato appetizer has become a popular request among them. I like to surround it with an array of dipping vessels: fresh bread, crackers, and endive leaves. Sometimes I'll make the tomatoes in advance and throw them in the oven for a few minutes before serving. This way the hot tomatoes and juices gently warm the ricotta and melt the honey. Whisking the ricotta for a few minutes enhances its creaminess and transforms it into a silky canvas for the blistered tomatoes.

Sanaë

Position a rack in the middle of the oven and preheat to 375°F (190°C). Line a half-sheet pan with parchment paper.

Prick the garlic cloves with a sharp paring knife and set on the prepared pan. Add the cherry tomatoes, drizzle with the oil, and sprinkle with the sugar. Using your hands, toss everything to coat. Season with kosher salt and pepper and arrange in a single layer.

Roast for 30 to 35 minutes, or until the tomatoes are softened and beginning to brown.

Remove the hot sheet from the oven and scatter the butter over the tomatoes. Return to the oven and roast for 5 minutes, or until the butter is completely melted.

In a large bowl, with a hand mixer on medium speed, whip the ricotta with a pinch of kosher salt until airy and smooth, 2 to 3 minutes.

Spoon the ricotta onto a plate or shallow bowl. Using the back of the spoon, spread in a circular motion. Lightly drizzle with some honey.

Once the tomatoes are done, squeeze the garlic out of their skins onto the tomatoes and stir together. Spoon the mixture onto the ricotta. Drizzle with the pan juices and sprinkle with the thyme and some flaky salt.

Serve with bread for sopping up all the goods, as well as crackers and endive spears, if desired, for scooping up.

Roasted Dates with Blue Cheese and Hot Honey

SERVES 4

16 large Medjool dates (see Hot Tip!)

2 to 3 ounces (57 to 85 g) sharp blue cheese, such as Stilton

2 tablespoons hot honey, such as Mike's, or regular honey, plus more (optional) for drizzling

½ teaspoon fresh thyme leaves, plus more (optional) for serving

¼ teaspoon crushed red pepper flakes (optional)

Dates are one of the MVPs of the pantry: They're a delicious snack, a lovely way to add sweetness without relying on processed sugar, and truly magical when hit with a bit of heat in the oven. There, the dates melt and become luxuriously soft, as well as caramelized. We like to off-set their innate sweetness with a punchy, creamy blue cheese, such as Stilton and a light sprinkling of fresh thyme (this is one of the recipes where dried thyme won't work). While these make terrific appetizers for guests, they also do well as a solo dinner with a glass of crisp white wine and some crackers or a slice of bread.

Olga + Sanaë

Position a rack in the middle of the oven and preheat to 400°F (200°C). Line a quarter-sheet pan with parchment paper.

Using a small paring knife or with your fingers, open each date length-wise just enough to remove the pit while leaving the date intact. Add a small piece of blue cheese to the cavity of each date and press the date together to return it to its original shape.

Transfer to the prepared sheet pan, drizzle with the honey, and sprinkle with the thyme and pepper flakes (if using).

Roast for 8 to 10 minutes, or until the cheese starts to melt and slightly ooze out.

Let cool slightly, drizzle with more honey and sprinkle with more thyme, if you like, and serve warm.

HOT TIP! Just as with olives, look for unpitted dates. They will be a lot fresher, softer, and more delicious. Already pitted dates are often dried out.

Ham and Cheese Puff Pastry Tart

MAKES ABOUT 20 SQUARES / SERVES 8 TO 10

One 14-ounce (397 g) sheet frozen all-butter puff pastry dough, such as Dufour, thawed in the refrigerator

⅓ cup (80 g) crème fraîche

1 tablespoon Dijon mustard

8 ounces (227 g) Gruyère or Comté cheese, coarsely grated (2½ cups)

2 tablespoons herbes de Provence

6 ounces (170 g) thinly sliced ham (6 slices)

Few of us may want to admit that what we really yearn for is a buttery, crisp pastry oozing with cheese instead of a platter of crudités. Don't get me wrong, I adore vegetables, but there's something undeniably irresistible—and a tad impressive—about starting the evening with a warm, indulgent appetizer. This ham and cheese tart is always a big hit and smells divine as it comes out of the oven.

I used to make the tart with two pieces of puff pastry, but I was inspired by food writer Sohla El-Waylly's brilliant method for her giant almond croissant in the *New York Times*. First you bake one piece of puff pastry on its own, then halve it horizontally and fill it like a sandwich, before returning it to the oven until deeply golden. This technique works like a dream for a savory pastry and means you only need one sheet of puff, which is great news as all-butter puff pastry can be expensive! I fill mine with ham, cheese, and a layer of crème fraîche and Dijon mustard.

Sanaë

Position a rack in the middle of the oven and preheat to 400°F (200°C). Cut a piece of parchment paper the size of a half-sheet pan.

Lightly roll out the puff pastry sheet on the parchment paper to flatten any wrinkles or folds. Transfer the puff pastry with the parchment paper to a half-sheet pan.

Bake for about 10 minutes, or until puffed and pale golden. Reduce the oven temperature to 350°F (180°C) and continue baking for 20 to 30 minutes, rotating the pan front to back halfway through, or until deeply golden.

Meanwhile, in a small bowl, stir together the crème fraîche and mustard. In a medium bowl, mix together the Gruyère and herbes de Provence.

Remove the hot sheet from the oven and allow the puff pastry to cool for a few minutes on a heatproof surface. Using a long, serrated knife, split the puff pastry horizontally into two thinner pieces, being careful not to burn yourself. Open it up like a sandwich. Spread the crème fraîche mixture over the bottom piece, leaving a ½-inch (1.3 cm) border around the edges. Sprinkle with one-third of the cheese-herb mixture and top with the ham. Sprinkle with another third of the cheese-herb mixture, then cover with the top piece of puff pastry. Sprinkle with the remaining cheese-herb mixture.

Return to the oven and bake for 30 to 35 minutes, or until the pastry is deeply golden brown. Allow to cool for a few minutes, then, using a sharp knife, cut into 20 squares. Serve warm or at room temperature.

HOT TIP! For a twist, you can swap out the ham for thin slices of Spanish chorizo and replace the herbes de Provence with dried oregano.

Roasted Shallots with Maple-Miso Butter

SERVES 4

1 stick (4 oz/113 g) unsalted butter, at room temperature

2 tablespoons shiro miso (white miso)

1 tablespoon maple syrup, plus more to taste

1 tablespoon white and black sesame seeds (optional)

1 pound (454 g) shallots, peeled and halved if large

Finely chopped fresh chives (optional), for garnish

Behold! I set before you an appetizer you'll wish to extend into your main course, consider not sharing with your guests, hoard the drippings as if they're buried treasure, and always feel like no matter how many of these you make, it'll never be enough. Here, shallots are slow-roasted in compound butter until they are falling apart, gloriously mellow and savory-sweet, thanks to the holy matrimony of maple syrup and miso. Outside of peeling the alliums—a laborious task I like to accompany with a good music mix—this recipe takes care of itself.

I like to make extra maple-miso butter to have on hand for spreading on toast, topping baked sweet potatoes, and finishing a steak.

Olga

In a medium bowl, stir together the butter, miso, and maple syrup until combined. Add the sesame seeds (if using) and mix to incorporate. Taste and add more maple syrup, if you'd like a little more sweetness. Transfer the butter to a piece of plastic wrap or wax paper and roll into a cylinder. Refrigerate or freeze until needed.

Position a rack in the middle of the oven and preheat to 325°C (160°C).

Place the shallots on a quarter-sheet pan and add pats of the miso-maple butter all around. Place in the oven for 5 minutes, or until the butter melts.

Gently shake the pan to coat the shallots in the butter, cover with foil, and return to the oven for about 1 hour, or until the shallots are tender and starting to collapse.

Lift the foil, baste with the melted butter, then re-cover and return to the oven for another 10 minutes, repeating the basting two more times, or until the shallots are lacquered and glistening.

Remove from the oven and let cool before serving warm or at room temperature, garnished with the chives, if you like.

Ginger-Lemongrass Meatballs

SERVES 4 TO 8

For the glaze

¼ cup (60 ml) Chinese dark soy sauce

1 tablespoon granulated sugar

1½ teaspoons grated ginger

1 teaspoon toasted sesame oil

1 garlic clove, minced

For the meatballs

Neutral oil, such as canola

1 pound (455 g) ground pork

1 stalk lemongrass, white part only, minced

2 scallions, minced, plus more thinly sliced for serving

2 tablespoons minced fresh cilantro, plus whole leaves for serving

1½ tablespoons soy sauce

2 teaspoons granulated sugar

2 teaspoons grated fresh ginger

1 garlic clove, minced

½ teaspoon kosher salt

½ teaspoon freshly ground black pepper

14 small lettuce leaves, such as Bibb or Boston

Sambal oelek, for serving

These flavorful meatballs make a delightful appetizer at parties. Lemongrass, scallions, and cilantro unite to lend an aromatic herbal note, while soy sauce and brown sugar balance one another for a savory-sweet, umami-rich bite. These meatballs look festive served on lettuce leaves, which also double as "cups" or wraps to help keep your fingers clean (if you care about that sort of thing). My family loves these so much, we'll often serve them for dinner, alongside rice and Quickles (page 273). If you're unfamiliar with Chinese dark soy sauce, I can't recommend it enough. Thicker than regular Chinese soy sauce, which is often labeled as "light soy sauce" in Asian markets—dark soy sauce frequently contains sugar or molasses and adds an earthy sweet note to dishes. It's great for adding to glazes or as a finishing touch.

Olga

MAKE THE GLAZE: In a small bowl, whisk together the dark soy sauce, sugar, ginger, sesame oil, and garlic until combined. Divide equally between two small bowls. Set one bowl aside to be the dipping sauce. Have the second bowl ready for glazing the meatballs.

MAKE THE MEATBALLS: Position a rack in the middle of the oven and preheat to 425°F (220°C). Lightly grease a half-sheet pan with some neutral oil.

In a large bowl, mix together the pork, lemongrass, minced scallions, cilantro, soy sauce, sugar, ginger, garlic, salt, and pepper until well combined. Roll the mixture into 1-inch (2.5 cm) balls and place on the prepared sheet pan.

Roast the meatballs for 10 minutes, then brush them with the glaze and roast for another 5 minutes. Glaze again and roast for a final 5 minutes, or until the meatballs are generously browned and cooked through (the internal temperature of the meatballs should reach 160°F/71°C).

TO SERVE: Line a platter with the lettuce leaves and arrange the warm meatballs on top. Garnish with the cilantro leaves, sliced scallions, and sambal oelek. Serve with the reserved dipping sauce on the side.

Roasted Carrots with Avocados and Furikake Seeds

SERVES 4

For the furikake seeds

3 tablespoons sunflower seeds

3 tablespoons pumpkin seeds

3 tablespoons furikake, plus more to taste

For the citrusy carrots

3 medium garlic cloves

1 teaspoon kosher salt, plus more as needed

1 teaspoon fennel seeds

1 teaspoon coriander seeds

1 teaspoon fresh thyme leaves or ½ teaspoon dried

½ teaspoon freshly ground black pepper, plus more as needed

¼ teaspoon crushed red pepper flakes

¼ cup (60 ml) plus 2 tablespoons extra-virgin olive oil

1 tablespoon red wine vinegar

1 pound (454 g) medium carrots, scrubbed

2 oranges, halved

2 lemons, halved

ingredients continued

The salad that inspired this recipe comes from a beloved New York City restaurant, ABC Kitchen. At the time when this salad became popular, the restaurant was helmed by the supremely talented chef Dan Kluger, who turned out vegetable-forward cooking when "vegetable-forward" wasn't even a term. One of the things that stands out is a combination of roasted and fresh citrus juices, which acts as a bright foil to the earthy sweetness of carrots. Crunchy seeds and furikake—we can never get enough of it—deliver delightful texture as well umami, while yogurt offers cooling tang. The list of ingredients may seem long, but comprises mostly spices and seasonings, which you can adjust to your liking or what you have on hand. And because the recipe makes more citrus juice than you'll need here, you can reserve the remainder for more dressing to drizzle on salads and vegetables for days to come.

Olga + Sanaë

MAKE THE FURIKAKE SEEDS: Position a rack in the middle of the oven and preheat to 350°F (180°C).

On a quarter-sheet pan, spread the sunflower and pumpkin seeds in a single layer. Toast, stirring occasionally, 5 to 7 minutes, or until lightly toasted and golden; don't let the seeds brown much. Transfer to a small bowl, stir in the furikake, and set aside.

Leave the oven on for the carrots.

MAKE THE CITRUSY CARROTS: Line a half-sheet pan with parchment paper.

In a mini food processor, combine the garlic, salt, fennel, coriander, thyme, black pepper, and pepper flakes. Pulse until the mixture looks roughly chopped, then add ¼ cup of the oil and the vinegar and process until the marinade is uniform. (If you don't have a mini food processor, finely chop the aromatics until almost uniform, then whisk together with the oil and vinegar in a small bowl until combined.)

continued

For serving

¼ cup (57 g) sour cream or whole-milk Greek yogurt

Flesh of 1 avocado, thinly sliced

3 handfuls of sprouts or microgreens (optional)

Arrange the carrots in a single layer on the prepared sheet pan. Spoon the marinade all over the carrots and roll them around until well coated.

Arrange 2 of the orange halves and 2 of the lemon halves over the carrots, cut side down. Roast for 40 to 50 minutes, or until the carrots are golden brown.

Transfer the carrots to a large serving platter and the roasted citrus to a plate and set aside until cool enough to handle.

Squeeze the roasted orange and lemon halves into a small jar, then squeeze in the remaining fresh citrus. You should have between ½ and ⅔ cup (120 and 180 ml) of blended citrus juice. Pour ¼ cup (60 ml) of the blended juice into a measuring cup (reserve the rest for another use—a vinaigrette, perhaps; it can be refrigerated for up to 4 days). Season the juice to taste with salt and pepper, and whisk in the remaining 2 tablespoons oil until emulsified. Drizzle half of the dressing over the carrots, reserving the rest for serving.

TO SERVE: Spread the sour cream on a large plate and top with the carrots, avocado, and sprouts (if using). Drizzle everything with the remaining dressing, sprinkle with the furikake seeds, and serve.

Potato and Ricotta Galette

SERVES 6 TO 10

For the crust

1½ cups (188 g) all-purpose flour, plus more for dusting

1 teaspoon kosher salt

1 teaspoon granulated sugar

10 tablespoons (5 oz/140 g) cold unsalted butter, cut into ½-inch (1.3 cm) pieces

4 to 5 tablespoons ice water

For the filling

1 large or 2 small russet potatoes (12 oz/340 g total), unpeeled, scrubbed, and thinly sliced

2 tablespoons extra-virgin olive oil, divided, plus more for drizzling

1 cup (220 g) whole-milk ricotta cheese, at room temperature

½ teaspoon kosher salt

¼ to ½ teaspoon crushed red pepper flakes

Freshly ground black pepper

1 large egg, whisked

Flaky sea salt, such as Maldon, for sprinkling

Freshly grated Parmigiano-Reggiano cheese, for sprinkling

This savory vegetarian galette can be served two ways: in small slices as an appetizer or alongside a green salad as a main course (in which case it serves 6). It's a crowd-pleaser and easily transportable, making it a terrific option for a potluck or picnic. You can replace the russet potatoes with Yukon Gold or sweet potatoes; just make sure to cut slices that are thin enough to bend but not look translucent, using a sharp knife or a mandoline. You could also sprinkle some chopped fresh herbs, such as thyme or rosemary, at the very end.

Keep in mind that the galette dough needs to rest for a few hours, so you'll want to plan ahead. The good news is that you can keep the dough for up to 3 days in the refrigerator, or freeze it for up to 3 months (thaw it overnight in the refrigerator).

While the galette is delicious at room temperature, I prefer to serve it warm, reheated in a 350°F (180°C) oven for about 10 minutes, or until the crust is fragrant and warm to the touch. Ideally, grate the Parmigiano-Reggiano cheese over the galette just as it comes out of the oven, right before serving. If you have leftovers, refrigerate them in an airtight container or wrapped in foil and reheat them in the oven for lunch or—my personal favorite—a savory breakfast.

Sanaë

MAKE THE CRUST: In a large bowl, whisk together the flour, salt, and sugar. Add the butter pieces and toss to coat. Incorporate the butter into the flour, pressing the pieces of butter between your fingers and tossing with the flour until the mixture resembles a coarse meal with some visible flat pieces of butter. Drizzle in the ice water, 1 tablespoon at a time, stirring with a fork, until a shaggy dough begins to form. It should just hold together when pressed between your fingers. Transfer to a large sheet of plastic wrap. Using the plastic, press with your knuckles to gather the dough into a disk. Tightly wrap in the plastic and refrigerate for at least 2 hours and up to 3 days. (You can also double-wrap the dough and freeze it for up to 3 months.)

When ready to bake, position a rack in the middle of the oven and preheat to 375°F (190°C).

continued

MAKE THE FILLING: In a medium bowl, toss the potato slices with 1 tablespoon of the oil until each slice is coated. In a small bowl, stir the ricotta with the remaining 1 tablespoon oil, the kosher salt, and pepper flakes (use ½ teaspoon for more heat). Season with black pepper and stir to combine.

Remove the dough from the refrigerator and let it sit at room temperature for 5 minutes. Cut a piece of parchment paper the size of a half-sheet pan.

Lightly flour the parchment and roll out the dough on it into a round roughly 15 inches (38 cm) in diameter. Don't worry if it's not perfect; galettes are forgiving and we love how the uneven edges look—part of their beauty is in their rustic appearance. Use the parchment to transfer the dough to a half-sheet pan.

Evenly spread the ricotta over the dough, leaving a 2-inch (5 cm) border. Arrange the potato slices over the ricotta, slightly overlapping. (The potatoes will shrink in the oven, so make sure to overlap the slices to prevent any gaps.) Drizzle with a little oil, then fold and pleat the outer edges of the dough over the potato filling, pressing gently on the pleats to seal. Brush the edges of the crust with the whisked egg. Sprinkle some flaky salt over everything, along with several grinds of black pepper.

Bake for 50 to 55 minutes, or until the crust is deeply golden. (Check the bottom by lifting a corner with a spatula.) Immediately sprinkle with some Parmigiano-Reggiano. Serve warm or at room temperature.

Scallion and Cheddar Tart with Honey

SERVES 6 TO 8

One 14-ounce (397 g) sheet frozen all-butter puff pastry dough, such as Dufour, thawed in the refrigerator

1 large egg, whisked

1 tablespoon white sesame seeds

1 bunch scallions (4 oz/113 g), root ends trimmed

2 tablespoons extra-virgin olive oil

¼ teaspoon kosher salt

Freshly ground black pepper

8 ounces (227 g) sharp white cheddar cheese, coarsely grated (2½ cups)

6 sprigs fresh thyme, leaves picked

1 tablespoon honey (see Hot Tip!)

HOT TIP! If you have hot honey and like some heat, add that instead of the regular honey in the last step.

I've made this tart countless times and it remains a favorite among my friends. I love how the large rectangle of puff pastry naturally accommodates the long scallions—no need to cut them into pieces, they can be strewn on top and will soften as they bake. A drizzle of honey at the end provides a hint of sweetness to balance the sharpness of cheddar. Try sprinkling some cheese onto the edges of the tart, where it'll melt over the sesame seeds for irresistible cheesy corners, which are my favorite part of the tart. They always remind me of these cheese twists my father would buy from our neighborhood bakery in Melbourne. I can still taste the buttery flakes laced with melted cheese.

Sanaë

Position a rack in the middle of the oven and preheat to 375°F (190°C).

Cut a piece of parchment paper the size of a half-sheet pan. Lightly roll the puff pastry sheet on the parchment to flatten any wrinkles or folds. Transfer the puff pastry with the parchment to a half-sheet pan.

Using a sharp paring knife, score a 1-inch (2.5 cm) border around the puff pastry sheet. Prick the inside of the border all over with a fork. Brush the edges of the pastry with the egg and sprinkle with the sesame seeds. (Don't worry if the sesame seeds spill into the inside of the puff pastry.) Bake for about 15 minutes, or until pale golden.

Meanwhile, cut the scallions lengthwise in half. (It's fine if some of the scallions break into smaller pieces.) In a large bowl, toss the scallions with the oil and salt, and season with pepper. In a medium bowl, stir together the cheddar and thyme.

If the pastry has puffed up, gently press down on its center (inside the border) with the back of a spoon. Sprinkle the pastry with half of the cheddar-thyme mixture and place the scallions on top. (Don't worry if they're sticking up, they'll collapse in the oven.) Sprinkle the scallions with the remaining cheese.

Bake for 30 to 35 minutes, or until the cheese is melted, the edges are deeply golden, and the scallions are softened and starting to brown. Immediately drizzle the tart with the honey and serve warm.

Chapter 3

From the Low Sky

Poultry

Roasted Chicken with Vegetables and Dijon Mustard

SERVES 3 TO 4

1 whole chicken (3 to 4 lb/ 1.4 to 1.8 kg), giblets removed

Kosher salt and freshly ground black pepper

1 small yellow onion (5 oz/ 140 g), quartered

4 sprigs fresh rosemary

4 sprigs fresh thyme

1 small head garlic, halved across its equator

½ lemon, halved

Extra-virgin olive oil

1½ pounds (680 g) Yukon Gold potatoes, cut into 1-inch (2.5 cm) pieces, or baby potatoes

6 shallots, peeled and quartered

2 carrots, peeled and cut on the bias into 2-inch (5 cm) pieces

1 small bunch lacinato kale, rinsed, thick ribs removed (optional), and cut into wide ribbons

2 tablespoons Dijon mustard, plus more as needed

I am always on the lookout for meals with a high ROI, and few things deliver like a perfectly roasted chicken. The crackling, crispy skin and the succulent, fragrant meat might be one of the loveliest comfort foods out there. And since you're roasting the chicken anyway, you might as well make it a complete meal. Here, the vegetables cook in flavorful chicken fat, but the ingredient that makes this recipe sublime is Dijon mustard. You add a heaping spoonful of it to the cooked, warm vegetables, and toss to coat. The chicken fat, along with drippings, mix with the mustard to form a warm dressing that infuses the vegetables with more zip and flavor. I can't think of a fancier-looking meal that takes so little effort to throw together and delivers such extraordinary results.

Olga

Position a rack in the middle of the oven, place a half-sheet pan on it, and preheat to 450°F (230°C).

Let the chicken sit on the counter for about 20 minutes—it will roast more evenly if it's allowed to lose that chill. Thoroughly pat the chicken dry and generously season it inside the cavity with salt and pepper. Place the onion quarters, rosemary sprigs, thyme sprigs, garlic halves, and lemon quarters inside. Truss the chicken (or just tie the drumsticks together), rub some oil all over the chicken skin, and generously season the outside of the chicken with salt and pepper.

Carefully remove the hot sheet from the oven and set the chicken breast side up in the center—it will sizzle loudly. Transfer the pan to the oven and roast for 15 minutes, or until the skin begins to brown and crisp up. (If you're like us and lack a hood over the oven, you may set off your smoke detector; turn on that kitchen fan to prevent such an ordeal.)

Pull the chicken out of the oven and add the potatoes, shallots, and carrots to the pan. Drizzle with a little oil and very lightly season with salt and pepper. Return to the oven and roast for about 45 minutes,

continued

or until the chicken skin is crisp and golden brown and the juices run clear. The internal temperature in the thickest part of the thigh should register around 160°F (71°C).

Remove the sheet pan from the oven and transfer the chicken to a carving board. Let it rest for about 10 minutes before carving. The internal temperature will continue to rise and should hit 165°F (74°C).

While the chicken rests, use a slotted spoon to transfer the roasted vegetables, along with any accumulated juices, to a large bowl. Add the kale and briefly toss to combine—the residual heat of the roasted vegetables will help the kale wilt. Add the mustard and toss until the vegetables are evenly coated.

Divide the vegetables among plates, carve the chicken, and serve.

Chicken with Clementines, Dates, and Capers

SERVES 4 TO 6

¼ cup (60 ml) fresh orange juice (from 1 orange)

¼ cup (60 ml) extra-virgin olive oil

¼ cup (60 ml) dry white wine (or half fresh orange juice and half fresh lemon juice)

3 tablespoons silan (date molasses/date syrup)

3 tablespoons fresh lemon juice (from 1 lemon)

2 tablespoons Dijon mustard

2 teaspoons kosher salt

1 teaspoon freshly ground black pepper

3 pounds (1.4 kg) bone-in, skin-on chicken (thighs, drumsticks, or a whole chicken cut up)

1 pound (453 g) cauliflower, cut into bite-size florets (optional)

4 clementines, unpeeled and sliced ¼ inch (6 mm) thick

1 fennel bulb, trimmed but core left intact, and cut into wedges ¼ inch (6 mm) thick

ingredients continued

If you don't own a copy of Yotam Ottolenghi's sublime cookbook *Jerusalem*, run, don't walk, to your nearest bookstore to grab a copy. I promise you'll cook from it so much that you'll have many pages with splatters and fingerprints. One of the dishes that has stayed with me through the years and I've recommended to friends, family, and colleagues is the roasted chicken with clementines and arak (an anise-flavored spirit). Not a fan of the latter, I've taken it out and replaced it with white wine and added silan (date molasses). Then I took this beloved dish in a different direction by adding whole dates, capers, onion, and, frequently, cauliflower— often moving the cauliflower to a separate sheet pan (see Hot Tip!) so the ingredients aren't so crowded—for sweet, salty, tart, and savory flavors mingling together in every bite. You can serve the chicken as is, for a low-carb meal, or alongside cooked rice or couscous.

Olga

In a large bowl, whisk together the orange juice, oil, wine, silan, lemon juice, mustard, salt, and pepper until combined. Add the chicken, cauliflower (if using), clementines, fresh fennel, onion, dates, capers, thyme, fennel seeds, and coriander and stir with your hands to ensure the chicken and vegetables are well coated in the marinade. Set aside while you preheat the oven. (For more flavor, and if you have time, cover, and refrigerate for at least 2 hours and up to overnight.)

When ready to roast, position a rack in the middle of the oven and preheat to 450°F (230°C).

Transfer the chicken, vegetables, and any accumulated juices, to one or two half-sheet pans (see Hot Tip!) and arrange in a single layer. (Make sure the chicken is facing skin side up.)

Roast for about 35 minutes, or until the chicken is cooked through (and registers 165°F/75°C on an instant-read thermometer) and the vegetables are tender and starting to caramelize in places.

continued

1 medium red onion (8 oz/
227 g), trimmed but root left
intact, and cut into wedges
¼ inch (6 mm) thick

7 Medjool dates (4 oz/113 g),
pitted and halved

2 tablespoons capers, drained

1 tablespoon fresh thyme
leaves or 1½ teaspoons dried

2 teaspoons fennel seeds

1 teaspoon coriander seeds

Chopped fresh flat-leaf
parsley, for serving

You can serve the chicken as is, with the pan juices, or opt to re-duce the sauce. To do so, transfer the chicken to a serving platter, cover, and keep warm. Strain the sauce into a small saucepan and bring to a boil over medium-high heat. Lower the heat so the sauce is at a lively simmer and cook until reduced by one-third, about ½ cup (120 ml). Pour the sauce over the chicken, garnish with pars-ley, and serve.

HOT TIP! If you have too much stuff to fit on a single half-sheet pan without steaming, divide the chicken and vegetables between two half-sheet pans and position two racks in the middle and lower third of the oven. Or simply keep the cauliflower separate from the outset, toss it with olive oil and a little salt and pepper, and roast on the lower rack. While roasting, switch racks and rotate the sheet pans front to back to ensure even cooking throughout.

Spiced Yogurt Chicken with Chickpeas and Eggplant

SERVES 4 TO 6

⅓ cup (82 g) plain whole-milk yogurt

¼ cup (30 g) almond flour

4 garlic cloves, finely chopped or grated

One 1-inch (2.5 cm) piece fresh ginger, finely chopped or grated

1 small yellow onion (6 oz/ 170 g), finely chopped

6 tablespoons extra-virgin olive oil, divided

1 tablespoon plus 1 teaspoon kosher salt, plus more as needed

2 teaspoons ground cumin

1 teaspoon ground coriander

¼ teaspoon ground turmeric

¼ teaspoon ground cinnamon

Freshly ground black pepper

3 pounds (1.4 kg) bone-in, skin-on chicken thighs

1 large eggplant (1 lb/454 g), cut into 1-inch (2.5 cm) pieces

One 15-ounce (425 g) can chickpeas, drained and rinsed, or 1½ cups cooked chickpeas

Fresh cilantro leaves and tender sprigs, for serving

This dish requires some planning as you'll marinate the chicken for at least 2 hours and salt the eggplant for 30 minutes (this draws out some of the moisture and results in a more concentrated flavor). But once the ingredients are in the oven, they need little attention. If you add some rice and a green salad, you can stretch this meal to serve 8, making it a lovely centerpiece for a dinner party.

Marinating the chicken in yogurt results in incredibly tender meat. We've never *ever* had dry chicken using this method. We added almond flour to the marinade—a technique we learned from Meera Sodha's brilliant cookbook, *Made in India*. It creates a super-flavorful crust over the chicken skin.

Sanaë + Olga

In a large bowl, mix together the yogurt, almond flour, garlic, ginger, onion, 3 tablespoons of the oil, 1 tablespoon of the salt, the cumin, coriander, turmeric, cinnamon, and several grinds of black pepper. Add the chicken and rub the mixture evenly over it, carefully getting it under the skin without removing it. Cover and refrigerate for at least 2 hours and up to overnight.

When ready to roast, position a rack in the middle of the oven and preheat to 425°F (220°C).

Place the eggplant in a colander and sprinkle with the remaining 1 teaspoon salt. Toss to coat and set aside to drain for 30 minutes. Pat dry with paper towels, absorbing any moisture.

On a half-sheet pan, toss the eggplant and chickpeas with the remaining 3 tablespoons oil. Lightly season with salt and pepper.

Scoop the chicken out of the marinade and nestle, skin side up, among the eggplant and chickpeas, keeping everything in an even layer. It will be snug—don't worry, the eggplant will shrink as it cooks. Spread any remaining yogurt marinade over the chicken skin.

Roast for about 1 hour, stirring the eggplant and chickpeas halfway through, or until the chicken is deeply golden brown and cooked through and the eggplant is completely softened and browning at the edges.

Remove from the oven, garnish with cilantro, and serve.

Chicken Legs with Carrots, Potatoes, and Apricots

SERVES 4

2 teaspoons kosher salt, plus more as needed

1½ teaspoons ground cumin

1 teaspoon ground coriander

¼ teaspoon ground cinnamon

Freshly ground black pepper

4 bone-in, skin-on chicken legs (3 lb/1.4 kg total)

4 medium carrots (8 oz/ 227 g total), cut into 1-inch (2.5 cm) pieces

1 pound (454 g) Yukon Gold potatoes (3 to 4 potatoes), cut into 1-inch (2.5 cm) wedges

5 tablespoons extra-virgin olive oil, divided

1 cup (6 oz/170 g) dried apricots

¼ cup (60 ml) boiling water

½ cup (75 g) Castelvetrano olives, pitted (see Hot Tip!)

½ cup (25 g) coarsely chopped fresh flat-leaf parsley leaves

¼ preserved lemon, seeds removed, finely chopped

This is my go-to entertaining dish that feels special enough for guests but requires minimal prep and effort. The colors are gorgeous displayed on a platter or served right on the sheet pan—for the latter, return the chicken legs to the pan after adding the parsley and preserved lemon. I love the combination of flavors: salty olives and preserved lemon, sweet plump apricots, gently spiced chicken. It's a delicious marriage, and I try to get a bit of everything on my fork with each bite. The dried apricots are soaked in boiling water before going into the oven to prevent them from burning. (I use the same method for prunes on page 89.) You could replace the apricots with another dried fruit, such as prunes or figs. And if you can't find preserved lemon—no worries!—add a squeeze of lemon instead.

Sanaë

Position a rack in the middle of the oven and preheat to 425°F (220°C).

In a small bowl, mix together the salt, cumin, coriander, cinnamon, and several grinds of black pepper. Sprinkle and rub the spice mixture all over the chicken. Set aside while the oven preheats.

On a half-sheet pan, toss the carrots and potatoes with 3 tablespoons of the oil. Season with salt and pepper. Make space for the chicken legs and add them to the sheet pan, skin side up. Drizzle the chicken with the remaining 2 tablespoons oil and rub the oil over the skin. Roast for 30 minutes.

Meanwhile, place the apricots in a heatproof medium bowl and pour the boiling water over them. Set aside, stirring from time to time.

After 30 minutes, flip the vegetables and scatter the apricots around the chicken and vegetables. Drizzle the apricot soaking liquid over everything.

Roast for 15 to 20 minutes more, or until the chicken is cooked through and the vegetables are softened and turning golden brown.

Turn on the broiler. Remove the hot sheet from the oven, scatter the olives over everything, and return the pan to the oven. Broil for 2 to 3 minutes, or until the chicken skin is very crispy and deeply golden brown. Remove the pan from the oven and transfer the chicken to a plate.

Add the parsley and preserved lemon to the sheet pan and stir to combine with the vegetables. Serve the vegetables and chicken on a platter, or return the chicken to the sheet pan and serve directly on it.

HOT TIP! For the best texture, we recommend buying whole olives rather than pitted. With pitted olives, the brine penetrates the flesh and makes it mushy. To remove the pit, press down on the olive with the flat side of a chef's knife blade. As you crush the olive with the blade, the pit should release from the olive flesh.

Homemade Shake 'n Bake

3 tablespoons extra-virgin olive oil, divided, plus more for the pan and drizzling

2 large sweet potatoes (1¾ lb/795 g total), peeled and cut into 1-inch (2.5 cm) pieces

1¾ teaspoons kosher salt, plus more as needed

¾ teaspoon freshly ground black pepper, plus more as needed

¼ cup (60 g) Dijon mustard

3 tablespoons plain whole-milk or low-fat Greek yogurt

1 tablespoon chopped fresh thyme leaves or 1½ teaspoons dried

2 large garlic cloves, minced or finely grated

1½ cups (150 g) panko bread crumbs

3 pounds (1.4 kg) bone-in, skin-on chicken thighs (about 8 large)

Simplest Arugula Salad (page 274)

I moved to the United States around age eleven and was soon after introduced to the temple of Shake 'n Bake. It might not be highbrow, but there's a reason it, like boxed cake mix, is still around. For the eleven-year-old me, throwing chicken drumsticks (cheapest chicken parts in the supermarket) into a bag of the flavorful spice mix was nothing short of magic. And the results were extremely tasty.

I didn't set out to re-create the boxed mix at home. It happened by accident when one night, feeling lazy, I stirred together a generous heap of Dijon mustard, Greek yogurt, olive oil, garlic, thyme, salt, and pepper. I slathered the resulting slurry on chicken thighs, pressed them into panko, and threw the whole thing in the oven. The meal was so good, my husband and I finished the whole thing in one sitting and since then, this sheet pan dinner became a weeknight go-to.

To make this a complete meal, I like to roast sweet potatoes alongside the chicken and serve both with peppery baby arugula.

Olga

Position two racks in the middle and lower third of the oven and preheat to 425°F (220°C). Set out two half-sheet pans. Lightly grease one with oil and lightly sprinkle it with salt.

In a large bowl, toss the sweet potatoes with 1 tablespoon of the oil and a generous pinch each of salt and pepper. Toss until the sweet potatoes are thoroughly coated in the oil and seasonings. Transfer the potatoes to the greased sheet pan and spread them out in a single layer, allowing for the pieces to have a little space around each one.

In the same large bowl, whisk together the mustard, yogurt, the remaining 2 tablespoons oil, the thyme, garlic, salt, and pepper until combined. Place the panko in a wide, shallow bowl.

Pat the chicken dry and add to the bowl with the mustard mixture. When dredging and coating chicken parts, it's good to have a mixing-dredging hand and a transfer hand. Mix with one hand (keep the other hand clean) or a large spoon until all the chicken pieces are well coated. Working with one piece at a time, dip each thigh, skin side down, into the panko, pressing on them to adhere. Using your clean hand, transfer to the other sheet pan, skin side up, and repeat with the remaining chicken. Drizzle the chicken with a little oil and transfer to the middle rack in the oven.

Roast on the middle rack for about 10 minutes, then add the pan of sweet potatoes to the lower rack and continue roasting for another 25 to 30 minutes, or until the chicken juices run clear, the coating is golden brown, and the sweet potato pieces are browned and can be easily pierced with a paring knife.

Serve right away, with the arugula salad.

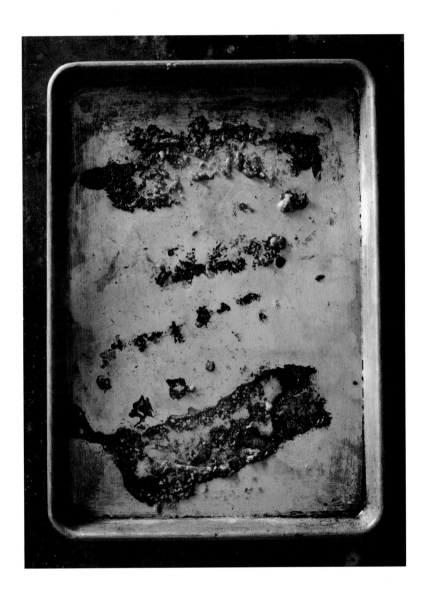

Chicken Legs with Prunes, Pancetta, and Potatoes

SERVES 4

5 tablespoons extra-virgin olive oil, divided

2 tablespoons herbes de Provence

1 tablespoon dark brown sugar

1 tablespoon sherry vinegar or red wine vinegar

2 teaspoons kosher salt, plus more as needed

Freshly ground black pepper

4 bone-in, skin-on chicken legs (about 3 lb/1.4 kg total)

12 ounces (340 g) small potatoes, such as fingerling or creamer potatoes, halved or quartered if large

3 shallots (7 oz/198 g), halved lengthwise and cut into ½-inch (1.3 cm) slices

4 ounces (113 g) pancetta cubetti or coarsely chopped bacon

1 cup (6 oz/170 g) prunes

¼ cup (60 ml) boiling water

This recipe is inspired by my paternal grandfather's chicken: *le poulet farci de Papy*. Every Christmas he would make a whole chicken—stuffed with prunes, chestnuts, shallots, and small pieces of ham—which he roasted with potatoes. He would start preparing in the afternoon, patiently peeling the chestnuts and potatoes, then slicing the shallots and ham. The chicken would be slathered in salted butter and roasted at a low temperature. I loved the combination of sticky sweet prunes and soft potatoes. I've taken those flavors—minus the chestnuts, which I only liked in small quantities anyway—and adapted them into this simpler dish that you could prepare for a weeknight or as the centerpiece of a dinner party. Regardless, I recommend serving it with our Simplest Arugula Salad (page 274).

Sanaë

Position a rack in the middle of the oven and preheat to 425°F (220°C).

In a medium bowl, combine 3 tablespoons of the oil, the herbes de Provence, brown sugar, sherry vinegar, salt, and lots of pepper. Add the chicken legs and mix to coat all over.

On a half-sheet pan, toss the potatoes, shallots, and pancetta with the remaining 2 tablespoons oil. Season lightly with salt and pepper and mix well to combine. Make room for the chicken legs and nestle them, skin side up, among the other ingredients on the sheet pan. Drizzle any remaining marinade over the chicken. Roast for 30 minutes.

Meanwhile, place the prunes in a heatproof medium bowl and pour the boiling water over them. Set aside, stirring from time to time.

After 30 minutes, stir the shallots and potatoes and add the prunes, scattering them around the chicken and potatoes. Drizzle the prune soaking liquid over everything.

Roast for 15 to 20 minutes more, or until the chicken is cooked through, the skin is browned, and the potatoes and shallots are tender and golden brown. Serve on a large platter or divide among four plates.

Crispy Chicken Paillards with Cucumber Salad

SERVES 4

For the chicken paillards

2 tablespoons extra-virgin olive oil, plus more for the pan

Half a 5.2-ounce (150 g) package Boursin Garlic & Fine Herbs cheese

1 tablespoon mayonnaise

Finely grated zest of 1 lemon

½ teaspoon kosher salt, divided

Freshly ground black pepper

½ cup (30 g) panko bread crumbs

¼ cup (25 g) finely grated Parmigiano-Reggiano cheese

2 large boneless, skinless chicken breasts (about 12 oz/ 340 g each)

For the cucumber salad

Juice of ½ lemon (use the lemon from the paillards)

1 teaspoon honey

2 tablespoons extra-virgin olive oil

Kosher salt and freshly ground black pepper

3 Persian (mini) cucumbers, thinly sliced

1 cup (50 g) fresh flat-leaf parsley leaves

These tender chicken paillards—chicken breasts that are halved and pounded into thin cutlets—are covered in a cheesy mixture that creates a soft layer beneath the ultracrispy panko topping. (I think it's the best of both worlds!) The secret ingredient is Boursin Garlic & Fine Herbs cheese, which provides creaminess and lots of flavor. Unlike other breaded cutlets, only the top gets covered in bread crumbs, so it feels less decadent, though no less crunchy. I love serving these paillards with a cucumber salad, or you can swap in a different crunchy vegetable, such as radishes and/or celery. For a slightly more elegant meal, make our Fennel and Citrus Salad (page 277).

Sanaë

MAKE THE CHICKEN PAILLARDS: Position a rack in the middle of the oven and preheat to 425°F (220°C). Lightly oil a half sheet pan.

In a small bowl, stir together the Boursin, mayonnaise, lemon zest, ¼ teaspoon of the salt, and a few grinds of black pepper.

In another small bowl, combine the panko, Parmigiano-Reggiano, oil, the remaining ¼ teaspoon salt, and a few grinds of black pepper. Mix well with your fingers until the bread crumbs are coated in oil. Set aside as you prepare the chicken.

Using a sharp knife, split the chicken breasts horizontally in half, with your knife blade parallel to the cutting board. (It'll be easier to split the chicken if you cut in long strokes.) You should have 4 pieces. Working with one piece at a time, cover the chicken with parchment paper or plastic wrap and use a meat mallet or heavy skillet to pound to ¼-inch (6 mm) thickness. Transfer to the prepared sheet pan.

Using a small spoon or flexible spatula, spread the Boursin mixture over the chicken to completely cover the top. Sprinkle the panko mixture over the chicken (don't worry if some falls onto the sheet pan) and gently press with your fingers to adhere.

Roast for 10 to 12 minutes, or until the chicken is cooked through and the topping is pale golden. Turn on the broiler and broil for 2 to 4 minutes, or until deeply golden.

MAKE THE CUCUMBER SALAD: While the chicken is cooking, in a medium bowl, stir together the lemon juice and honey. Drizzle in the oil, whisking until smooth. Season with salt and pepper. Add the cucumbers and parsley and toss to coat in the dressing.

Serve the cucumber salad alongside the crispy chicken paillards with the remaining zested lemon half for squeezing over.

Chicken Faux-gine with Olives, Dates, and Preserved Lemon

SERVES 4 TO 6

1 teaspoon saffron threads (optional)

4 tablespoons extra-virgin olive oil, divided, plus more as needed

2 tablespoons mayonnaise

2 tablespoons ground coriander

2 teaspoons ground ginger

2 teaspoons kosher salt, divided

1 teaspoon ground white pepper

1 teaspoon garlic powder

½ teaspoon ground turmeric

3 pounds (1.4 kg) bone-in, skin-on chicken thighs (about 8 large)

1 large yellow onion (12 oz/340 g), halved and thinly sliced

3 to 4 medium carrots, halved crosswise and quartered lengthwise

1 small lemon, thinly sliced, seeded, and chopped

6 Medjool dates (3½ oz/100 g), pitted and sliced, or 6 to 8 dried apricots, coarsely chopped

½ cup (75 g) mixed olives (about 10 olives)

ingredients continued

Tagine purists, look away! Not only is this not made in a traditional tagine pot, but it's a sheet pan adaptation. Still, I wanted to capture all the flavors of a tagine but (!) with crispy skin to boot. I riffed on a recipe I adapted from San Francisco chef Mourad Lahlou, but added garlic powder (for a mellow garlic flavor that won't burn in the oven) and a touch of mayonnaise—like I said, purists, avert your gaze—to create an emulsion for coating the chicken and for helping the skin get really browned and crispy. I mixed in lots of thinly sliced onions and quartered carrots, the latter of which stay crisp-tender (no mushy carrots here). And because I'm a sucker for sweet-and-salty combinations, I tossed in a handful of dates and olives, and let the former caramelize, delivering candy-like bites of sweetness. At home, I make it with lemony, herby orzo to sop up the delicious pan juices, but you're welcome to serve it however you like.

Olga

Position a rack in the middle of the oven and preheat to 425°F (220°C).

If using saffron, in a small bowl, combine the saffron with an ice cube and let it melt; this will bloom the saffron.

In a large bowl, stir together 2 tablespoons of the oil, the mayonnaise, coriander, ginger, 1½ teaspoons of the salt, the white pepper, garlic powder, and turmeric. Add the chicken to the bowl and rub the pieces all over with the mixture, including under the skin. Transfer the chicken to a half-sheet pan, placing them skin side up and ensuring the pieces aren't touching one another.

Using the same bowl, toss the onion and carrots with the remaining 2 tablespoons oil and the remaining ½ teaspoon salt. Arrange the vegetables around the chicken, and scatter the chopped lemon over everything. If using saffron, drizzle with the saffron water.

Roast for 25 minutes.

Remove the hot sheet from the oven, scatter the dates (or apricots) and olives all over the pan and dot the mixture with the butter. Return

continued

3 tablespoons (1½ oz/43 g) unsalted butter or vegan butter, cut into small pieces

2 tablespoons chopped or whole leaves fresh flat-leaf parsley (optional)

2 tablespoons chopped or whole leaves fresh mint (optional)

Lemony Orzo (optional; recipe follows), for serving

to the oven and roast for about 15 minutes more, or until the chicken is cooked through.

Transfer the contents of the sheet pan to a large platter. Garnish with the parsley and mint, if desired, and serve immediately, with the orzo on the side.

Lemony Orzo

SERVES 6

One 1-pound (454 g) box orzo

¼ cup (60 ml) extra-virgin olive oil

Finely grated zest and juice of 1 large lemon

Pinch of kosher salt

Coarsely ground black pepper

A handful of chopped fresh tender herbs, such as flat-leaf parsley, mint, or a combination

Cook the orzo according to package instructions.

Drain, then return to the pot and drizzle with the oil, stirring to combine. Add the lemon zest, lemon juice, salt, a generous few grinds of black pepper, and the fresh tender herbs. Stir to combine and serve immediately.

Roasted Duck with Salted Maple Butter

SERVES 2 TO 3

For the duck

1 whole duck (5 lb/2.25 kg)

2 teaspoons kosher salt, plus a generous pinch for the glaze

1 teaspoon five-spice powder

1 teaspoon finely grated orange zest

¾ teaspoon freshly ground black pepper

2 tablespoons (1 oz/28g) unsalted butter, at room temperature

2 teaspoons maple syrup, plus more to taste

For the vegetables

1½ pounds (680 g) fingerling potatoes

2 medium red onions (1 lb/ 454 g total), halved and sliced into ½-inch (1.3 cm) wedges

2 tablespoons extra-virgin olive oil

¾ teaspoon kosher salt

¼ teaspoon freshly ground black pepper

People are often intimidated by cooking duck, but here's a secret: It's actually easier than chicken thanks to duck's rich fat reserves, which not only keep the meat from drying out but also reward you with rendered fat. I strain the rendered fat into a jar and keep it on hand for roasting vegetables (hello, duck fat–roasted potatoes!) or frying eggs—an excellent way to stretch a pricey ingredient. Here, the duck is first doused with boiling water to tighten the skin, which makes scoring it easier, and the quick blast of high heat in the oven also helps the skin to crisp up better. Toward the end of roasting, I baste the skin with salted maple butter, which complements the duck's richness and adds caramel notes. To serve more than three, either roast two ducks or make lots of sides for a single bird. Ideally, try to season the duck about a day in advance and let it cure in the refrigerator to help the skin dry out.

Olga

PREPARE THE DUCK: The day before you plan to roast the duck, bring about 3 quarts (3 liters) of water to a boil. While you wait for the water to boil, remove the giblets and neck from the duck cavity and reserve for another use. (I sear the liver with a little salt and pepper as a cook's snack, and poach the gizzards and neck in water and give the broth and the meat to our dog, Latke, as a treat.) Trim any excess fat around the cavity and the neck; discard the fat or render it to use for cooking. Place a wire rack in the sink and set the duck, breast side up, on top. Pour half of the boiling water over the duck, then carefully turn over the bird and pour the remaining water over—this helps to tighten the skin for easier scoring. Let the duck cool and dry for about 10 minutes.

Using a very sharp paring knife—you may need to sharpen it first—score the duck breast in a ½-inch (1.3 cm) crosshatch pattern, being careful to only cut into the skin and not the meat. Avoid scoring the legs. Turn over the duck and score the back as well. Thoroughly pat the duck dry, inside and out, with paper towels.

In a small bowl, mix together the salt, five-spice powder, orange zest, and pepper until combined. Season the bird all over, including inside the cavity, with the salt mixture. Place a wire rack in a half-sheet pan, set the duck on top, breast side up, and refrigerate, uncovered, for at least 12 hours and up to 24 hours.

continued

When ready to roast, let the duck sit on the counter while you preheat the oven. Position racks in the middle and lower third of the oven and preheat to 450°F (230°C).

Pour ½ cup (120 ml) water into the sheet pan around the duck, being careful not to get any water on the bird. Roast on the middle rack for 30 minutes. (The high heat will help jump-start the rendering to crisp up the skin, and the added water will prevent the rendered fat from splattering all over your oven.)

Once the duck goes in the oven, in a small bowl, use a fork to mash and stir together the butter, maple syrup, and a pinch of salt until thoroughly combined. Set the maple butter aside.

PREPARE THE VEGETABLES: While the duck is roasting, in a large bowl, toss together the potatoes, onions, oil, salt, and pepper. Spread the vegetables out on another half-sheet pan in a single layer.

After the first 30 minutes, remove the duck from the oven and set the sheet pan on a heatproof surface. Reduce the oven temperature to 350°F (180°C). Carefully prick the top of the duck skin with the tip of a sharp paring knife; you should see rendered fat oozing out.

Return the duck to the middle rack in the oven and place the sheet pan with the vegetables on the lower rack. Roast for another 30 minutes.

Gently shake the sheet pan with the vegetables. Set the sheet pan with the duck on a heatproof surface and again use the tip of the paring knife to prick the skin all over. Lightly brush the duck with some of the maple butter and return to the oven for another 10 minutes. Prick and glaze again and give it another 10 minutes in the oven. Glaze for a final time and return to the oven for a final 10 minutes, or until the duck reaches the internal temperature of 160°F (71°C) when an instant-read thermometer is inserted into the thickest part of the thigh without hitting the bone. (Depending on the size of the bird, you may need to roast it up to another 30 minutes. If that's the case, remove the vegetables from the oven and check on the duck every 10 minutes or so.)

Remove the duck and vegetables from the oven. Let the duck rest for 10 to 15 minutes before carving and serving alongside the roasted potatoes and onions.

Chicken "Stir-Fry" with Green Beans and Bell Peppers

SERVES 4

3 tablespoons soy sauce

1 tablespoon toasted sesame oil

1½ teaspoons granulated sugar

1 teaspoon balsamic vinegar

2 garlic cloves, finely grated

One 1-inch (2.5 cm) piece fresh ginger, finely grated

1½ pounds (680 g) boneless, skinless chicken thighs, cut into 1-inch (2.5 cm) pieces

8 ounces (227 g) green beans, trimmed

1 small yellow onion (6 oz/ 170 g), halved and thinly sliced

1 red bell pepper, thinly sliced

3 tablespoons extra-virgin olive oil or neutral oil, such as canola or grapeseed

Kosher salt and freshly ground black pepper

1 tablespoon cornstarch

1 scallion, thinly sliced

Short-Grain White Rice (page 271), for serving

Aside from some prep for making the marinade and slicing the vegetables, this is an exceedingly simple and hands-off "stir-fry" where a blistering oven does all the work. First get the rice started (either on the stove or in your electric rice cooker), then marinate the chicken while you chop the vegetables and wait for the oven to preheat. When broiling, make sure you check every minute or so, as broilers vary in intensity. I recommend scraping up every last bit of the sweet-savory sauce from the sheet pan for drizzling over the rice—it's the best part and every drop should be savored. (I'll use a flexible spatula and tip the sheet pan, allowing the sauce to pool at one corner of the pan for easier spooning.)

Sanaë

Position racks in the lower and upper thirds of the oven and preheat to 425°F (220°C).

In a medium bowl, whisk together the soy sauce, sesame oil, sugar, vinegar, garlic, and ginger. Add the chicken and mix well to combine. Set aside.

On a half-sheet pan, toss together the green beans, onion, bell pepper, and oil. Season with salt and pepper and spread in an even layer. Roast on the lower rack for about 10 minutes, or until starting to sizzle and soften.

Sprinkle the cornstarch over the chicken and stir to combine. Remove the hot sheet from the oven, stir the vegetables, and place the chicken over the vegetables in a single layer. Drizzle any remaining marinade over everything.

Return to the oven on the lower rack and roast for about 10 minutes, or until the chicken is cooked through.

Turn on the broiler and move the sheet pan to the upper rack. Broil for 2 to 5 minutes, or until the chicken and vegetables are browned in spots.

Top with the sliced scallion and serve with rice.

Chapter 4

From the Land

Beef, Lamb, Pork

Cuban-Style Roast Pork with Mojo

For the pork

¼ cup (34 g) kosher salt

¼ cup (55 g) packed dark brown sugar

Finely grated zest of 2 limes

Finely grated zest of 2 oranges

5 garlic cloves, minced or finely grated

1½ tablespoons finely chopped fresh oregano or 2½ teaspoons dried

2 teaspoons ground cumin

¾ teaspoon freshly ground black pepper

½ teaspoon cayenne pepper (optional)

One 7-pound (3.2 kg) boneless pork shoulder with fat cap

1 cup (240 ml) fresh orange juice (from 2 to 3 oranges)

For the mojo

⅓ cup (80 ml) extra-virgin olive oil

4 large garlic cloves, minced or finely grated

¼ cup (60 ml) fresh orange juice

ingredients continued

This is one of those weekend project dishes, one you cook for a larger gathering—or a small one if you like leftovers like we do—but most of the time spent on it is hands-off. It's important that you get a pork shoulder with a fat cap, which will protect the meat from drying out, and also produce crispy skin, which, in my opinion, is the best part. A citrusy, herby sauce such as mojo cuts through the richness of the meat, and here the sauce incorporates peach nectar. While not traditional, the sweeter peach nectar gives the mojo a rounder, more balanced flavor. If I'm feeling extra, I make a pot of black beans from scratch and serve it along with the pork and white rice. Otherwise, canned beans, zhuzhed up with a little cumin, garlic, oil, and oregano work in a pinch.

Olga

MARINATE THE PORK: In a small bowl, stir together the salt, brown sugar, lime zest, orange zest, garlic, oregano, cumin, black pepper, and cayenne (if using) until combined. Using a sharp knife, trim the fat cap on the pork to about ¼ inch (6 mm) thick, then score the remaining fat in a crosshatch pattern, ½ inch (1.3 cm) apart. Place the pork in a large bowl and rub the salt-sugar mixture all over the meat. Cover the bowl and refrigerate for at least 8 hours and up to 48 hours.

ROAST THE PORK: Cover a half-sheet pan with a double layer of heavy-duty foil and set a wire rack in it. Remove the meat from the refrigerator, set it fat side up on the rack, and let sit on the counter for about 2 hours; this will take the chill off and ensure even cooking as well as dry out the fat, which will help it crisp in the oven.

Position a rack in the middle of the oven and preheat to 325°F (160°C).

Pour the orange juice and 1 cup (240 ml) water around the meat. Cover the shoulder with a large piece of heavy-duty foil and transfer to the oven. Roast for 2½ to 3 hours, or until the meat registers 175°F (80°C) on an instant-read thermometer inserted in the middle of the roast.

continued

¼ cup (60 ml) fresh lime juice

¼ cup (60 ml) peach nectar

2 tablespoons minced fresh cilantro

2 tablespoons minced fresh mint

1 tablespoon brown sugar (any kind), honey, or maple syrup

1 teaspoon fresh oregano

Kosher salt and freshly ground black pepper

For serving

Short-Grain White Rice (page 271) or No-Rinse Basmati-Cumin Rice (page 272)

Cooked black beans

Uncover the pork and continue roasting for another 1 to 2 hours, or until it registers 190°F (90°C) in the center. The meat should be tender and a knife should easily slide in and out of it. Transfer the pork to a carving board, tent with foil, and let sit for at least 30 minutes and up to 1 hour.

MAKE THE MOJO: While the pork is resting, in a small saucepan, combine the oil and garlic and heat until the oil is fragrant, about 3 minutes. Remove from the heat and let cool completely.

Just before serving, whisk in the orange juice, lime juice, peach nectar, cilantro, mint, brown sugar, and oregano until combined. Season to taste with salt and pepper.

To serve, thinly slice the pork, or shred it using two forks, and transfer to a serving platter. Drizzle with the mojo and serve with rice and beans.

Sausages with Fennel, Peaches, and Spinach

SERVES 4

1 large fennel bulb (12 oz/ 340 g), trimmed and fronds reserved (see Hot Tips!)

1 large red onion (12 oz/ 340 g), halved and cut into slices ½ inch (1.3 cm) thick

10 ounces (283 g) frozen sliced peaches

¼ cup (60 ml) extra-virgin olive oil, plus more as needed

½ teaspoon kosher salt, plus more as needed

Freshly ground black pepper

4 sausages (4 oz/113 g each), such as chorizo, spicy or sweet Italian, or bratwurst

5 ounces (142 g) baby spinach (1 clamshell)

1 teaspoon balsamic vinegar, plus more to taste (see Hot Tips!)

¼ cup (10 g) fresh basil leaves

¼ teaspoon crushed red pepper flakes, or more to taste

This meal is inspired by a recipe from my friend, the extraordinary cookbook author and recipe developer Dawn Perry. My first job out of grad school was as a recipe editor at Martha & Marley Spoon (the meal kit delivery service) with Dawn, who taught me so much of what I know about cooking, and who showed me the true potential of a sheet pan. In our first months of working together, Dawn dreamed up a delicious and incredibly easy roasted sausage dish with fennel, onions, and peppers. She wilted an entire 5-ounce box of baby spinach on the sheet pan. I've borrowed her method for my own spin, replacing the peppers with peaches for a sweeter combination. I've been making a version of this for a decade—sometimes it's a quick weeknight meal, other times it's served for guests on a platter with toasted slices of sourdough. Regardless, it's one of those recipes I return to time and again, always reminding me of how much I adore Dawn and her cooking.

Sanaë

Position a rack in the middle of the oven and preheat to 425°F (220°C).

Halve the fennel bulb through the core and cut lengthwise into ½-inch (1.3 cm) wedges. On a half-sheet pan, toss together the fennel, onion, peaches, and oil. Season with the salt and several grinds of black pepper and toss to combine. Arrange in an even layer (don't worry if it's snug—the vegetables will shrink in the oven).

Roast for about 10 minutes, or until the fennel and onion start to soften.

Prick the sausages all over with a sharp paring knife. Remove the pan from the oven and place the sausages on top of the fennel, onion, and peaches. Return to the oven and roast for about 25 minutes, flipping the fennel, onion, and peaches (especially those nearer the edges of the pan; see Hot Tips!) halfway through, or until the sausages are cooked through and everything is softened and golden brown.

continued

Transfer the sausages to a plate. Scatter the baby spinach over the fennel-onion-peach mixture and return to the oven for about 3 minutes, or until the spinach is wilted.

Remove from the oven, drizzle with the balsamic vinegar, and season with salt and pepper. Drizzle with a little oil, if desired, and toss to combine. Taste and drizzle with more balsamic vinegar, if desired.

Return the sausages to the sheet pan, or transfer everything to a serving platter. Top with the basil leaves and sprinkle with the pepper flakes to taste.

HOT TIPS! If your fennel has nice fronds, reserve a few small ones to garnish the dish. (If the fronds are large, tear them into smaller sprigs.)

The ingredients at the edges of the sheet pan tend to brown faster, so I like to flip them and/or move them around halfway through cooking.

For a sweeter version, you could replace the balsamic vinegar with a generous drizzle of balsamic glaze.

Gochujang Steak Fajitas with Kimchi, Onions, and Peppers

SERVES 4

2 tablespoons gochujang

3 tablespoons neutral oil, such as canola or grapeseed, divided

1 tablespoon dark brown sugar or honey

1½ teaspoons kosher salt, divided, plus more to taste

½ teaspoon ground coriander

½ teaspoon ground cumin

¾ teaspoon freshly ground black pepper, divided

1 pound (454 g) skirt or flank steak, thinly sliced across the grain

3 large bell peppers (a mix of colors is nice)

1 large red onion (12 oz/ 340 g), halved

8 fajita-size flour tortillas

Napa cabbage kimchi, for serving

Sour cream, for serving

Lime wedges, for serving

Hot sauce, for serving

Ever since I worked on a cookbook with Mother-in-Law's Kimchi founder, Lauryn Chun, gochujang (Korean chile paste) and kimchi have become my pantry staples. Here, I take a twist on fajitas by marinating the steak in gochujang and honey. Broiling the vegetables and steak—all on one sheet pan, no less—makes quick work for a weeknight dinner that tastes like you've put in a lot more effort.

Olga

Position racks in the lower and upper thirds of oven. Turn on the broiler. Place a half-sheet pan on the top rack.

In a large bowl, combine the gochujang, 1 tablespoon of the oil, the brown sugar, 1 teaspoon of the salt, the coriander, cumin, and ½ teaspoon of the pepper. Add the steak and toss to coat. Set aside.

Cut the bell peppers and onion into slices ¼ inch (6 mm) thick. Transfer them to another large bowl, drizzle with the remaining 2 tablespoons oil, season with the remaining ½ teaspoon salt and ¼ teaspoon pepper, and toss to combine.

Carefully remove the hot sheet from the oven. Spread the vegetables on it in a single layer. Broil for 5 to 8 minutes, or until the vegetables start to brown and soften. (Watch carefully, as the vegetables can burn within seconds.)

Remove from the oven and push the vegetables to one side of the pan. Arrange the steak in an even layer on the other side. Wrap the tortillas in foil.

Return the sheet pan to the top rack under the broiler. Place the package of tortillas on the lower rack. Broil for about 5 minutes, or until the steak is browned and cooked through. The tortillas should be warmed through, but if not, return them to the oven for another 1 to 2 minutes.

Serve the steak and vegetables with the warmed tortillas, kimchi, sour cream, lime wedges, and hot sauce alongside. Build your fajitas as you eat.

Dumpling Filling Meatloaf with Sweet Potatoes and Quickles

SERVES 6 TO 8

¼ cup (60 ml) hoisin sauce

1 tablespoon mirin

1 tablespoon Chinese light soy sauce

1 tablespoon honey

1 teaspoon ground ginger

1 teaspoon garlic powder

2 pounds (907 g) ground pork or dark meat turkey

One 14-ounce (397 g) package firm tofu, squeezed in cheesecloth and finely crumbled

½ cup (50 g) finely chopped Chinese chives or scallions

½ cup (30 g) panko bread crumbs

2 large eggs, lightly beaten

2 tablespoons finely grated fresh ginger

2 tablespoons toasted sesame oil

2 teaspoons kosher salt, plus more as needed

Neutral oil, such as canola

2 large sweet potatoes (1¾ lb/795 g total), preferably Japanese, peeled and cut into ¾-inch (2 cm) cubes

Freshly ground black pepper

Quickles (page 273), for serving

Inspired by Ina Garten's turkey meatloaf recipe, here's meatloaf that tastes like the filling of pork dumplings. I lighten the meat with tofu, a trick I picked up from Lauryn Chun, founder of Mother-in-Law's Kimchi, when we were working on a cookbook together, and use scallions, ginger, and toasted sesame oil. Since no meatloaf is complete without a ketchup topping, this one goes in a more sweet-and-savory direction, thanks to soy sauce and honey. If you're lucky enough to have leftover meatloaf and quickles, make a play on banh mi: Get a baguette, slide a gently warmed slice of meatloaf and cold quickles in the middle, add sprigs of cilantro, and finish with thin slices of jalapeño and a drizzle of sriracha.

Olga

Position a rack in the middle of the oven and preheat to 350°F (180°C).

In a medium bowl, whisk together the hoisin sauce, mirin, soy sauce, honey, ground ginger, and garlic powder until combined. Set the glaze mixture aside.

In a large bowl, gently mix together the pork, tofu, chives, panko, eggs, fresh ginger, sesame oil, and salt until combined.

Lightly grease a half-sheet pan with neutral oil and shape the meat mixture into a loaf. Brush with the glaze mixture. Scatter the sweet potatoes around the meatloaf and drizzle with a little more oil, using your hands to ensure the sweet potato is evenly coated. Lightly season with salt and pepper and transfer to the oven. (A pan of hot water under the meatloaf in the oven will help keep the top from cracking.)

Roast for 1 hour, or until the internal temperature of the meatloaf registers 145°F (63°C). Once or twice throughout the cooking, stir the sweet potatoes.

Remove the meatloaf from the oven and let sit for 5 minutes. Slice the meatloaf and divide it and the sweet potatoes among plates. Serve with quickles on the side.

Japanese Oven Burgers with Cabbage Salad

MAKES 10 BURGERS / SERVES 5

For the burgers

1 pound (454 g) ground beef
(80% lean/20% fat)

6 ounces (170 g) ground pork
(see Hot Tip!)

1 small yellow onion (7 oz/
198 g), very finely chopped
(see Hot Tip!)

½ cup (30 g) panko bread
crumbs

3 tablespoons whole milk

1 large egg

1¼ teaspoons kosher salt

1 teaspoon Dijon mustard

Pinch of freshly grated nutmeg

Freshly ground black pepper

1 tablespoon neutral oil, such
as canola or grapeseed

For the ketchup sauce

⅓ cup (95 g) ketchup

1 tablespoon Dijon mustard

2 teaspoons Worcestershire
sauce

2 teaspoons soy sauce

2 teaspoons dark brown sugar

2 tablespoons (1 oz/28 g)
unsalted butter, cut into small
pieces

ingredients continued

These Japanese burgers, known as *hambāgu* in Japanese, are such a comforting, nostalgic meal for me. My mother would make them with a red wine and ketchup sauce that was especially delicious, as it soaked into the short-grain rice. Because my kitchen has no ventilation—it's awkwardly placed in the middle of the apartment, the farthest point from all the windows—I particularly appreciate making patties in the oven on a sheet pan. I can make a big quantity (ten!) without setting off the fire alarm. The ketchup sauce is the best part and gets made right on the hot sheet pan as you scrape up bits and pieces and mix everything together. If you're not in the mood for cabbage, you can also serve the burgers and rice with a different vegetable, such as blanched broccoli, our Simplest Arugula Salad (page 274), or even some sliced cucumbers sprinkled with a little salt and vinegar.

Sanaë

Position a rack in the middle of the oven, set a half-sheet pan on it, and preheat to 425°F (220°C).

MAKE THE BURGERS: In a large bowl, combine the beef, pork, onion, panko, milk, egg, salt, mustard, nutmeg, and several grinds of black pepper. Using your hands, gently mix until fully combined. Refrigerate for 15 minutes.

Divide the burger mixture into 10 portions (about 3⅓ oz/95 g each) and shape into balls (yes, the patties are shaped like balls—Japanese burgers are thicker than American patties!).

Use an oven mitt to remove the hot sheet from the oven and add the neutral oil. Tilt the sheet pan to distribute the oil. Place the patties on the sheet pan, spacing them about 1 inch (2.5 cm) apart. Gently press your thumb into the center of each patty to slightly indent. Roast for 10 minutes, or until the edges are sizzling and the tops are opaque.

Using a thin metal spatula, flip the patties and roast for 6 to 8 minutes more, or until cooked through. (An instant-read thermometer inserted into the middle should register 160°F/71°C and the juices should run

continued

For the cabbage salad

¼ head green cabbage (about 10 oz/283 g)

1 tablespoon white wine vinegar

1½ teaspoons soy sauce

½ teaspoon Dijon mustard

3 tablespoons extra-virgin olive oil

Kosher salt

Short-Grain White Rice (page 271), for serving

clear.) If the burgers don't look browned enough, turn on the broiler and broil for 2 to 3 minutes, or until browned.

MAKE THE KETCHUP SAUCE: While the burgers cook, in a small bowl, stir together the ketchup, mustard, Worcestershire sauce, soy sauce, and brown sugar. Add the pieces of butter and set aside.

MAKE THE CABBAGE SALAD: Fill a large bowl with cold water. Remove the core from the cabbage and thinly slice the leaves. Place the cabbage in the cold water and set aside to soak for 5 minutes. Drain the cabbage and dry in a salad spinner. (If you don't have a salad spinner, drain in a fine-mesh sieve and pat dry with paper towels or clean kitchen towels.)

Dry the bowl from the cabbage. Add the vinegar, soy sauce, and mustard, and stir to combine. Whisk in the olive oil. Add the cabbage and toss to coat with the dressing. Taste and season with salt.

When the burgers are cooked, immediately transfer them to a plate. Add the ketchup sauce to the hot sheet and return to the 425°F (220°C) oven or with the broiler turned on for 1 to 2 minutes, or until the butter is completely melted and starts to foam.

Remove the pan from the oven. Using a silicone or wooden spatula, stir the sauce along the entire surface of the sheet pan, scraping up and mixing in any bits of meat until the sauce is smooth and combined.

Spoon the sauce over the burgers and serve alongside the cabbage salad and rice. Leftover burgers can be refrigerated in an airtight container for up to 3 days. I like to slather each burger with some sauce before storing. Reheat the burgers (with the sauce) in the oven or microwave.

HOT TIPS! Since the onion goes into the burger mixture raw, I like to chop it as finely as possible to avoid any larger raw pieces. You could also use a food processor to finely chop it.

You can use all ground beef for the burgers, though I find the combination of beef and pork to yield the juiciest patties.

Oven Milanesas with Tomato Salad

SERVES 2

For the milanesas

2 tablespoons extra-virgin olive oil, plus more for drizzling

Two 6-ounce (170 g) beef sirloin steaks

2 large eggs

¼ cup (60 ml) whole milk

½ cup (25 g) fresh flat-leaf parsley leaves, finely chopped

1 garlic clove, finely chopped

1½ teaspoons kosher salt, divided

Freshly ground black pepper

1 cup (112 g) fine dried bread crumbs

For the tomato salad

12 ounces (340 g) cherry or cocktail tomatoes, halved

½ medium red onion, thinly sliced (see Hot Tip!)

1 cup (50 g) fresh flat-leaf parsley leaves

1 tablespoon extra-virgin olive oil

2 teaspoons sherry vinegar or red wine vinegar

Kosher salt and freshly ground black pepper

For serving

1 lemon (optional)

My Japanese mother moved to Buenos Aires in her early twenties and stayed there for almost two decades. She married her first husband, had my brother, divorced, met my French father, and followed him to Paris. Although most of her cooking is Japanese, there are notable influences from her time in Argentina, such as these *milanesas*, which are my brother's favorite. It always felt like such a special occasion whenever we'd see her making bread crumbs from scratch (always with day-old baguette—probably because we lived in France!), pounding the beef, and mashing potatoes to serve on the side. Traditionally, milanesas are deep-fried, but my mother prefers to make them in the oven. The half-sheet pan is just the right size and the perfect vehicle for two large milanesas. My recipe makes two portions, but you could double the amounts and cook four milanesas on two sheet pans—just make sure to position the racks in the lower and upper thirds of the oven and to switch the sheet pans from top to bottom halfway through. Or you could cut each piece of beef in half to make four smaller milanesas. In which case, add a side of mashed potatoes to complete the meal for four.

Sanaë

MAKE THE MILANESAS: Position a rack in the middle of the oven and preheat to 425°F (220°F). Coat a half-sheet pan with the 2 tablespoons of oil.

Working with one at a time, place a steak between two pieces of plastic and, using a meat mallet or heavy skillet, pound to about a ⅛-inch (3 mm) thickness. (It's okay if some parts are even thinner, especially the edges, as they'll make for crispy pieces!)

In a large bowl, whisk together the eggs, milk, parsley, garlic, 1 teaspoon of the salt, and several grinds of black pepper. Add the beef and turn to coat. Set aside to soak for 30 minutes.

In a quarter-sheet pan or on a large plate, stir together the bread crumbs, the remaining ½ teaspoon salt, and several grinds of black pepper. Working with one at a time, lift a piece of beef, allowing the

continued

excess liquid to drip back into the bowl. Place in the bread crumbs and flip to coat all over, pressing to adhere and flipping again. The beef should be completely covered in bread crumbs. Transfer to the prepared half-sheet pan. Lightly drizzle each milanesa with some oil.

Bake the milanesas for about 15 minutes, or until sizzling and starting to brown at the edges and cooked through.

Turn on the broiler and broil for about 3 minutes, or until golden brown all over. Remove from the oven. Line two large plates with paper towels and transfer the milanesas to the plates. (This absorbs a little of the excess oil; you can skip this step if the milanesas don't look "oily.")

MAKE THE TOMATO SALAD: In a large bowl, toss together the tomatoes, onion, parsley, oil, and vinegar. Season with salt and pepper. Cut the lemon into wedges.

Serve the milanesas with the tomato salad and the lemon wedges, if you like, for squeezing over.

HOT TIP! My mother always soaks raw onion in cold water for 5 minutes before serving, which mellows its bite. If you have time, I recommend trying this extra step: Soak the sliced onion, then drain and pat dry before adding to the salad.

Merguez Meatball Pitas with Herby Yogurt

SERVES 4

For the merguez meatballs

1 pound (454 g) ground lamb

2 tablespoons finely chopped fresh cilantro

1 tablespoon finely chopped fresh mint

2 garlic cloves, minced or finely grated

1½ teaspoons kosher salt

1 teaspoon smoked paprika

½ teaspoon ground cumin

½ teaspoon ground coriander

½ teaspoon ground fennel

½ teaspoon cayenne pepper, or more to taste

For the herby yogurt

1 cup (255 g) whole-milk Greek yogurt

2 teaspoons chopped fresh cilantro

2 teaspoons chopped fresh mint

2 teaspoons chopped fresh dill

2 teaspoons harissa, plus more as needed

1 teaspoon finely grated lemon zest

2 tablespoons fresh lemon juice

ingredients continued

Merguez is a flavorful spiced lamb or beef sausage that has its origins in the Maghreb region and is popular throughout North African countries as well as the Middle East and France. Easy to make at home, even on a weeknight, I've often shaped the mixture into patties and seared them in a skillet. But because I loathe cleaning up oil splatters post frying—raise your hand if that's you, too—and because things are cuter when made small, I now shape the mixture into adorable little meatballs and roast them. Have a kid who hates burger patties or meatloaf? Turn them into meatballs and watch the little spheres vanish before your eyes. The added benefit of a meal that practically cooks itself is having the freedom to relax a bit. While the meatballs are roasting, make the salad, stir together the yogurt sauce, and pour yourself a glass of wine or sparkling water—you earned it!

Olga

MAKE THE MERGUEZ MEATBALLS: In a large bowl, combine the lamb, cilantro, mint, garlic, salt, smoked paprika, cumin, coriander, fennel, and cayenne and, using your hands, gently mix until thoroughly incorporated. Form the mixture into meatballs the size of golf balls and place on a half-sheet pan. Freeze for 10 minutes before cooking; it helps the meatballs keep their shape. (If you're not cooking the meatballs right away, cover and refrigerate for up to 4 days, or flash-freeze on the sheet pan before wrapping tightly and freezing for up to 3 months.)

Position a rack in the middle of the oven and preheat to 425°F (220°C).

MAKE THE HERBY YOGURT: While the meatballs are chilling and the oven is preheating, in a quart deli container (or a similar-sized container with tall sides), stir together the yogurt, cilantro, mint, dill, harissa, lemon zest, and lemon juice until combined. Using an immersion blender, process the mixture until smooth with tiny green flecks. Refrigerate until ready to use.

continued

For serving

4 pitas, halved and opened

1 cup (135 g) grape tomatoes, halved

½ small red onion (2 oz/60 g), thinly sliced

2 Persian (mini) cucumbers, halved lengthwise and sliced crosswise

4 to 6 radishes, sliced

A handful of fresh herbs and their tender stems, such as parsley, mint, cilantro, and dill

Roast the meatballs for about 12 minutes, or until cooked through and the centers are no longer pink.

TO SERVE: Divide the pitas and meatballs among four plates. Divide the yogurt sauce among small bowls and set them on each plate. Have each person assemble their own pita pockets by stuffing them with the meatballs, drizzling with the yogurt sauce, and adding vegetables and herbs to their sandwiches.

Open-Face Croque-Monsieur

SERVES 6

⅔ cup (150 g) crème fraîche

1 cup (50 g) fresh basil leaves, finely chopped

Finely grated zest of 1 lemon (see Hot Tip!)

2 teaspoons smoked paprika

½ teaspoon kosher salt

Freshly ground black pepper

6 slices milk bread or soft white bread, such as sandwich bread or brioche

2 tablespoons (1 oz/28 g) unsalted butter, at room temperature

6 ounces (170 g) sliced ham

2 cups (4 oz/113 g) grated Gruyère cheese

Cornichons (optional), for serving

Simplest Arugula Salad, for serving (optional; page 274)

> **HOT TIP!** If you are making the arugula salad to go with this, reserve the zested lemon and use its juice to dress the salad.

We love a croque-monsieur, but often find that it's too much bread and we don't particularly like the richness of béchamel. We wanted all those delicious flavors without the feeling of a brick in our stomachs. Our solution was an open-face sandwich (the sheet pan allows you to make 6 in one go!) and using thick slices of milk bread, though any soft bread would work nicely. Instead of béchamel, a crème fraîche mixture flavored with lemon zest, paprika, and basil melts right into the bread and feels indulgent without being too heavy. The bottom of the bread gets golden and toasted, the middle remains soft, while the top bubbles into a cheesy crust. It's a splendid contrast of textures.

If you have leftover milk bread, it makes for the most delicious breakfast toast. Sanaë's favorite toppings are salted butter, tahini, and honey, or just salted butter and fruit preserves (ideally, cherry!).

Sanaë + Olga

Position a rack in the middle of the oven and preheat to 400°F (200°C).

In a small bowl, stir together the crème fraîche, basil, lemon zest, smoked paprika, and salt. Season with a few grinds of black pepper and stir to combine.

Line a half-sheet pan with parchment paper. Working with one at a time, butter one side of each slice of bread, edge to edge. Place the slices, buttered side down, on the prepared sheet pan. Spread the crème fraîche mixture on the bread, about 2 tablespoons per slice, spreading from edge to edge. Top with the ham, folding the slices in half to fit on the bread, if needed. Sprinkle the Gruyère over the ham.

Bake for 10 to 14 minutes, or until the cheese is melted and the bottom of the bread is golden (lift a corner with a spatula to check). Turn on the broiler and broil for 2 to 3 minutes, or until the cheese is golden brown.

Serve immediately. If desired, accompany with cornichons and arugula salad.

Rack of Lamb with Baby Potatoes

SERVES 4 TO 6

4 large garlic cloves

3 sprigs fresh rosemary, leaves picked and finely chopped, divided

1 tablespoon plus ¾ teaspoon kosher salt

½ teaspoon freshly ground black pepper

⅓ cup (80 g) Dijon mustard

1½ tablespoons honey, plus more to taste

Two 1½-pound (680 g) racks of lamb, thoroughly patted dry and fat cap scored

2 tablespoons extra-virgin olive oil, plus more for the pan

2 pounds (900 g) baby potatoes, halved if large

HOT TIP! Out of Dijon mustard, as I once was while testing this recipe? Don't panic and, instead, use 1½ teaspoons mustard powder and 2 to 3 tablespoons extra-virgin olive oil. (The other paste ingredients stay the same.) Process in the food processor to form a smooth paste and proceed without anxiety.

This might be my go-to impress-your-guests-who-eat-meat recipe because it takes about half an hour and makes me look like a fancy-pants chef. While roasting a rack of lamb and potatoes is not exactly new—nor is pairing them with rosemary—the honey-Dijon mustard paste that flavors the lamb will steal the scene. Score the lamb so the fat can render and roast the meat fat cap side up. I love using teeny tiny baby potatoes for this, but if you can't find those, halved small potatoes work well, too—just be sure to roast them cut side down.

Olga

In a food processor, pulse together the garlic, two-thirds of the rosemary, 1 tablespoon of the salt, and the pepper until the rosemary leaves are minced and the mixture is paste-like. Add the mustard and honey and process until completely uniform, about 1 minute more. Taste and add more honey if the flavors aren't quite balanced.

Spread the mustard mixture all over the lamb—aim for about one-third of the mixture to coat the bottom side (the non-fat cap part) and the remaining two-thirds to cover the fat-cap side.

Lightly grease a half-sheet pan with oil and transfer the lamb to it, fat cap up; set aside while you preheat the oven. (You can also prepare the lamb and refrigerate it, uncovered, for up to 8 hours.)

Position racks in the middle and lower third of the oven and preheat to 450°F (230°C).

On another half-sheet pan, toss the potatoes with the 2 tablespoons oil, the remaining ¾ teaspoon salt, and the remaining rosemary until evenly coated.

Transfer the lamb to the middle rack and the potatoes to the lower rack and roast for 25 to 30 minutes, or until the internal temperature of the lamb reaches about 125°F (52°C) on an instant-read thermometer for medium-rare. The potatoes should be tender and browned in spots.

Remove from the oven, cover the lamb with foil, and let rest for 15 minutes.

Cut into individual ribs—at my house, we call these lamb-sicles—and serve.

Lamb-Stuffed Tomatoes with Fancy Hats (Tomates Farcies)

10 medium tomatoes on the
vine (3½ lb/1.6 kg total)

2 teaspoons kosher salt, plus
more as needed

1 large red onion (12 oz/340 g)

3 tablespoons extra-virgin
olive oil

Freshly ground black pepper

1 cup (50 g) fresh flat-leaf
parsley leaves, finely chopped

½ cup (60 g) crumbled feta
cheese

½ cup (30 g) panko bread
crumbs

½ cup (25 g) fresh mint leaves,
finely chopped, or 1 teaspoon
dried

¼ cup (60 ml) heavy cream

2 large egg yolks

¼ cup (40 g) dried currants or
⅓ cup (60 g) golden raisins

2 garlic cloves, finely chopped

Finely grated zest of 1 lemon

1 teaspoon ground cumin

½ teaspoon ground coriander

1 pound (454 g) ground lamb

I love *tomates farcies*—stuffed tomatoes in French, or tomatoes with fancy hats as Olga likes to call them—in the late summer when tomatoes are at their ripest. But sometimes I'll make them in the middle of winter with greenhouse tomatoes because I long for their concentrated sweetness and the gently spiced lamb filling. This recipe is a labor of love—I don't recommend it for a weeknight when you want to quickly put dinner on the table. Though not technically difficult, it requires some patience and time: You will scoop out the insides of 10 tomatoes, taking care not to break their skin, and fill them one by one. The result is so delicious and impressive that I think it's well worth the effort. The leftovers keep for up to 4 days and can be reheated in the oven. If anything, I find the flavors improve over time.

Most traditional recipes have you cook the filling first on the stove, but I wanted the oven to do all the work, so I created a tender filling with egg yolks and a bit of heavy cream. Don't worry if some of the tomatoes burst in the oven, it'll give them more character. I love to serve these with Short-Grain White Rice (page 271) or simply dressed greens.

Sanaë

Position a rack in the middle of the oven and preheat to 400°F (200°C). Set a wire rack inside a half-sheet pan.

Using a sharp paring knife, cut off the tops of the tomatoes. Don't discard the tops—they will be the "hats" for the stuffed tomatoes. Set a fine-mesh sieve over a large bowl. Using the knife and a small spoon, and working over the sieve, scoop out the seeds and flesh from the tomatoes. (Be careful not to tear the skin.) Transfer the emptied tomatoes to the wire rack set inside the sheet pan. Salt the tomato "hats" and insides of the emptied tomatoes and place them upside down on the rack to drain.

Drain the scooped tomato insides in the sieve. Discard the liquid and most of the seeds, keeping only the flesh. Coarsely chop any large pieces and transfer to another half-sheet pan.

Thinly slice half of the onion and transfer to the sheet pan with the tomato flesh. Add the oil, season lightly with salt and pepper, and stir to combine. Spread in an even layer and set aside.

Chop the remaining onion half as finely as possible (to avoid big pieces of raw onion in the filling!), and transfer to a large bowl. Add the parsley, feta, panko, mint, cream, egg yolks, currants, garlic, lemon zest, the 2 teaspoons salt, cumin, coriander, and lots of pepper. Mix well to thoroughly combine. Add one-third of the ground lamb and mix thoroughly to combine. Add the remaining lamb and, using your hands, gently mix until just combined. (Do not overmix.)

Flip the tomatoes so they are cut side up. Using paper towels or a clean kitchen towel, gently pat the tomatoes dry (they will have released some liquid). Fill the tomatoes with the lamb mixture, mounding on the top. Arrange the stuffed tomatoes on the sheet pan with the tomato flesh and onions. Cover with the reserved tomato "hats." (If you have leftover filling, you can make meatballs and bake them on the sheet pan alongside the stuffed tomatoes.)

Bake the tomatoes for 40 to 45 minutes, stirring the onion-tomato mixture halfway through, or until the filling is cooked through and the tomato skins are wrinkled. The internal temperature of the filling should reach 145°F (63°C). Set aside for 5 minutes (the filling will be piping hot) before serving.

Quick Sheet Pan Chili

SERVES 6

4 tablespoons olive oil, divided

1 pound (454 g) ground beef (93% lean/7% fat; see Hot Tip!)

Kosher salt and freshly ground black pepper

1 medium yellow onion (8 oz/227 g), chopped

2 green bell peppers, chopped

2 garlic cloves, minced

1 tablespoon chili powder

1 teaspoon ground cumin

1 teaspoon dried oregano

One 28-ounce (794 g) can chopped tomatoes, preferably fire-roasted, with their juices

One 15-ounce (425 g) can black beans, drained and rinsed

1 cup (240 ml) amber ale

½ cup (120 ml) brewed coffee

¼ cup (55 g) packed brown sugar, any kind

1 tablespoon unsweetened cocoa powder

¼ cup (10 g) chopped fresh cilantro

Chopped avocado, chopped scallions, shredded cheese, and/or sour cream, for serving

I learned to make chili in college, and it was a budget meal that never disappointed. One of my friends taught me to add coffee, amber beer, and unsweetened cocoa powder—ingredients that reward you with deeply flavorful results. In my house, we eat our chili with rice, which is untraditional, but it really hits the spot.

Olga

Position a rack in the middle of the oven and preheat to 375°F (190°C).

Spread 2 tablespoons of the oil on a half-sheet pan. Add the beef and lightly season with salt and black pepper. Roast for 5 minutes, or until the beef has very little pink remaining.

Add the onion, season with a pinch each of salt and pepper, and roast for about 10 minutes, or until the onion starts to brown. Add the bell peppers, garlic, chili powder, cumin, and oregano and stir to combine. Drizzle with the remaining 2 tablespoons oil and return to the oven. Roast for another 10 minutes, or until the peppers soften.

Add the tomatoes, beans, beer, coffee, brown sugar, cocoa powder, and salt to taste and stir to combine.

Carefully, using oven mitts, cover the sheet pan with foil and secure the edges by crimping around (you can also cover it with a turned-over sheet pan, if you like). Return to the oven and roast for about 40 minutes, or until the chili looks stewy and saucy and the vegetables are soft.

Remove the foil or top sheet pan and roast for another 10 to 15 minutes, or until the chili thickens. Remove from the oven, taste, and season with more salt and/or pepper, if desired.

Divide the chili among six bowls, top with the cilantro, avocado, scallions, cheese, and/or sour cream, and serve hot.

HOT TIP! Chili lends itself spectacularly to different proteins. In place of beef, use ground chicken or turkey, or keep the dish vegetarian or vegan with plant-based ground meat, lentils, tempeh, diced tofu (add that alongside the beans), double the amount of beans, or opt for chickpeas.

Crispy Ramen with Cabbage and Bacon

SERVES 4 TO 6

1¼ pounds (567 g) green cabbage, cut into 1-inch (2.5 cm) pieces (½ head)

6 scallions, cut into 1-inch (2.5 cm) pieces

1 large carrot (4 oz/113 g), thinly sliced on the bias

4 slices bacon (3 oz/85 g), cut crosswise into 1-inch (2.5 cm) pieces

One 2-inch (5 cm) piece fresh ginger, cut into thin matchsticks (see Hot Tip! on page 148)

3 tablespoons extra-virgin olive oil

Kosher salt and freshly ground black pepper

3 tablespoons toasted sesame oil

2 tablespoons oyster sauce

2 tablespoons soy sauce

1 tablespoon Worcestershire sauce

20 ounces (567 g) fresh ramen noodles, such as Sun Noodle Kaedama

Furikake (optional), for serving

This is one of my favorite recipes in the book. It's an ode to all the crispy noodles my mother made for me throughout my childhood. She always prepared hers with lots of scallions and ginger and seasoned them with soy sauce. I'd sneak back into the kitchen and scrape the pan for the crunchiest remains, while she'd chastise me for wanting to eat the "burnt" parts. I've expanded on my memory of her recipe, adding bacon and cabbage, and of course achieving crispiness on a sheet pan. The sheet pan does double duty, first softening the cabbage and rendering the bacon pieces, and then crisping up a large portion of noodles. You'll have to boil them on the stove first, but since they're fresh, it will only take a few minutes. The sprinkle of furikake at the end is optional, but it's become my preferred way of serving this dish. The inspiration came from my friend Fernanda, who ate most of the leftovers as I was developing recipes. One day, she was eating the fourth iteration of these noodles and had the brilliant idea to season them with furikake.

Sanaë

Position two racks in the middle and lower third of the oven and preheat to 425°F (220°C). Bring a large pot of water to a boil.

On a half-sheet pan, toss together the cabbage, scallions, carrot, bacon, ginger, and olive oil. Season with salt and pepper and stir to combine. Roast on the middle rack for 15 to 20 minutes, or until the cabbage starts to soften and brown.

Meanwhile, in a small bowl, stir together the sesame oil, oyster sauce, soy sauce, and Worcestershire sauce. Set aside.

Add the ramen noodles to the boiling water and cook according to the package directions. Drain and rinse under cold water. (This helps keep the noodles separate.)

Remove the hot sheet from the oven and add the noodles and sauce. Toss everything to coat well; I find it easiest to use chopsticks or tongs. Spread in an even layer, pushing some of the noodles to the edges (they'll get very crispy there).

continued

HOT TIPS! If you can't find fresh ramen noodles, replace them with 12 ounces (340 g) of spaghetti. Boil until al dente, rinse and drain, and add to the sheet pan, following the same directions as for the ramen.

Roast on the lower rack for 25 to 30 minutes, or until the noodles are browned and crispy at the edges. Using a metal spatula, turn and toss the noodles to reveal the crispy pieces. (For even crispier noodles, re-spread in an even layer and roast for 5 minutes more.)

Sprinkle with the furikake, if desired, and serve immediately.

FOR VEGETARIAN CRISPY NOODLES, replace the bacon with 7 ounces (198 g) fresh shiitake and/or maitake mushrooms, quartered or torn into bite-size pieces, and add an additional 1 tablespoon sesame oil to the sauce.

Roasted Cabbage with Sausages and Orange

SERVES 4

1½ pounds (680 g) Savoy or green cabbage

1 medium red onion (7 oz/ 198 g), halved and cut into slices ½ inch (1.3 cm) thick

1 navel orange (see Hot Tip!)

¼ cup (60 ml) extra-virgin olive oil

1 teaspoon kosher salt, plus more to taste

Freshly ground black pepper

1 pound (454 g) mild or spicy Italian sausage

Fresh flat-leaf parsley or oregano leaves, for serving

HOT TIP! Yes, you're only using the zest of the orange here. Please don't throw out the flesh! I usually snack on the orange while the oven is doing all the work, or I'll save it for a sweet after-dinner treat.

Roasted cabbage and sausage is one of my favorite combinations. The cabbage softens and chars while the sausage pieces turn crisp and golden. If you have a big cabbage head, weigh it and cut it down, otherwise it'll be too much vegetable for the sheet pan and it will steam rather than caramelize. (Tightly wrap any remaining cabbage and refrigerate. It will keep for a while; just trim any browned parts.) I like to squeeze the sausage from its casings to make small "meatballs" that get very crispy in the oven. Keep in mind that the edges of the sheet pan get hotter than the center. I always place bigger pieces of cabbage, like the thick rib or core, close to the edges, as those take longer to cook.

Sanaë

Position racks in the lower and upper thirds of the oven and preheat to 450°F (230°C).

Cut the cabbage through the core into quarters, then cut away the thick center core. Cut into 1-inch (2.5 cm) wedges. On a half-sheet pan, arrange the cabbage and onion in an even layer. Using a vegetable peeler, peel strips of orange zest onto the sheet pan. Drizzle everything with the oil and season with the salt and lots of pepper. Gently toss the ingredients and flip the cabbage to coat in the oil, doing your best not to break apart the wedges too much. Place the thicker pieces of cabbage close to the edges of the pan.

Squeeze the sausage out of its casings onto the sheet pan into about 1-tablespoon amounts, evenly placing the "meatballs" between and over the cabbage and onions. For even crispier bits, make the sausage pieces smaller.

Roast on the lower rack, flipping the cabbage halfway through, for 25 to 35 minutes, or until the cabbage softens, the onions caramelize, and the sausage starts to brown.

Turn on the broiler and move the sheet pan to the top rack. Broil for 2 to 3 minutes, or until everything is deeply golden and the cabbage is starting to char.

Sprinkle with the parsley, season with more salt if desired, and serve.

Vietnamese Caramel Pork Chops with Snow Peas

SERVES 4

¼ cup (55 g) plus
2 tablespoons dark brown
sugar, plus more to taste

1 teaspoon ground fennel

1 teaspoon kosher salt

½ teaspoon ground white
pepper

¼ teaspoon ground cloves

4 boneless pork loin chops
(6 oz/170 g each), ¾ to 1 inch
(2 to 2.5 cm) thick, patted dry

Neutral oil, such as grapeseed
(ideal for high-heat cooking)

½ cup fresh lime juice (from
3 to 4 limes)

3 tablespoons fish sauce, plus
more to taste

1 small garlic clove, minced or
finely grated

¼ bird's eye chile, minced
(optional)

½ small head red cabbage,
shredded

12 ounces (340 g) snow peas

2 tablespoons tamarind
concentrate

Fresh cilantro leaves, for
serving

Cooked jasmine rice
(optional), for serving

The combination of sweet, salty, sour, and spicy is one I can never resist. And when I made pork chops this way, the result was succulent meat with bright, assertive flavors. To make nuoc cham, one of the foundational sauces in Vietnamese cuisine—I learned mine from cookbook author Andrea Nguyen—use a quality fish sauce, such as Red Boat, as you'll really taste its flavor here. Another useful tip from Andrea: To find a juicy lime, look for fruit with smooth, shiny skin. Use leftovers in a salad or a grain bowl. Throwing a shredded carrot into leftover nuoc cham will give you delicious quickles (see page 273).

Olga

In a small bowl, combine ¼ cup (55g) of the brown sugar, the fennel, salt, white pepper, and cloves. Rub the mixture all over the pork and cure for 1 hour at room temperature, or cover and refrigerate for up to 10 hours.

When ready to cook, position racks in the middle and upper third of the oven (about 6 inches away from the broiler) and preheat to 450°F (230°C). Grease a half-sheet pan with some oil and place the pork chops on it. Lightly brush the meat with oil.

In a small bowl, whisk together the lime juice, the remaining 2 tablespoons brown sugar, the fish sauce, garlic, and chile (if using). This is your nuoc cham dipping sauce. Taste and add more sugar, chile (if using), and/or fish sauce until your nuoc cham tastes bright and balanced. Drizzle each pork chop with 1 tablespoon of the sauce and transfer to the oven.

Roast for about 7 minutes, or until the meat starts to brown.

Meanwhile, toss the cabbage with 1 tablespoon of the nuoc cham and a drizzle of oil. Taste and add more nuoc cham, if desired. Set aside.

Turn on the broiler. Add the snow peas to the sheet pan, drizzle with a little oil, and gently stir to coat. Brush the pork chops with the tamarind concentrate. Return the sheet pan top rack of the oven. Broil for 2 to 3 minutes, watching carefully, or until the meat is caramelized and the snow peas start to blister and brown.

Remove from the oven and immediately scatter the cilantro leaves over the meat, letting them slightly wilt in the heat. Let the pork chops sit undisturbed for about 10 minutes before serving with the cabbage and nuoc cham. If desired, serve with rice.

Chapter 5

From the Sea

Fish and Shellfish

Hot Maple-Coconut Shrimp with Mango and Broccoli

SERVES 4

1 pound (454 g) large shrimp, peeled and deveined, tails left on

1 lime

3 tablespoons coconut oil, divided, plus more as needed

1 pound (454 g) broccoli, cut into florets

½ teaspoon kosher salt, plus more as needed

¼ teaspoon freshly ground black pepper, plus more as needed

2 tablespoons maple syrup

1 tablespoon sambal oelek, plus more for serving

½ teaspoon ground ginger

½ teaspoon ground coriander

¼ teaspoon garlic powder

⅛ teaspoon cayenne pepper, or more to taste

Fresh cilantro sprigs, Thai basil leaves, and/or mint leaves, for serving

Flesh of 1 mango, roughly chopped, for serving

Toasted coconut chips, for serving

Cooked jasmine rice, for serving

Shrimp and broccoli are a classic pairing and I have lots of sheet pan permutations of it, but this is probably my favorite. There was a time when hot honey was all the rage (it still might be, I no longer know what's trendy) and was drizzled on anything from toast to pizza. I'm always a sucker for a sweet-hot combination, and here I wanted to combine it with shrimp and broccoli. Serving this with fresh, room-temperature mango and cooked rice makes for a simple dinner that somehow feels brighter and more festive than the ingredients let on. Don't use frozen shrimp for this dish—they release too much liquid even after thawing. (And, yes, I'm aware that most shrimp is flash-frozen and thawed before we buy it but somehow it makes a difference.) Leave the shell on the shrimp tails to protect the tender meat from drying out.

Olga

Position a rack in the middle of the oven and preheat to 475°F (250C).

Thoroughly pat the shrimp dry on all sides with paper towels or clean kitchen towels. Using a rasp grater such as a Microplane, zest the lime into a medium bowl; reserve the lime.

Add 2 tablespoons of the coconut oil to a half-sheet pan and place in the oven for 1 minute, or until it melts. Remove the hot sheet from the oven and carefully tilt it around to spread the melted oil so it covers the bottom of the pan, then set on a heatproof surface. Add the broccoli, season with the salt and black pepper, and toss to combine. Transfer to the oven and roast for about 7 minutes, or until starting to brown and crisp up in places.

Meanwhile, to the bowl with the lime zest, add the maple syrup, sambal oelek, ginger, coriander, garlic powder, cayenne pepper, a generous pinch of salt, and a few grinds of black pepper and stir until combined. Add the shrimp and toss to combine.

Remove the sheet pan from the oven and move the broccoli to one side of the pan. Spread the shrimp out in a single layer on the other

continued

side, making sure the shrimp aren't touching. Dot the shrimp with the remaining 1 tablespoon coconut oil. Roast for about 5 minutes, or until the shrimp turn pink and opaque.

While the shrimp are roasting, cut the zested lime into wedges.

Remove the shrimp and broccoli from the oven and immediately top with the herbs, letting them slightly wilt in the heat.

Divide among four bowls, garnish with the mango and coconut chips, and serve with the rice and lime wedges for squeezing over.

Oven Fish Tacos with Avocado, Radishes, and Cumin-Lime Crema

SERVES 4

For the fish

Neutral oil, such as canola or grapeseed for the pan

1 pound (454 g) flaky fish fillets, such as tilapia, cod, or haddock

1 teaspoon kosher salt

½ teaspoon ground cumin

½ teaspoon chili powder

½ teaspoon chipotle chile powder

¼ teaspoon freshly ground black pepper

For the guacamole

3 medium avocados, halved and pitted

¼ cup (40 g) chopped tomato

2 tablespoons finely chopped white onion

2 tablespoons chopped fresh cilantro leaves

½ jalapeño, seeded for less heat and finely chopped

Kosher salt and freshly ground black pepper

Juice of ½ lime, plus more to taste

ingredients continued

Years ago, I went over to my friends Jane and Geoff's house for a dinner party and was excited to learn we were having fish tacos. But I felt bad for Geoff, the main cook in the family, because I imagined he would be stuck in the kitchen most of the night cooking fish for a hungry group of ten adults. My mind was completely blown when Geoff informed us that when he's serving a group, the fish for the tacos goes in the oven. It was such a smart and practical approach that whenever I get asked for a recommendation to serve a crowd, fish tacos is one of the first things I mention. In addition to feeding a crowd—this recipe doubles easily for a dinner party—you avoid the splatter messes that come with frying, and it frees you up to make guacamole and cumin-lime crema, or mix up a batch of margaritas or mint limeade.

Olga

ROAST THE FISH: Position a rack in the middle of the oven and preheat to 425°F (220°C). Lightly grease a half-sheet pan with oil.

Pat the fish fillets dry. In a small bowl, stir together the salt, cumin, chili powder, chipotle powder, and black pepper. Rub the spice mixture all over the fillets and place them on the prepared sheet pan.

Roast for 12 to 14 minutes, or until the fish is fully cooked through and just flakes when tested with a fork.

MAKE THE GUACAMOLE: While the fish is roasting, scoop out the avocado flesh into a medium bowl and lightly mash with a fork or a potato masher (you want the avocado to retain enough texture to keep it interesting). Add the tomato, onion, cilantro, and jalapeño. Season to taste with salt and black pepper and gently stir to combine. Add the lime juice and give another gentle stir to combine. Taste and adjust the seasonings as needed. Cover the bowl with a plate while you wait for the fish to cook through.

continued on page 144

For the cumin-lime crema

½ cup (113 g) sour cream

½ teaspoon finely grated lime zest

¼ teaspoon ground cumin

A squeeze of fresh lime juice

Pinch of kosher salt

For assembly

Warmed corn tortillas

Jalapeño-Onion Quickles (page 273)

Radishes, cut into matchsticks

Fresh cilantro leaves

MAKE THE CUMIN-LIME CREMA: In a small bowl, stir together the sour cream, lime zest, cumin, lime juice, and salt until combined.

ASSEMBLE THE TACOS: When the fish is done, serve it tableside on the sheet pan set over a trivet. Be careful, the sheet pan will be hot. (Alternatively, you can transfer the fish to a serving platter.) Set up a station so everyone can assemble their own tacos: warm tortillas, guacamole, crema, quickles, radishes, and cilantro.

Oven Paella with Chicken, Chorizo, and Shrimp

SERVES 6

4 tablespoons extra-virgin olive oil, divided, plus more for drizzling

3 teaspoons sweet paprika, divided

2 teaspoons kosher salt, plus more as needed

Freshly ground black pepper

2 to 2½ pounds (1 kg) boneless, skinless chicken thighs

One 14.5-ounce (411 g) can diced tomatoes

1 large white or yellow onion (10 oz/283 g), halved and thinly sliced

3 ounces (85 g) cured Spanish chorizo, thinly sliced

3 garlic cloves, thinly sliced

Pinch of saffron threads (about ⅛ teaspoon), crumbled

¼ cup (60 ml) dry white wine (see Hot Tips!)

¼ cup (60 ml) clam juice, preferably from a glass bottle

1 cup (215 g) bomba or Arborio rice (see Hot Tips!)

8 ounces (227 g) large shrimp, peeled and deveined, tails left on

ingredients continued

This is not a traditional paella—you won't get the same layering of flavor and the iconic crispy *socarrat* bottom throughout. However, the flavors are reminiscent of a paella and utterly scrumptious, and the rice along the edges of the sheet pan gets caramelized and crispy. Every time I make this dish, I find myself standing by the stove, scraping up and eating the remains from the sheet pan with a spoon. Since you'll have plenty of saltiness from the chorizo and olives, go light on the seasoning throughout. You can always season to taste at the end.

If you are making this paella for guests and don't want to be cooking when they arrive, you could prepare the chicken and rice up to an hour before serving. Keep the sheet pan covered with foil or another sheet pan at room temperature. Then preheat the oven to 425°F (220°C), add the peas and shrimp, and return the paella to the oven. By the time the shrimp is cooked, the rice will be heated through.

Sanaë

Position a rack in the bottom third of the oven and preheat to 425°F (220°C).

In a medium bowl, stir together 2 tablespoons of the oil, 2 teaspoons of the paprika, the salt, and several grinds of black pepper. Add the chicken and coat well in the mixture.

On a half-sheet pan, toss together the tomatoes with their juices, onion, chorizo, garlic, 1 tablespoon of the oil, and the remaining 1 teaspoon paprika. Lightly season with salt. Place the chicken over the mixture.

Roast for about 25 minutes, or until the onions are softened and the chicken is cooked through.

Meanwhile, in a large spouted measuring cup or bowl, combine the saffron with 1½ cups (350 ml) water. Add the wine and clam juice and stir to combine.

continued

1 cup (140 g) frozen peas

1 cup (50 g) fresh flat-leaf parsley leaves, coarsely chopped

⅓ cup (65 g) pimiento-stuffed green olives

1 lemon, cut into wedges

When the chicken is cooked, remove the hot sheet from the oven and transfer the chicken to a plate. Evenly sprinkle the rice over the tomato-chorizo mixture, season with salt, and stir well to combine. Spread the rice-tomato-chorizo mixture into an even layer. Return the chicken to the pan, placing it over the rice mixture. Drizzle the saffron water mixture over the rice and around the chicken, making sure that each grain of rice is a little submerged in liquid.

Return the pan to the oven and bake for about 5 minutes, or until the liquid at the edges is bubbling.

Cover the sheet pan of paella with a second turned-over sheet pan (carefully slide it onto the lower sheet pan) and bake for about 25 minutes, or until the rice is tender and the liquid is absorbed. (If you don't have a second sheet pan, tightly cover the pan with aluminum foil, being careful not to burn yourself.)

Meanwhile, thoroughly pat the shrimp dry on all sides. In a medium bowl, toss the shrimp with the remaining 1 tablespoon oil and season with salt and pepper.

Remove the top sheet pan (or foil). Scatter the peas over the rice and add the shrimp. Drizzle with a little oil and bake for about 8 minutes, or until the shrimp is opaque and just cooked through.

Top with the parsley and olives. Serve with the lemon wedges for squeezing over.

HOT TIPS! You can replace the white wine with 2 tablespoons white wine vinegar plus 2 tablespoons water.

If you can't find bomba or Arborio rice, use sushi rice, though the texture will be a bit different.

Fish over Cabbage with Sambal Oelek Sauce

SERVES 4

½ head green cabbage
(1¼ lb/567 g)

One 1½-inch (4 cm) piece
fresh ginger, cut into thin
matchsticks (see Hot Tip!)

3 tablespoons extra-virgin
olive oil

Kosher salt and freshly ground
black pepper

1 large cod fillet (1½ lb/680 g)

12 sprigs fresh cilantro, plus
more for garnish

For the sambal oelek sauce

2 tablespoons sambal oelek

2 tablespoons toasted
sesame oil

2 teaspoons soy sauce

2 teaspoons rice vinegar

2 teaspoons dark brown sugar

Short-Grain White Rice (page
271), for serving

> **HOT TIP!** To cut
> ginger into thin
> matchsticks, thinly
> slice it, then stack
> the slices and thinly
> slice again.

I can't get enough of roasted cabbage, so forgive me for yet another cabbage recipe, but I love how it transforms in the oven—its natural sweetness enhanced, the thicker ribs soft enough to break apart with a fork, the curled edges charred and crispy. Plus, it pairs so well with ginger and fish for this easy weeknight meal. With the oven's high heat, the large cabbage leaves collapse and become pliable enough to wrap around the fish and rice. As a result, my favorite way of eating this dish is using chopsticks to make little cabbage/fish/rice packets, so I get all the flavors in one bite. Sambal oelek, an Indonesian chile paste, provides a welcome lingering heat. Taste it first and add as much or as little as you like depending on how spicy you prefer your food.

Sanaë

Position a rack in the middle of the oven and preheat to 425°F (220°C).

Cut the cabbage half in half through the core. Cut out the thick core and separate the leaves. On a half-sheet pan, toss the cabbage leaves with the ginger and olive oil and season with salt and pepper. Place the thicker leaves and ribs closer to the edges of the sheet pan.

Roast for about 10 minutes, or until the cabbage is starting to wilt and brown at the edges. Remove from the oven, stir the cabbage, and redistribute in an even layer.

Season the fish on both sides with salt and pepper. Place the cilantro sprigs on the cabbage in the center of the sheet pan. Place the fish over the cilantro. Return to the oven and roast for 12 to 15 minutes, or until the fish is cooked through and just flakes when tested with a fork. (The cooking time will vary depending on the thickness of the fillet.)

MAKE THE SAMBAL OELEK SAUCE: While the fish cooks, in a small bowl, stir together the sambal oelek, sesame oil, soy sauce, vinegar, and brown sugar until combined.

Divide the rice, cabbage, and fish among four plates or bowls. Garnish with cilantro sprigs and serve with the sambal oelek sauce for drizzling over everything.

Branzino with Asparagus and Scallions

SERVES 4

12 ounces (340 g) asparagus, woody ends trimmed

2 bunches scallions, white and light-green parts only, left whole

2 tablespoons plus 4 teaspoons extra-virgin olive oil, plus more for drizzling

½ teaspoon kosher salt, plus more for the fish

¼ teaspoon freshly ground black pepper, plus more for the fish

2 head-on whole fish (2 lb/ 1 kg each), such as branzino, gutted and scaled (see Hot Tip!)

8 thin lemon slices, plus lemon wedges for squeezing

8 sprigs fresh flat-leaf parsley, plus more (optional) for garnish

4 sprigs fresh oregano, rosemary, or thyme

2 garlic cloves, thinly sliced

Flaky sea salt, for sprinkling

> **HOT TIP!** How to tell if your whole fish is fresh? Start by looking at its eyes: They should be clear. The fish should smell pleasantly of the sea and the scales should be intact.

Few things are easier to pull off in the kitchen—and look more impressive—than a whole roasted fish. It takes minutes to throw together, needs minimal ingredients to taste amazing (provided, of course, your fish is fresh), and comes together in a flash. Here, you do barely any chopping as you prep the vegetables, which you spread out in a layer before topping them with the whole fish. They cook together and are ready at the same time. All under 20 minutes. I know that some folks are put off by a head-on fish, but then you miss out on the tastiest morsel—the fish cheeks (and yes, for branzino, they are *tiny*!). A little of your best olive oil—the kind you'd want to sip—goes a long way, as does a squeeze of lemon and a pinch of flaky sea salt right before serving. It turns an ordinary meal into something that truly sings.

Olga

Position a rack in the middle of the oven and preheat to 450°F (230°C). Line a half-sheet pan with parchment paper.

Add the asparagus and scallions to the sheet pan and drizzle with 2 tablespoons of the oil, shaking the pan lightly until well coated. Season with the kosher salt and pepper and set aside.

Pat the fish dry and drizzle with the remaining 4 teaspoons oil. Generously season the inside and outside of each fish with kosher salt and pepper. Dividing evenly, stuff the fish cavities with the lemon slices, parsley, oregano, and garlic. You can use kitchen twine to tie the fish so it stays more intact.

Set the fish atop the vegetables. Transfer to the oven and roast for 12 to 15 minutes, or until the fish skin starts to blister, its flesh turns opaque and just flakes when tested with a fork, and the asparagus tips start to crisp up.

Garnish the fish and vegetables with a sprinkling of parsley, if you like, and serve with lemon wedges, extra-virgin olive oil, and flaky sea salt alongside for squeezing, drizzling, and sprinkling.

Salmon with Baby Bok Choy and Soy-Ginger Sauce

SERVES 4

1 pound (454 g) baby
bok choy

6 scallions, root ends trimmed

4 tablespoons extra-virgin
olive oil, divided

Kosher salt and freshly ground
black pepper

One 2-inch (5 cm) piece
fresh ginger

Juice of ½ lemon

2 tablespoons soy sauce

4 skin-on salmon fillets
(6 oz/170 g each)

Short-Grain White Rice
(page 271)

I've always loved the combination of extra-virgin olive oil and soy sauce (see our soy sauce and olive oil dip for focaccia on page 44). In fact, my childhood breakfast of choice was a steamed bun dipped in a bowl of olive oil mixed with soy sauce. It's my Japanese mother's signature blend, and one I've incorporated into my own cooking.

In this recipe, the fruitiness of olive oil brings out the concentrated umami of soy sauce, and if you stir in fresh ginger and lemon juice something magical happens. The bright citrus and lingering heat of ginger create a perfect balance of flavors—a glorious concoction you'll want to drizzle over everything. As you whisk the sauce together, let the oven do the rest of the work. Scallions soften and caramelize, the leafy greens of bok choy crisp up like kale chips while the bulbs retain a crunchy texture, and salmon roasts alongside without demanding your attention. This is the weeknight dinner I turn to after a long day of work, when I'm feeling particularly tired and uninspired, and my stomach is howling for a nourishing meal! (Just remember to spoon the sauce over the rice, too.)

Sanaë

Position a rack in the middle of the oven and preheat to 400°F (200°C).

Halve the bok choy through the bulb (or quarter, if large) and wash well to remove any grit between the leaves. Cut the scallions lengthwise in half.

On a half-sheet pan, drizzle the bok choy and scallions with 2 tablespoons of the oil. Season with salt and pepper and toss with your hands to coat. Arrange in a single layer, with the bok choy cut side down. Roast for 10 to 12 minutes, or until the vegetables are starting to wilt.

Meanwhile, finely grate the ginger over a plate. Using your fingers, squeeze the ginger juice into a small bowl; discard the pulp. Add the lemon juice, soy sauce, and the remaining 2 tablespoons oil. Whisk to combine and set aside.

Cut a piece of parchment paper half the size of a half-sheet pan (about 9 × 13 inches/23 × 33 cm). Push the bok choy and scallions to one side of the sheet pan (they will have wilted and reduced in size) and place the piece of parchment paper on the other side (this is to prevent the salmon from sticking to the sheet pan). Place the salmon fillets on the parchment, skin side down. Season with salt and pepper and return to the oven.

Roast for 10 to 12 minutes, or until the salmon is opaque and just flakes when tested with a fork.

Serve the salmon and vegetables with the rice. Drizzle the soy-ginger sauce to taste over everything.

Whole Fish with Chermoula and Baby Potatoes

SERVES 4

For the chermoula

¼ cup (60 ml) extra-virgin olive oil

1 bunch fresh flat-leaf parsley (2½ oz/70 g), finely chopped

2 garlic cloves, finely chopped

½ preserved lemon, finely chopped

Finely grated zest of 1 lemon

Juice of ½ lemon

2 teaspoons sweet or smoked paprika

2 teaspoons ground cumin

1 teaspoon kosher salt

Freshly ground black pepper

For the fish and potatoes

1 large whole fish (2¾ lb/ 1.25 kg), such as red snapper, or 2 small whole fish (1 to 1½ lb/454 to 680 g each), such as branzino, gutted and scaled

1 pound (454 g) baby potatoes, halved

1 tablespoon extra-virgin olive oil

Kosher salt and freshly ground black pepper

Lemon wedges from the leftover ½ zested lemon, for squeezing

This recipe calls for an entire bunch of finely chopped parsley. Of course, you could use a food processor if you prefer the ease, but one of my favorite activities in the kitchen is chopping this herb. There's something satisfying and meditative about the task. You could replace half of the parsley with cilantro, though I almost always have parsley on hand—I take after my mother, who throws it into almost every dish—and I love how it keeps for (almost) ever in the fridge. Wash it the way you would leafy greens: Soak the parsley in cold water, dry thoroughly (use a salad spinner if you have one), loosely wrap in paper towels or a clean kitchen towel, and store in a resealable plastic bag in the fridge. Then you'll make chermoula, a vibrant and pungent North African marinade, that I find pairs especially well with whole fish. I've folded in preserved lemon and lemon zest to balance the richness of olive oil. I encourage you to eat the fish with its skin, as that's where the chermoula will have crisped up and become extra flavorful. When serving the fish, use the back of a large spoon to gently lift the flesh from the bones.

Sanaë

Position a rack in the middle of the oven and preheat to 425°F (220°C). Line a half-sheet pan with parchment paper.

MAKE THE CHERMOULA: In a medium bowl, stir together the oil, parsley, garlic, preserved lemon, lemon zest, lemon juice, paprika, cumin, salt, and several grinds of black pepper.

ROAST THE FISH AND POTATOES: Pat the fish dry and slather with the chermoula inside and out. Place the fish in the center of the prepared sheet pan.

Take the bowl you used for the chermoula, add the potatoes and oil, season with salt and pepper, and toss to combine. Transfer the potatoes to the sheet pan, cut side down, arranging around the fish in a single layer.

Roast for 20 to 25 minutes, or until the fish is cooked through and just flakes when tested with a fork and the potatoes are tender and browning. Serve the fish and potatoes with the lemon wedges for squeezing over.

Lemony Cod over Pommes Anna

SERVES 4

6 tablespoons ghee, melted and divided, plus more as needed (can substitute extra-virgin olive oil)

2 pounds (910 g) russet potatoes (4 to 5 medium), peeled and very thinly sliced (see Hot Tip!)

2 teaspoons finely chopped fresh thyme leaves, plus more for garnish

1¼ teaspoons kosher salt, plus more as needed

½ teaspoon freshly ground black pepper, plus more as needed

4 skinless cod or other firm, flaky fish fillets (6 oz /170 g each), about 1 inch (2.5 cm) thick

2 lemons, 1 halved and 1 cut into wedges

Extra-virgin olive oil (optional), for drizzling

HOT TIP! To get your potato slices to look like flower petals, you will need to use a mandoline in order to make slices that are so thin they are translucent.

The original idea for this dish was inspired years ago by a Mark Bittman recipe for roasted cod over potatoes. For someone from Eastern Europe, it's hard for me to overstate my love of potatoes, especially when cooked in a way to yield lots of crispy, browned bits. When I developed a lazy pommes Anna recipe for the *Washington Post*, I relied on not having to flip the potatoes (which is the traditional method) and this yielded a beautiful, almost flower-like dish that was easy to put together but looked artfully arranged (see Hot Tip!). When the potatoes are nearly done, you top them with pieces of cod, broil everything, and a few minutes later, dinner is ready. If you want, a light salad will round out the meal, but we won't judge you if you want to just stick to the ingredients below.

Olga

Position a rack in the middle of the oven and preheat to 400°F (200°C). Grease a quarter-sheet pan with ghee.

In a large bowl, toss the potatoes, 4 tablespoons of the ghee, and the thyme until evenly coated. Season the potatoes with the salt and pepper, gently toss again, and arrange in shingled layers over the greased sheet pan—you should be able to get at least four layers. Don't worry so much about getting the perfect shingling effect—it will wind up looking rustic and beautiful when fully cooked.

Transfer to the oven and roast for about 25 minutes, or until the potatoes start to brown and crisp on top and are tender when pierced with a sharp paring knife. (As the potatoes roast, check on them a couple of times; if they're browning too fast, tent around with foil.) Remove the hot sheet from the oven and set on a heatproof surface.

Position a rack 6 inches from the broiling element and turn on the broiler.

Thoroughly pat the fish dry and place on top of the potatoes, drizzle with the remaining 2 tablespoons ghee, squeeze the 2 lemon halves over the fish, and season liberally with salt and pepper. Broil for 5 to 8 minutes, depending on the thickness of the fillets, or until the fish is cooked through and just flakes when tested with a fork. Watch the pan carefully—if the potatoes start to burn, move the oven rack lower.

Divide among plates, drizzle with a little oil, if desired, garnish with thyme, and serve hot, with the lemon wedges for squeezing over.

Ritzy Fish and Chips

SERVES 4

For the potatoes and fish

2 tablespoons extra-virgin olive oil, plus more for the pan

1 pound (454 g) Yukon Gold potatoes, cut into wedges

Kosher salt and freshly ground black pepper

1 lemon

2 ounces (60 g) Ritz crackers, or another butter-flavored cracker (about 20 crackers)

2 ounces (60 g) potato chips

4 tablespoons (2 oz/57 g) unsalted butter, melted, divided

¼ cup (11 g) minced fresh chives or 2 tablespoons dried

¼ cup (13 g) minced fresh dill or 2 tablespoons dried

1 teaspoon onion powder

1 teaspoon garlic powder

¼ teaspoon cayenne pepper (optional)

4 skinless flaky fish fillets (6 oz/170 g each), such as cod, hake, or flounder, patted dry

For the ranch dip

¼ cup (57 g) plain whole-milk Greek yogurt or sour cream

¼ cup (57 g) mayonnaise

1 teaspoon apple cider vinegar

I believe it was cookbook author Julia Turshen who first inspired me to use Ritz crackers as a crunchy, buttery fish coating. These fish and chips came together when I discovered, in medias rec(ipe), that I didn't have quite enough Ritz crackers, because I suspect my husband had eaten them, not realizing I was saving them for a dish. Contemplating a workaround, I spied a partially consumed bag of potato chips in the pantry, with just enough chips to make up the difference, resulting in a serendipitous play on fish and chips. I added potato wedges to roast alongside for a complete meal. And while waiting on my dinner, I threw together a little homemade ranch dip, as I prefer it to tartar sauce. If you don't want to add any MSG—a trick I learned from my *Washington Post* colleague Aaron Hutcherson to deeply enhance the umami of your dip—skip it, but know that this unfairly maligned ingredient may transport you to when you were a kid and likely dipped everything in ranch. If you want to hew closer to tradition, serve this dish with malt vinegar for sprinkling.

Olga

ROAST THE POTATOES AND FISH: Position a rack in the middle of the oven and preheat to 425°F (220°C). Lightly grease a half-sheet pan with a little oil.

In a large bowl, drizzle the potatoes with the oil and lightly season with salt and pepper, then toss until well coated. Transfer the potatoes to the prepared sheet pan and arrange them on half of the sheet, allowing for a little breathing room. The potatoes should be snug, but they should all fit. (Hold on to the bowl you used for the potatoes.)

Transfer to the oven and roast for 20 minutes, or until you can disengage the potatoes from the sheet pan.

Meanwhile, finely grate the zest of the lemon into a food processor. (Set the now-naked lemon aside.) To the processor, add the crackers, chips, 3 tablespoons of the melted butter, the chives, dill, onion powder, garlic powder, and cayenne (if using). Pulse until the crumbs are evenly moistened and resemble wet sand. (If you don't have a food processor, place the crackers and chips in a resealable bag, and use a rolling pin, meat tenderizer, or empty wine bottle to crush until they form fine crumbs. Transfer the crumbs to a bowl and combine with the

1 tablespoon finely chopped fresh chives or 1½ teaspoons dried

1 tablespoon finely chopped fresh dill or 1½ teaspoons dried

½ teaspoon onion powder

½ teaspoon garlic powder

¼ teaspoon MSG (optional)

¼ teaspoon kosher salt

¼ teaspoon freshly ground black pepper

remaining coating ingredients from above.) Transfer the crumb mixture to the same bowl you used for the potatoes.

After the potatoes have been in for 20 minutes, remove the sheet pan from the oven (keep the oven on). Taking care since the pan will be hot, gently push the potatoes to one side of the pan. Place the fish on the other side and lightly season the tops of the fish with a little salt and pepper (remember that both the crackers and chips will add saltiness). Mound the cracker-chip mixture on top of each of the fish pieces; it's okay if some of the crumb coating falls off. Drizzle with the remaining 1 tablespoon melted butter.

Return the sheet pan to the oven and roast for 12 to 15 minutes, depending on the thickness of the fish pieces, or until the fish is cooked through and just flakes when tested with a fork. The potato wedges should be gloriously burnished and boast a thick, crunchy bottom. While both are roasting, cut your naked lemon into wedges.

MAKE THE RANCH DIP: While the fish and potatoes are roasting, in a small bowl, whisk together the yogurt, mayonnaise, vinegar, chives, dill, onion powder, garlic powder, MSG (if using), salt, and pepper until combined. Refrigerate until ready to use (you can also make this a few days ahead, and if you want it to become a dressing, loosen with a few tablespoons of buttermilk, half-and-half, or milk—whatever you've got on hand).

Divide everything among four plates and serve with the lemon wedges for squeezing over.

Coconut Fish en Papillote with Cherry Tomatoes

SERVES 2

12 ounces (340 g) cherry tomatoes

1 tablespoon extra-virgin olive oil, plus more for drizzling

Kosher salt

8 ounces (227 g) skinless salmon, halibut, or cod, cut into 1-inch (2.5 cm) pieces

1 shallot (2 oz/57 g), thinly sliced

One 1-inch (2.5 cm) piece fresh ginger, cut into thin matchsticks (see Hot Tip! on page 148)

Freshly ground black pepper

1 teaspoon garam masala

½ cup (120 ml) canned full-fat coconut milk

12 sprigs fresh cilantro

1 lime, cut into wedges

Short-Grain White Rice (page 271), for serving

I've been eating fish en papillote—wrapped in parchment paper—for years. It's a popular method for cooking fish (and other ingredients) in France, and my go-to weeknight dinner for two when I want to make something easy and a bit special. And while this recipe is exceedingly simple, it does require some assembly and patience when folding the parchment to create little boat-shaped packets. I learned this particular technique for papillote from my friend Rie McClenny, the cookbook author of *Make It Japanese*. It works every single time and looks beautiful out of the oven when you unwrap the packet. Sealing the ingredients in parchment mimics steaming (so the fish remains incredibly tender—no evaporation or dry flakes) and allows the flavors to infuse and meld. I love the pairing of salmon with coconut milk, but another thick firm-fleshed fish, such as halibut or cod, works beautifully, too.

You'll want to slice the shallots and ginger as thinly as possible, so they can soften in the time it takes to cook the fish.

Sanaë

Position a rack in the middle of the oven and preheat to 400°F (200°F).

In a medium bowl, toss the cherry tomatoes with the oil and season with salt. Season the fish all over with salt.

Tear off two 13-inch (33 cm) squares of parchment paper. Position the squares like a diamond, with a corner facing you (1). Dividing evenly, place the shallots and ginger in the center of each parchment square. Lightly drizzle with oil and season with salt and pepper (2). Divide the fish between the squares, placing it over the shallots and ginger. Sprinkle ½ teaspoon garam masala over the fish in each packet (3). Using a spoon, drizzle ¼ cup (60 ml) coconut milk over the fish in each packet (4)—don't worry if it spreads a little onto the parchment—and top with the cilantro (5). Working with one parchment square at a time, take two opposite corners of the parchment paper, press them together (6), and fold over several times to seal (7 and 8). Tightly twist the remaining two ends of the parchment to completely seal the packet (9). The parchment packet should look like a boat or candy wrapper.

continued

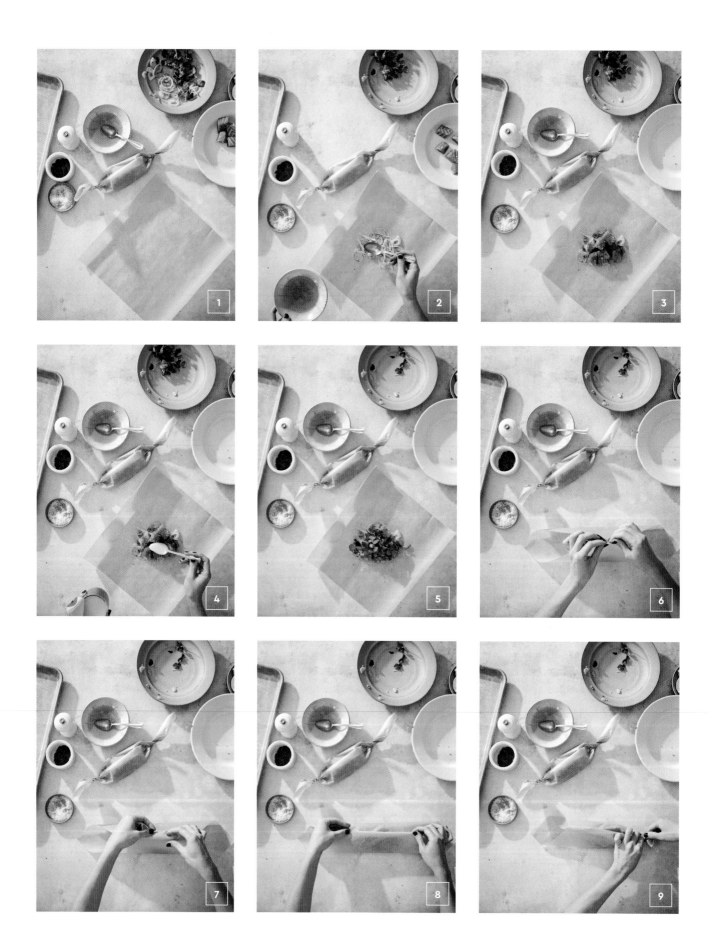

Place the parchment packets on a half-sheet pan. Arrange the cherry tomatoes between the packets, avoiding the edges of the pan where the tomatoes are more likely to burn (10). Bake for about 20 minutes, or until the tomatoes are bursting and starting to caramelize. (The fish will be cooked through.)

Place a packet on each plate. Carefully open them (the steam will be hot!) and season with several grinds of black pepper. Spoon the tomatoes into the packets, squeeze the lime wedges over the fish, and serve with the rice.

HOT TIP! You could double the recipe to serve four, in which case I would keep the same amount of cherry tomatoes—it will be plenty—and double everything else.

Arctic Char with Buttery Herb Sauce, Broccolini, and Potatoes

SERVES 4

1 bunch Broccolini, thick stems halved lengthwise

1 pound (454 g) baby potatoes, halved or quartered if large

3 tablespoons extra-virgin olive oil

Kosher salt and freshly ground black pepper

1½ pounds (680 g) arctic char fillet

2 tablespoons drained capers

1 teaspoon coriander seeds, crushed (see Hot Tip!)

2 cups (100 g) tender herb leaves (such as parsley, dill, basil, or tarragon), coarsely chopped

4 tablespoons (2 oz/57 g) unsalted butter, melted

1 lemon, cut into wedges

HOT TIP! To crush coriander seeds, place them on a large cutting board. Press down with the flat side of the blade of a chef's knife until they crack. (Alternatively, you can use a mortar and pestle.)

This is one of the prettiest sheet pan dishes: The sheet's large rectangular shape easily accommodates a long fillet of arctic char surrounded by potatoes and Broccolini. The fish gets covered in a blanket of herbs that are soaked in butter. Capers and crushed coriander seeds are hidden beneath the herbs, providing intense pops of flavor with every bite. This recipe also happens to be my best friend's favorite, so I've gotten into the habit of preparing it whenever she comes over for dinner, and then sending her home with any leftovers. Using arctic char makes for a stunning centerpiece that can easily stretch to six people if you accompany it with a salad (see Simplest Arugula Salad, page 274, or Fennel and Citrus Salad, page 277). In that case, just make sure to add an extra lemon for serving. This recipe works just as well with salmon, if that is your preferred fish or you're unable to find arctic char.

Sanaë

Position a rack in the middle of the oven and preheat to 400°F (200°C).

On a half-sheet pan, toss the Broccolini and potatoes with the oil. Season with salt and pepper. Push the vegetables to the sides of the sheet pan, making room for the arctic char in the center. Place the artic char, skin side down, in the center of the sheet pan. (You can place the potatoes cut side down in a single layer and arrange the Broccolini among and over the potatoes.)

Season the fish with salt and pepper and scatter the capers and coriander seeds on top. Cover the fish with the fresh herbs and drizzle with the melted butter.

Roast for about 20 minutes, or until the fish is cooked through and just flakes when tested with a fork, the potatoes are tender when pierced with a knife, and the Broccolini florets are starting to brown and crisp up.

Serve with the lemon wedges for squeezing over the fish.

Baked Potatoes with Smoked Trout Crème Fraîche and Trout Roe

SERVES 2 TO 4

4 large russet potatoes (9 oz/ 255 g each), scrubbed

1 tablespoon extra-virgin olive oil

Kosher salt

One 7- to 8-ounce (198 to 227 g) container crème fraîche

6 to 8 ounces (170 to 227 g) smoked trout or another hot-smoked fish

3 tablespoons finely chopped fresh dill, plus more for serving

2 scallions, thinly sliced, plus more for serving

Freshly ground black pepper

Trout or salmon roe, for serving (optional, but highly recommended)

Don't you love finding a recipe so smart you wish you had thought of it? It instantly becomes part of how you start rethinking ingredients or techniques. These baked potatoes were inspired by cookbook author Ali Slagle. She shared with us at the *Washington Post* a recipe for genius compound smoked fish butter on baked potatoes—all the familiar flavors I grew up eating in Russia. I wanted to re-create this at home for my family, so, I made a twist on Ali's recipe, subbing in crème fraîche for butter, and the results were so delicious I had to share them here. In another nod to my childhood, I added a dollop of smoked trout roe (salmon roe also works well). For a humble baked potato, it turned into a surprisingly elegant and luxurious dish that takes little effort to put together, and tastes both comforting and familiar, yet exciting and new.

Olga

Position a rack in the middle of the oven and preheat to 400°F (200°C).

Use a fork to pierce the potatoes in several places all over. In a medium bowl, toss the potatoes with the oil and a pinch of salt until coated. Transfer to a half-sheet pan and roast for about 1 hour, or until the potatoes can be easily pierced with a paring knife.

Using the same bowl, combine the crème fraîche, smoked trout, dill, and scallions. Use a fork to mash and stir to create a uniform mixture. Season to taste with pepper. Because the fish is salty and the crème fraîche is tangy, you may not need any additional salt.

When the potatoes are done, remove from the oven and let sit for about 5 minutes. Using a sharp paring knife, make a deep incision on top of each potato, leaving about ½ inch (1.3 cm) uncut on each end. Using a kitchen towel on both ends, gently push the ends in to crack each potato open. Use a fork to scrape and fluff the cooked interior, then let sit for another 5 minutes.

Add 2 to 3 tablespoons of the crème fraîche mixture on top. If desired, add a dollop of roe. Garnish with more dill and scallions, and serve immediately.

Roasted Red Peppers and Onions with Tuna and Feta

2 red bell peppers (1 lb/
454 g total), cut into slices
¼ inch (6 mm) wide

1 large red onion (12 oz/
340 g), halved and cut into
slices ¼ inch (6 mm) thick

6 sprigs fresh thyme, leaves
picked

¼ cup (60 ml) extra-virgin
olive oil, plus more for
drizzling

1 teaspoon sweet or
smoked paprika

1 teaspoon ground cumin

1 teaspoon kosher salt, plus
more as needed

Freshly ground black pepper

6 ounces (170 g) feta cheese,
broken into 1-inch (2.5 cm)
pieces

6 to 8 ounces (170 to
227 g) oil-packed canned
tuna, drained

1 cup (20 g) fresh flat-leaf
parsley leaves

1 lemon, cut into wedges
(optional)

Toasted bread, orzo, rice, or
couscous, for serving

I have a soft spot for all canned fish, and especially adore the pairing of tuna with caramelized bell peppers and onions. This is a meal I throw together when I have impromptu guests over for lunch on a weekend. It easily feeds a crowd—double all the ingredients and use two sheet pans with racks in the lower and upper thirds of the oven, switching the pans from top to bottom halfway through—and the bright colors are beautiful displayed in a large bowl or platter alongside thick slices of toasted bread. (You could even ask your guests to pick up a fresh loaf on their way over.) I'll toast the bread in the oven in the last 5 minutes of cooking, then drizzle it with olive oil and sprinkle with flaky sea salt.

It's best to serve this dish right away, when the feta is warm and easily spreads onto the bread. That said, you can roast the peppers and onions (minus the feta) up to 2 hours in advance. Keep them covered at room temperature, then when you're ready to serve, add the feta and return the sheet pan to a preheated oven for those final 10 minutes.

Sanaë

Position a rack in the middle of the oven and preheat to 400°F (200°C).

On a half-sheet pan, toss together the peppers, onion, thyme, oil, paprika, cumin, and salt. Season with several grinds of black pepper.

Roast, stirring halfway through, for about 30 minutes, or until the vegetables are softened and turning golden brown at the edges.

Remove the hot sheet from the oven. Scatter the feta over the peppers and onion and drizzle with a little oil. Return the pan to the oven for about 10 minutes, or until the feta is softened and turning golden on the bottom.

Remove the pan from the oven and scatter the tuna and parsley over everything. Season to taste with salt and pepper. Serve in a large bowl or platter with the lemon wedges, if you like, and toasted bread.

Chapter 6

From the Garden

Plant-Based

Arrabbiata and White Bean Cheesy Ravioli

SERVES 4 TO 6

1 cup (4 oz/113 g) shredded low-moisture mozzarella cheese

½ cup (1¾ oz/50 g) finely grated Parmigiano-Reggiano cheese

One 10-ounce (283 g) package fresh or frozen ravioli (no need to thaw)

One 15.5-ounce (439 g) can cannellini beans, drained and rinsed

¼ cup (35 g) golden raisins

2 tablespoons extra-virgin olive oil

1½ tablespoons drained capers

Kosher salt and freshly ground black pepper

⅓ cup (80 ml) heavy cream

2 cups (16 oz/454 g) store-bought arrabbiata, or your favorite jarred tomato sauce

Fresh basil leaves, for serving

Simplest Arugula Salad (optional; page 274), for serving

This baked ravioli dish requires almost no prep. The oven does most of the work, and since you'll be using store-bought ravioli and tomato sauce, most of the "cooking" is simple assembling. The ravioli simmer directly in the arrabbiata and cream, while the top transforms into a gloriously golden crust. Raisins soften and plump in the sauce and add subtle sweetness to complement the heat. When Olga cooked through this recipe, she suggested adding capers for bursts of salinity, and now I can't imagine the ravioli without them. If you don't like spicy dishes, or for a more kid-friendly version, you can replace the arrabbiata with tomato-basil, marinara, or your favorite jarred pasta sauce. I like to use a simple cheese ravioli for this recipe, but of course, feel free to play around with your preferred fillings. This recipe scales up nicely to make a larger portion for a crowd: Simply double all the ingredients and bake in a half-sheet pan.

Sanaë

Position a rack in the middle of the oven and preheat to 400°F (200°C).

In a medium bowl, stir together the mozzarella and Parmigiano-Reggiano. In a large bowl, mix together the ravioli, cannellini beans, golden raisins, oil, and capers. Lightly season with salt and pepper and toss again to combine.

Transfer the ravioli and bean mixture to a quarter-sheet pan and spread in an even layer. Drizzle the cream over everything. Using a large spoon, spread the arrabbiata over the ravioli to completely cover, and top with the cheese mixture. Place the quarter-sheet pan on a half-sheet pan to catch any overflow.

Bake for 30 to 40 minutes, or until golden and bubbling.

Remove from the oven and let rest for 5 minutes. Top with the basil and serve with the arugula salad, if desired.

Cauliflower Steaks with Parsley-Shallot Sauce

SERVES 2 TO 4

For the cauliflower

1 large, dense head cauliflower (3 lb/1.4 kg)

2 tablespoons extra-virgin olive oil

Kosher salt and freshly ground black pepper

For the parsley-shallot sauce

¾ cup (40 g) lightly packed fresh flat-leaf parsley leaves

1 small shallot, coarsely chopped

2 tablespoons Dijon mustard

Finely grated zest and juice of ½ lemon

Pinch of kosher salt

Pinch of freshly ground black pepper

1 tablespoon extra-virgin olive oil

During winter months, it's rare that our kitchen is without a head or two of cauliflower in our fridge. We often roast it as florets with a little salt, pepper, and za'atar, but we also love to give it the "steak" treatment. Cut into thick slabs and roasted, the crucifer doesn't try to mimic meat, but instead offers a satisfying, flavorful, and filling alternative to animal protein. Cooking the cauliflower in the top third of the oven helps with better browning without needing to flip, which can cause the slabs to fall apart. Served with a genius lemon/parsley/shallot sauce I adapted from cookbook author and *Washington Post* columnist Ellie Krieger, it's bound to win over even the biggest cauliflower skeptics. Accentuated with punchy Dijon mustard, it's a sauce you'll want to put on everything, including scrambled eggs, as a sandwich spread, or even as a dip for french fries.

Olga

ROAST THE CAULIFLOWER: Position a rack in the upper third of the oven and preheat to 425°F (220°C).

Trim any green leaves surrounding the cauliflower and, using a sharp chef's knife, trim the cauliflower stem to create a flatter surface. Set the cauliflower on a cutting board, stem side down, and slice it into 1-inch-thick (2.5 cm) slabs. Arrange the slabs on the prepared sheet pan and brush with some of the oil. Gently flip over and brush with the oil on the other side. Season with salt and pepper.

Transfer the pan to the oven and roast without flipping for 30 to 35 minutes, or until the cauliflower slabs are golden brown.

MAKE THE PARSLEY-SHALLOT SAUCE: While the cauliflower roasts, in a mini food processor or blender, combine the parsley, shallot, mustard, lemon zest, lemon juice, salt, and pepper and process until mostly smooth (small bits of parsley are fine). Transfer to a small jar and stir in the oil. Let the flavors meld until ready to serve.

Transfer the roasted cauliflower to a large platter and serve right away, with the sauce on the side for spooning over the slabs.

Crispy Tofu with Turnips, Shiitakes, and Carrot-Ginger Dressing

SERVES 4

For the tofu and vegetables

3 tablespoons neutral oil, such as canola or grapeseed, divided, plus (optional) more for the pan

One 14- to 16-ounce (397 to 454 g) package firm tofu

1 tablespoon soy sauce

1 tablespoon cornstarch

1 pound (454 g) turnips (4 medium), peeled and cut into eighths

5 ounces (142 g) sliced fresh shiitake mushrooms

1 bunch scallions (6 to 8 scallions), trimmed and cut into 2-inch (5 cm) pieces

Kosher salt and freshly ground black pepper

For the carrot-ginger dressing

1 large carrot (4 oz/ 115 g), scrubbed and roughly chopped

1 small shallot (2 oz/60 g), roughly chopped

2 tablespoons roughly chopped fresh ginger

1½ tablespoons rice vinegar, plus more to taste

This is the kind of dish I want to eat every day: Healthful without trying and bursting with flavor. You can make it faster in two sheet pans (see recipe directions below) or, use one sheet pan and take a little longer. My favorite way of roasting tofu—besides coating it in a little cornstarch, which helps it crisp up—is to tear it into bite-size pieces the same way you would with bread if you were making croutons. The scraggly bits of tofu get nice and crispy in the oven, a little chewier and meatier, and all those crevices here and there make the pieces especially good at taking on flavoring.

And while turnips, along with rutabaga, will never win any beauty contests, few vegetables are so near and dear to my heart (and I really, truly, deeply love vegetables). Roasting turnips releases their mild earthy sweetness, which pairs beautifully with shiitakes and scallions. But the entire enterprise truly sings when drizzled with the bright—both in color and flavor—carrot ginger dressing and topped with optional (but highly recommended) chili crisp. I know it's an unusual combination, but trust me, it works. My tofu-loving kid gave it two thumbs up and my tofu-skeptical husband gave it an 8 out of 10, which is as good as it gets around here.

Olga

ROAST THE TOFU AND VEGETABLES: Position a rack in the middle of the oven and preheat to 400°F (200°C). Line a half-sheet pan with parchment paper (or lightly grease it with oil).

Pat the tofu dry and tear it, much like you'd tear bread, into bite-size pieces. As you tear the tofu, place the pieces in a large bowl. Add 1 tablespoon of the oil and the soy sauce and gently toss to coat. Using a fine-mesh sieve, sift in the cornstarch—this will ensure even distribution and prevent the cornstarch from caking in one place—and gently toss again to coat.

Transfer the tofu to the prepared sheet pan and roast for 15 minutes, or until the tofu starts to turn golden.

1½ tablespoons mirin, plus more to taste

1 tablespoon shiro miso (white miso)

2 teaspoons toasted sesame oil

¼ cup (60 ml) neutral oil, such as canola or grapeseed

For serving

Short-Grain White Rice (page 271) or a grain of your choice

Chili crisp (optional; I love the Momofuku and Fly by Jing brands)

Meanwhile, in the same bowl, combine the turnips, shiitakes, scallions, and the remaining 2 tablespoons oil. Lightly season with salt and pepper and gently toss to coat.

Remove the hot sheet from the oven and move the tofu over to one side of the pan—it should take up about one-third of the area. Add the vegetables to the other side. (You can also speed this up and roast the tofu on one sheet pan and the vegetables on another.)

Return the pan to the oven and roast for another 15 to 20 minutes, shaking it halfway through, or until the turnips start to brown and become tender, the shiitakes shrink considerably, and the scallions lose their verdant color. (If you find you need to cook down the vegetables more after this time frame, transfer the tofu to a bowl, spread the vegetables across the entire sheet pan, and roast for another 10 minutes, or until they are further cooked and a little more browned.)

MAKE THE CARROT-GINGER DRESSING: Meanwhile, in a mini food processor or blender, pulse the carrot, shallot, and ginger until finely chopped. Scrape down the sides of the bowl or pitcher; add the vinegar, mirin, miso, and sesame oil and process until mostly smooth. With the machine running, slowly drizzle in the neutral oil, followed by 2 tablespoons water, and process until fully incorporated. Taste and season with more vinegar and/or mirin, if you like—the dressing should taste equal parts sweet, tart, and bright. You should have a generous 1½ cups (360 ml). Process until smooth, pausing to scrape the sides and bottom of the processor bowl.

TO SERVE: Serve the tofu and vegetables with rice and chili crisp (if using), and the carrot-ginger dressing.

HOT TIP! Not a fan of mushrooms? Toss in drained canned chickpeas to get more heft. Can't find turnips? Try radishes or even rutabaga (you know you want to!). Out of scallions? A sliced onion (any color) will do.

Curry Gratin Dauphinois

**SERVES 6 AS A MAIN
OR 8 AS A SIDE**

2 pounds (908 g) Yukon Gold
potatoes, peeled and very
thinly sliced

3 tablespoons (1½ oz/43 g)
unsalted or salted butter,
melted

2 teaspoons curry powder

1 garlic clove, thinly sliced

Kosher salt and freshly ground
black pepper

1 cup (240 ml) heavy cream

½ cup (55 g) coarsely grated
Gruyère cheese

½ cup (56 g) shredded low-
moisture mozzarella cheese

HOT TIPS! You could
use all Gruyère or
all mozzarella as the
topping, or any other
melting cheese like
cheddar.

For a more traditional
gratin, replace the
curry powder with
a pinch of freshly
grated nutmeg.

If you have one, use a
mandoline to slice the
potatoes.

Gratin dauphinois is one of my favorite French potato dishes. My father also adores it, but we mostly make it for special occasions and serve it in small portions as it's quite rich from all the cream. This recipe is far from traditional, and not just because it's made in a sheet pan. I've always loved the combination of curry with cream and potatoes, and a gratin seemed like the perfect application for allowing those three ingredients to shine. The potatoes are coated in curry powder, which infuses them with a little heat and spice. They soften directly in the cream without any parcooking, and you'll be impressed by how the slices melt together to create the most luscious gratin. (If you can, use a mandoline when slicing the potatoes for thin, even slices.) I like to serve this as a side for a feast— think Thanksgiving, Christmas, or another special occasion—or as a vegetarian main accompanied by one of our salads (see pages 274 and 277).

Sanaë

Preheat the oven to 425°F (220°C). Set a quarter-sheet pan inside a half-sheet pan to catch any overflow.

In a large bowl, toss together the potatoes, melted butter, curry powder, and garlic. Season with salt and pepper. (I like my potatoes on the saltier side, so I usually season with about 1½ teaspoons salt. For a less salty version, start with 1 teaspoon.) Using your hands, toss the potatoes, making sure each slice is coated. Transfer the potato mixture to the quarter-sheet pan and arrange in an even layer.

Drizzle the cream evenly over the potatoes, then gently tip the pan to distribute it. Tightly cover the quarter-sheet pan with foil.

Bake for 30 minutes. Remove the foil and sprinkle the potatoes with the Gruyère and mozzarella. Return to the oven, uncovered, and bake for about 15 minutes, or until the potatoes are softened (they should be easily pierced with a knife) and the cheese is deeply golden brown.

Remove from the oven and let rest for 10 minutes before serving.

Quesadilla for a Crowd (or Hangry Kids)

SERVES 4 TO 6

One 15.5-ounce (439 g) can black beans, drained and rinsed (see Hot Tips!)

Neutral oil, such as canola or grapeseed, for the pan

8 burrito-size flour tortillas

8 ounces (227 g) coarsely shredded Mexican blend cheese or queso Oaxaca or Chihuahua

Sliced avocado, sour cream or crema, chipotles in adobo, lime wedges, and/or hot sauce, for serving

"What's for dinner?" might be my least favorite phrase. While I make my living developing and editing recipes, dinner on weeknights feels like a race I'm destined to lose, where I'm darting in the kitchen, feeding the dog and the cat, helping our son, Avi, with his homework, checking in on work, and trying to tidy around. Like many children, Avi's tastes change faster than TikTok trends, and a dish that was a hit a week ago is likely a dud now. Thus, finding a dinner option that's reliable, made with refrigerator and pantry staples, is like spotting a unicorn. Enter this low-lift quesadilla, which never fails at our house. While we most often use canned black beans for this, we sometimes have leftover chicken from roasting or poaching, and this is a terrific way to give it a new life.

Olga

Position a rack in the middle of the oven, set a half-sheet pan on it, and preheat to 450°F (230°C).

Spread the black beans over a clean kitchen towel and, using another clean kitchen towel, thoroughly pat them dry.

Take the hot sheet out of the oven and set it on a heatproof surface. Carefully, as the pan will be searing-hot, brush the sheet pan with a little oil and place 2 tortillas, slightly overlapping (like a Venn diagram) along one long side of the sheet pan with half hanging over the rim; repeat with 2 more tortillas on the other long side of the pan. Place 1 tortilla, also half hanging over, at each short end, and finish with 1 tortilla in the center so the whole bottom of the sheet pan is covered.

Scatter the cheese and beans over the tortillas. (Resist piling on fillings or your quesadilla will have that problem where everything falls out of it when you try to eat it. Practice restraint for quesadilla Zen.) Fold the overlapping edges of the tortilla over the filling until you get an almost tortilla galette. Place the last tortilla in the center and brush with more oil on top. Place another sheet pan, bottom side down, over the giant quesadilla you just made and transfer to the oven.

continued

Bake for 20 to 25 minutes, or until the tortilla is crisp and golden on the outside (it's okay to peek).

Using a pizza cutter, slice the quesadilla into desired-size pieces. Serve with sliced avocado, sour cream, chipotles in adobo, lime wedges, and hot sauce.

HOT TIPS! In place of beans, use shredded cooked chicken. I like to add about 1½ cups of it scattered over the cheese—not too much, not too little—and it melts into the cheese for a filling, satisfying result.

If using black beans, be sure to spread them out on a towel and carefully pat them dry—you don't want any excess moisture in there. Not a fan of beans? Try cooked mushrooms! Want a little green in there? Toss in a handful of spinach leaves. You can also add frozen roasted corn and/or roasted poblano peppers, patted dry.

Any leftover quesadilla pieces can be refrigerated for up to 3 days. Reheat them in a toaster oven or regular oven at 350°F/180°C until warmed through and crisp. I know it sounds insane to say the leftovers are better than the original, but that double-toasted crispy tortilla makes me so excited when we have a piece or two left over—which means a terrific lunch the following day.

Eggplant with Grapes, Feta, and Lemony Tahini

SERVES 4

For the eggplant

¼ cup (60 ml) extra-virgin olive oil, plus more as needed

2 medium globe eggplants (1½ lb/680 g total)

1 teaspoon ground sumac, plus more as needed

Kosher salt and freshly ground black pepper

8 ounces (227 g) seedless grapes, preferably green

1 large red onion (12 oz/ 340 g), halved and sliced

1 fresh red chile, such as Fresno, halved and finely chopped

Juice of 1 lemon

3 ounces (85 g) feta cheese, crumbled

For the spiced tahini

½ cup (112 g) well-stirred tahini

¼ cup (60 ml) fresh lemon juice (from 1 to 2 lemons)

2 garlic cloves, minced or finely grated

1 teaspoon ground coriander

1 teaspoon ground sumac

ingredients continued

If you're reading this book, chances are you cook. Not just for yourself, but for others, too. And when we cook for friends and family, we have to take into consideration dietary restrictions as well as likes and dislikes. But what if an ingredient you love is wildly unpopular with your household? In my case, I live among ardent eggplant haters. I, on the other hand, find eggplant a versatile player in the kitchen, standing in for meatier dishes and transforming into silky purees such as baba ghanoush. One day, in an effort to clean out my fridge, I roasted eggplants with wilted grapes and a wrinkly chile, topped them with feta, fresh herbs, pine nuts, pomegranate, and hot honey, and finished it all off with a drizzle of lemony, spiced tahini dressing. I didn't actually expect anyone to try it—my then eight-year-old refused to even *smell* the dish—but when I saw my husband spooning an entire eggplant half onto his plate, I was speechless. I was further shocked into silence when he proclaimed, "I don't even like eggplant, and I love this dish." Which, if the ingredients in this recipe don't convince you, that sentence speaks for itself.

Olga

MAKE THE EGGPLANT: Position a rack in the middle of the oven and preheat to 425°C (220°C). Lightly grease a half-sheet pan with oil.

Halve the eggplants lengthwise and score a diamond pattern into the flesh of each half on the cut surface; don't cut all the way through. Set the eggplants, cut side up, on the sheet pan and generously drizzle with the oil, turning the eggplants over so they are glistening all over. Sprinkle the eggplants with the sumac and generously season with salt and pepper (they can take aggressive seasoning), then turn them over, cut side down, on the sheet pan. Arrange the grapes among the eggplant halves, then nestle the onion slices and chile among them. Drizzle everything lightly with oil and use your hands to ensure that all the ingredients are coated.

Roast for 25 to 30 minutes, or until the onion starts to char. Scoop the onions, grapes, and chile onto a serving platter.

continued

½ teaspoon kosher salt

½ teaspoon freshly ground black pepper, or more to taste

For serving (optional)

Generous handful of fresh tender herbs (such as mint, cilantro, parsley, and/or dill), roughly chopped or torn

Toasted pine nuts

Pomegranate arils

Hot honey, for drizzling

Return the sheet pan to the oven for another 10 to 15 minutes, or until the eggplants are really tender and starting to brown. Gently turn the eggplants over, cut side up, drizzle with the lemon juice and top with the feta. Return the pan to the oven for another 10 minutes, or until the feta starts to melt. Transfer to a wire rack and let cool for a few minutes or completely (depending on if you prefer eating this warm or at room temperature).

MAKE THE SPICED TAHINI: While the eggplants are roasting, in a small bowl, whisk together the tahini, lemon juice, garlic, coriander, sumac, salt, and pepper. The sauce should be the consistency of a creamy dressing; if it's too thick, whisk in 2 to 4 tablespoons water, 1 tablespoon at a time, until it's to your liking.

TO SERVE: When ready to serve, set the roasted eggplant atop the onions and grapes and generously drizzle with the tahini sauce. (Alternatively, if you wish to serve on the sheet pan, keep the eggplants on it, and return the onion, grapes, and chile to the pan, spooning the sauce over and around the eggplant.) If desired, sprinkle with herbs, pine nuts, and pomegranate arils. Finish with a thin drizzle of hot honey.

Halloumi Kebabs with Grapes and Chile-Mint Sauce

SERVES 3 TO 4

For the kebabs

1 tablespoon extra-virgin olive oil, plus more for the pan

Two 8-ounce (227 g) blocks Halloumi cheese, cut into 1-inch (2.5 cm) cubes

2 medium red onions (1 lb/ 454 g total), sliced into ½-inch (1.3 cm) wedges

About 50 seedless grapes (13 oz/370 g)

Kosher salt and freshly ground black pepper

For the chile-mint sauce

1 cup (40 g) fresh cilantro leaves

1 cup (50 g) fresh mint leaves

1 serrano chile, stemmed

1 small garlic clove

½ teaspoon ground cumin

⅛ teaspoon kala namak or ¼ teaspoon kosher salt

¼ cup (64 g) whole-milk Greek yogurt

Juice of ½ lime, plus more as needed

We're obsessed with Halloumi for its texture, ability to withstand high heat, and pleasantly rubbery squeak against our teeth. Halloumi delivers a salty bite that marries well with sweet fruit and might be the ideal summer grilling cheese, especially if it gets the skewer treatment. Here, we thread it with crunchy onions, juicy grapes (though frozen peaches work in the dead of winter, too), and an aromatic chile-mint sauce that's good enough to mix into rice or use as a salad dressing or dip for vegetables.

Kala namak, black salt mined in the Himalayas, has a funky, sulfuric note and imbues food with its pungency. If you've ever had a salty lassi, there's a good chance it was seasoned with kala namak!

Olga + Sanaë

MAKE THE KEBABS: Position a rack in the middle of the oven and preheat to 450°F (230°C). Line a half-sheet pan with foil and generously brush with oil. Soak 12 wooden skewers in water for at least 20 minutes.

In a large bowl, toss the Halloumi, onions, and grapes with the oil and a pinch each of salt and pepper (don't oversalt, as the Halloumi is quite salty). Alternating the Halloumi, onion, and grapes, thread a piece at a time onto each skewer until full; you should be able to get 3 or 4 iterations of each. Place the skewer on the prepared sheet pan and repeat with the remaining ingredients and skewers.

Roast for 15 to 20 minutes, or until the Halloumi pieces are generously browned and starting to crisp.

MAKE THE CHILE-MINT SAUCE: Meanwhile, in the bowl of a mini food processor, combine the cilantro, mint, chile, garlic, cumin, and salt and pulse until finely chopped. Add the yogurt, lime juice, and 1 tablespoon water and process until smooth. You should have about ½ cup.

To serve, transfer the skewers to a serving platter, drizzle with about ¼ cup (60 ml) of the sauce, and serve the remaining sauce on the side.

All-the-Crispy-Bits Mac and Cheese

4 tablespoons (62 grams) unsalted butter, melted, plus more for the sheet pan

12 ounces (340 g) sharp cheddar cheese, coarsely grated

12 ounces (340 g) Gruyère cheese, coarsely grated (see Hot Tip!)

Generous 1 cup (65 g) panko bread crumbs

⅓ cup (33 g) finely grated Parmigiano-Reggiano cheese

¼ teaspoon kosher salt

Pinch of cayenne pepper

Freshly ground black pepper

1 pound (454 g) cavatappi or other twisty pasta

3 cups (710 ml) whole milk

2 teaspoons smoked paprika

HOT TIPS! Did you grab a bag of pasta that's 17.6 ounces (500 g)? Increase the milk to 4 cups (950 ml) and decrease the water to 2 cups (475 ml) for cooking the noodles.

Not a fan of Gruyère? Use all cheddar instead.

When we started talking about mac and cheese for this book, we immediately agreed that the ratio of creamy to crispy in traditional casseroles was not to our liking. Just as we're always angling for that corner piece of lasagna, we're also fans of the textural bits from crisped cheese, noodles, and a bread crumb topping. So, we found a way to our platonic ideal of the beloved American classic. While you do use your stovetop briefly to cook the noodles, we promise it's worth it. Simmering the pasta in milk and water ensures creaminess without the effort required by béchamel. The noodles get covered in cheese and panko (our preferred bread crumbs for their large, airy flakes), so every bite has the perfect balance of soft, cheesy, and super crispy.

Sanaë + Olga

Position a rack in the middle of the oven and preheat to 425°F (220°C). Generously butter a half-sheet pan and line with parchment paper.

In a large bowl, mix together the cheddar and Gruyère. Measure out 3 cups (375 g) of the cheese mixture and set aside for the topping. Set the large bowl with the remaining cheese near the stovetop.

In a small bowl, combine the panko, Parmigiano-Reggiano, melted butter, salt, and cayenne. Generously season with black pepper and stir until the bread crumbs are evenly coated.

In a large pot, combine the pasta, milk, and 2½ cups (600 ml) water. Set the pot over medium-high heat and bring to a lively simmer, stirring occasionally. Reduce to a gentle simmer and cook, stirring often, until al dente, 3 to 4 minutes. Remove from the heat and stir in the smoked paprika. Add the cheese mixture from the large bowl, one handful at a time, stirring to melt after each addition. Generously season with black pepper and stir to combine.

Transfer the mixture to the prepared sheet pan and spread in an even layer. Cover with the reserved cheeses and sprinkle with the bread crumb mixture. Bake for 20 to 30 minutes, rotating the pan front to back halfway through, or until deeply golden and crispy. Let sit for 10 minutes before serving.

Mushroom Parmigiana

SERVES 4 TO 8

Extra-virgin olive oil

1 teaspoon kosher salt, divided, plus more as needed

8 large portobello mushroom caps

Freshly ground black pepper

1½ cups (375 g) store-bought or homemade marinara sauce

1¼ cups (5 oz/140 g) shredded low-moisture mozzarella cheese

⅔ cup (65 g) grated Parmigiano-Reggiano cheese, plus more for serving

⅔ cup (55 g) panko bread crumbs

1 garlic clove, minced or finely grated

¼ cup (10 g) fresh basil leaves, cut into chiffonade, plus whole leaves for serving

2 tablespoons finely chopped fresh flat-leaf parsley

While I love a good chicken or eggplant Parm, I don't make them often. It's a bit of a production and isn't realistic on a weeknight. Enter portobello caps, which appeal even to mushroom skeptics. This oven version is easy to prepare and short of a few times of removing the sheet pan from the oven to add another layer, the dish is hands-off. One of the reasons for this seemingly finicky layering process is to guarantee a mushroom Parm that's "meaty," satisfying, and not soggy. Let each component dry out a bit, which will intensify its flavors. Our favorite way to serve this is with arugula dressed with lemon juice and olive oil.

Olga

Position a rack in the middle of the oven and preheat to 425°F (220°C). Coat a half-sheet pan with a little oil and use a pastry brush to coat the bottom of the pan with it. Sprinkle the sheet pan with ½ teaspoon of the salt.

Place the mushroom caps on the prepared sheet pan, gill side up, transfer to the oven, and roast for 13 to 15 minutes, or until they dry out a bit. It's okay if a little liquid remains pooled in some of the gills; you can gently pour it off.

Remove the hot sheet from the oven, generously drizzle each mushroom with oil, and season with a little salt and pepper. Divide the marinara over each mushroom cap. Return to the oven and roast for 10 to 12 minutes, or until the sauce thickens slightly.

Remove the pan from the oven and top with the mozzarella. Return to the oven and roast for about 10 minutes, or until the cheese melts and starts to brown and bubble.

Meanwhile, in a small bowl, combine the Parmigiano-Reggiano, panko, garlic, basil, parsley, and the remaining ½ teaspoon salt. Drizzle with a little oil and stir; the mixture should look slightly moistened.

Remove the pan from the oven and top the mushrooms with the panko mixture. Return to the oven and roast for another 5 to 7 minutes, or until the panko is golden.

Divide the mushrooms among the plates, top with a sprinkling of Parmigiano-Reggiano, and garnish with a few basil leaves.

Twice-Baked Potatoes with Shiitakes and Miso

SERVES 3 TO 6

3 russet potatoes (2 lb/ 908 g total), scrubbed

4 tablespoons extra-virgin olive oil, divided, plus more for rubbing

Kosher salt

6 scallions

½ cup (30 g) panko bread crumbs

Freshly ground black pepper

7 ounces (200 g) fresh shiitake mushrooms, stems discarded, caps cut into slices ¼ inch (6 mm) wide

½ cup (120 g) sour cream

4 teaspoons shiro miso (white miso)

4 ounces (113 g) low-moisture mozzarella cheese, cut into ½-inch (1.3 cm) pieces

I love these potatoes and never tire of them despite eating them count-less times as I fine-tuned the recipe. A marriage between a twice-baked potato and a Japanese-style gratin, they are ideal for a winter eve, when you need something filling. Unlike most Japanese gratins, there's no bé-chamel in this recipe, but you will have ample creaminess from the sour cream and melted pockets of mozzarella. The miso adds depth of flavor, saltiness, and a hint of sweetness. If you're worried about the amount of miso used here, you can go down to 1 tablespoon, or taste the filling and adjust to your preference. (If using less miso, you may need to season with salt.)

This recipe takes a while because you first bake the potatoes for an hour before filling them and baking them a second time; but there's noth-ing technically difficult here, it just requires some patience and a gentle touch when scooping out the potato flesh. Plus, you can refrigerate left-overs for up to 3 days. Just reheat in the oven until hot and crisp.

Sanaë

Position racks in the middle and lower third of the oven and preheat to 400°F (200°C).

Using a fork, poke holes all over the potatoes. Place the potatoes in a large bowl and rub with a little oil and salt.

Line a half-sheet pan with foil and place on the lower rack to catch any drippings from the potatoes. Place the potatoes directly on the middle rack. (Reserve the bowl for later—no need to clean.) Bake for 1 hour to 1 hour 10 minutes, or until easily pierced with a sharp knife.

Meanwhile, cut the scallion whites into ½-inch (1.3 cm) pieces and set aside. Thinly slice the greens and set aside. In a small bowl, stir together the panko and 1 tablespoon of the oil. Season with salt and pepper, stir to combine, and set aside.

When the potatoes are cooked through, use tongs, oven mitts, or two large spoon to carefully transfer them to a large plate or cutting board and set aside to cool.

Remove the hot sheet from the oven and discard the foil. Immediately add the remaining 3 tablespoons oil to the pan and carefully tip to entirely coat the bottom. Add the scallion whites and shiitakes, season with salt, and toss to combine. Roast on the middle rack, stirring halfway through, for about 15 minutes, or until golden and starting to crisp.

In the large bowl that you used for the potatoes, stir together the sour cream and miso until combined. Add the mozzarella, scallion greens, and roasted shiitakes and scallion whites. Reserve the sheet pan for the potatoes (no need to clean it).

Using a sharp, preferably serrated knife, cut the potatoes in half lengthwise. With a spoon, gently scoop out the flesh and transfer to the large bowl with the other ingredients. (Leave a thin layer of potato flesh clinging to the skin.) Stir to combine all the ingredients, then use a metal spatula or wooden spoon to chop the potato flesh into smaller pieces. Chop and stir until the potato flesh is broken down but still has visible chunky pieces.

Place the potato skins on the sheet pan, like little boats, and evenly divide the filling among the potato skins, mounding the top. Sprinkle the tops with the panko mixture.

Roast on the middle rack for 20 to 25 minutes, or until the cheese is melted and bubbling and the panko is golden. For more color, turn on the broiler and broil for 2 to 3 minutes, or until the topping is deeply golden brown.

Set aside for 10 minutes before serving.

HOT TIP! If you don't like mushrooms, you could replace them with 4 ounces (113 g) bacon cut into small pieces. Just make sure to adjust the seasoning, as bacon will be salty.

Cheesy Orzo with Mushrooms

SERVES 6 TO 8

12 to 16 ounces (340 to 454 g) sliced fresh mushrooms, such as Baby Bella, button, or shiitake

1 large yellow onion (12 oz/ 340 g), halved and sliced

3 tablespoons extra-virgin olive oil

1 teaspoon kosher salt, plus more to taste

½ teaspoon freshly ground black pepper, plus more to taste

3 cups (720 ml) vegetable broth, hot, plus more as needed

1½ tablespoons Dijon mustard

1 pound (454 g) orzo

One 8-ounce (115 g) ball fresh mozzarella cheese, torn into pieces

1 cup (4 oz/113 g) shredded low-moisture mozzarella cheese

1 cup (3½ oz/100 g) grated Parmigiano-Reggiano cheese, divided, plus more (optional) for serving

Small handful of fresh flat-leaf parsley leaves, for serving

Lemon wedges, for serving

I've long admired food writer Ruby Tandoh, not only for her approachable and unfussy recipes, but also for her ability to arrange the most ordinary words in the most extraordinary way. I was especially taken with her 2022 cookbook, *Cook As You Are*, which made me feel seen as an exhausted food writer who has grown to detest cooking weeknight dinners. Sometimes, you just want to butter a piece of toast and call it a night. If you've been there, Tandoh sees you. One evening, I came upon this oven orzo bake, which I immediately wanted to adapt for our book in a sheet pan—Tandoh uses a deeper 9 × 13-inch (23 ×33 cm) roasting pan. I swapped out broccoli and zucchini for mushrooms, increased quantities of everything to fit a sheet pan, and added a couple of cheeses to make the dish comforting and fitting for a cold wintry night.

Olga

Position a rack in the middle of the oven and preheat to 400°F (200°C).

In a large bowl, toss together the mushrooms, onion, and oil until combined. Season with the salt and pepper and toss again. Spread the mixture on a half-sheet pan (don't clean the bowl; you'll use it again) and roast for about 25 minutes, or until the mushrooms and onions start to caramelize. Transfer to a heatproof surface.

In the same bowl, whisk together the broth and mustard until combined. Add the orzo and the broth mixture to the sheet pan and carefully stir to incorporate. Pat down the orzo to ensure it's completely submerged in the broth, adding more broth if needed. Scatter both kinds of mozzarella and half of the Parmigiano-Reggiano on top.

Return to the oven and bake for 20 to 25 minutes, or until the liquid is mostly absorbed and patches of cheese become burnished.

Once the pasta is cooked (it might be slightly al dente but should not be too firm/crunchy), remove from the oven, scatter the remaining Parmigiano-Reggiano over, and top with the parsley. Squeeze the lemon wedges over everything and season to taste with more salt and pepper. Serve right away, with more Parmigiano-Reggiano on the side, if desired.

Roasted Greek-ish Salad with Halloumi

SERVES 4

3 tablespoons extra-virgin olive oil, plus more for the pan

Kosher salt and freshly ground black pepper

1 large red bell pepper, cut into strips

1 pint cherry tomatoes, halved

1 medium red onion (8 oz/ 225 g), halved and sliced

½ cup (75 g) Kalamata olives, pitted and halved

Juice of 1 lemon, plus more as needed

2 teaspoons dried oregano

½ teaspoon crushed red pepper flakes (optional)

8 ounces (227 g) Halloumi cheese, cut into slices ¾ inch (2 cm) thick

½ cup (123 g) plain whole-milk yogurt

1 Persian (mini) cucumber, peeled and coarsely grated

1 tablespoon finely chopped fresh parsley, dill, and/or mint, plus more for garnish

This play on Greek salad takes its raw ingredients—minus the cucumber—and roasts them on a sheet pan. Something about roasting makes this dish feel more substantial, more like a main course than a starter, and every ingredient blossoms in the oven: The tomatoes become jammy; the red onion fades in color while its earthy sweetness grows; the bell peppers turn silky; the briny olives get pleasantly chewy. And although feta is traditional in Greek salad, I swapped it out for Halloumi, my husband's favorite. A splash of acid, such as lemon juice or red wine vinegar, brings everything together. While the ingredients are roasting, you can throw together a cucumber-yogurt drizzle to serve alongside. Serve with Lemony Orzo (page 94), couscous, or No-Rinse Basmati-Cumin Rice (page 272).

Olga

Position a rack in the middle of the oven and preheat to 400°F (200°C). Brush a half-sheet pan with oil and lightly sprinkle with salt and pepper.

Add the bell pepper, tomatoes, onion, and olives to the sheet pan, drizzle with the lemon juice, and sprinkle with the oregano and pepper flakes (if using). Lightly season with salt and black pepper (the olives are quite salty so don't overdo it), drizzle with the oil, and gently shake the pan so the ingredients get evenly coated in the oil and flavorings. Nestle the Halloumi slices in between the vegetables.

Roast for 20 to 25 minutes, stirring halfway through but without moving the Halloumi, or until the onions and peppers start to crisp and char and the tomatoes become jammy.

While the vegetables and halloumi are roasting, in a small bowl, whisk together the yogurt, cucumber, 1 to 2 teaspoons lemon juice, and the herbs. Lightly season with salt and pepper. Set aside until serving (or refrigerate if making well in advance).

Remove the sheet pan from the oven and garnish with additional parsley. Serve the yogurt drizzle alongside.

Vegetable Rice Bowls with Sweet Gochujang Sauce

SERVES 4

For the gochujang sauce

2 tablespoons gochujang

1 tablespoon brown sugar, any kind

1 tablespoon toasted sesame oil

For the mushrooms and vegetables

1 delicata squash (1 lb/454 g), seeded and cut into slices ¼ inch (6 mm) thick

4 tablespoons extra-virgin olive oil, divided

Kosher salt and freshly ground black pepper

7 ounces (200 g) fresh mushrooms, such as oyster, maitake, or shiitake, torn into bite-size pieces

1 tablespoon soy sauce

5 ounces (142 g) baby spinach

For serving

Short-Grain White Rice (page 271)

4 fried eggs (optional)

Black sesame seeds (optional), for sprinkling

I developed a version of this recipe when I worked in the test kitchen of Martha Stewart & Marley Spoon (a meal kit delivery service). The original calls for crisping rice in a nonstick skillet with a little oil, which you're welcome to do. I always feel nourished and satisfied after eating this bowl. The egg is optional, but highly recommended for how the warm yolk soaks into the rice. If you can't find delicata squash, use sweet potatoes, as they'll impart a similar sweetness.

Sanaë

MAKE THE GOCHUJANG SAUCE: In a small bowl, stir together the gochujang, brown sugar, sesame oil, and 2 tablespoons water until combined. Set aside.

MAKE THE MUSHROOMS AND VEGETABLES: Position racks in the upper and lower thirds of the oven and preheat to 425°F (220°C).

On a half-sheet pan, toss the squash with 2 tablespoons of the olive oil and season with salt and pepper. Arrange in a single layer.

In a medium bowl, toss the mushrooms with the remaining 2 tablespoons oil and the soy sauce. Arrange in a single layer on a second half-sheet pan.

Roast the squash on the bottom rack and the mushrooms on the top rack for about 10 minutes, or until starting to brown. Flip the mushrooms and squash and continue roasting for 10 to 15 minutes more, or until golden brown.

Remove the sheet pan with the squash from the oven and set it aside. Remove the other sheet pan with the mushrooms from the oven and evenly scatter the spinach over the mushrooms. Return to the oven on the top rack for about 3 minutes, or until the spinach is starting to wilt. Remove from the oven and stir together to finish wilting the spinach. Taste and season with salt, if desired.

TO SERVE: Divide the rice among four bowls. Top each bowl with the vegetables and a fried egg (if using) and drizzle with the sweet gochujang sauce. If desired, sprinkle with sesame seeds.

Sheet Pan "Fried" Rice

For the rice

2 tablespoons neutral oil, such as canola or grapeseed

1½ tablespoons Chinese light soy sauce

¾ teaspoon toasted sesame oil

½ teaspoon kosher salt

4 to 5 generous cups (680 to 850 g) leftover cooked rice

One 16-ounce (454 g) bag frozen mixed vegetables (no need to thaw)

3 large eggs, lightly beaten

For the sauce

2 tablespoons dark soy sauce

1 to 2 tablespoons honey, to taste

1 to 2 teaspoons Chinkiang vinegar, to taste

1 teaspoon grated fresh ginger

For serving

Thinly sliced scallions (optional)

Furikake (optional)

Chili crisp (optional)

Consider this recipe one that checks all the boxes on winning the weeknight dinner lottery: Fast, flavorful, and customizable. And while it's technically not fried rice, it's a hands-off method for making lots of crispy rice at once. Normally, I cobble together bits and bobs of frozen vegetables from my freezer, but if you don't have an assortment to choose from, the premixed bag of carrots, corn, peas, green beans, and lima beans comes to the rescue. But perhaps the most winning quality of this dish is the amount of audibly crispy bits that it produces.

Olga

MAKE THE RICE: Position a rack in the middle of the oven, place a half-sheet pan on it, and preheat to 450°F (230°C).

In a large bowl, whisk together the neutral oil, light soy sauce, sesame oil, and salt. Add the rice and toss to combine. The rice should be evenly coated in the oil but will have some darker clumps where the soy sauce penetrated and white clumps where it didn't—that's okay. Remove the hot sheet from the oven, set on a heatproof surface, and, carefully transfer the rice mixture to it. Spread out in an even layer and return to the oven. Roast for 15 minutes, or until the rice starts to crisp up and turn light golden.

Remove the pan from the oven, add the frozen vegetables, and carefully—the pan will be searing hot—stir to distribute. Return to the oven for another 15 minutes, or until the rice is rich golden brown and the vegetables are tender.

Remove the pan from the oven and push the rice and vegetables out to the sides, creating an empty space in the center. Pour the eggs in the space and return the sheet pan to the oven for 2 to 3 minutes, or until the eggs are cooked through and opaque. Remove from the oven and break up the egg, stirring it into the rice and vegetables.

MAKE THE SAUCE: While the rice and vegetables are roasting, in a small bowl, whisk together the dark soy sauce, honey, vinegar, and ginger until combined. Taste and adjust the sweetness and/or acidity to your liking, if needed.

TO SERVE: Divide among shallow bowls and drizzle with the sauce. Top with scallions, furikake, and chili crisp, if you like.

Gnocchi with Broccoli and Lemony Ricotta

SERVES 4

One 17.6-ounce (500 g) package shelf-stable or refrigerated potato gnocchi

1 pound (454 g) broccoli florets

3 tablespoons extra-virgin olive oil, plus more for drizzling

2 teaspoons dried oregano

1 teaspoon kosher salt, plus more as needed

¼ teaspoon crushed red pepper flakes

Freshly ground black pepper

⅓ cup (80 ml) heavy cream

1 cup (250 g) whole-milk ricotta cheese

1 lemon

½ cup (50 g) finely grated Parmigiano-Reggiano cheese

Fresh basil leaves, for garnish

This recipe came to me late in the process of writing our cookbook. I happened to have the ingredients on hand and threw them together for lunch. The result was so delicious—and the recipe so easy and quick—that I found myself remaking it again and again. First you cover the sheet pan so both the gnocchi and broccoli steam and soften, then everything gets sprinkled with Parmigiano-Reggiano and bakes until golden. A drizzle of heavy cream encourages caramelization along the edges that reminds me of a gratin, without ever feeling too rich. The star, though, is the lemony ricotta, which gets dolloped onto the gnocchi right as they come out of the oven. It melts just slightly from the residual heat to coat everything in an unctuous, bright sauce.

Sanaë

Position a rack in the middle of the oven and preheat to 400°F (200°C).

In a large bowl, mix together the gnocchi, broccoli, oil, oregano, salt, and red pepper flakes. Generously season with black pepper. Spread in a single layer on a half-sheet pan. Drizzle the heavy cream over everything, followed by ¼ cup (60 ml) water. Cover tightly with foil. Bake for 10 minutes.

Meanwhile, place the ricotta in a small bowl. Grate the lemon zest into the bowl and season to taste with salt and pepper. Stir to combine. Cut the zested lemon into wedges and set aside.

Remove the hot sheet from the oven, uncover (discard the foil), and sprinkle the Parmigiano-Reggiano over everything. Return to the oven and bake for about 15 minutes, or until the gnocchi and broccoli are starting to brown. Turn on the broiler and broil for 2 to 4 minutes, or until everything is golden brown.

Dollop the lemony ricotta over the gnocchi and broccoli. Garnish with basil leaves and serve with the lemon wedges for squeezing over.

Stewy Chickpeas and Tomatoes in Coconut Curry

SERVES 4

2 tablespoons coconut oil

2 pints (600 g) cherry or grape tomatoes

6 shallots, halved if large, and cut into wedges ¼ inch (6 mm) thick

3 garlic cloves, unpeeled

1 teaspoon kosher salt

½ dried bird's eye chile, crushed, or more to taste

Two 14-ounce (400 ml) cans full-fat coconut milk

2 tablespoons Thai curry paste (any kind)

1 tablespoon fish sauce or liquid aminos, plus more to taste

Juice of 1 lime

Two 15-ounce (425 g) cans chickpeas, drained and rinsed, or 3 cups cooked chickpeas

1 bell pepper (any color but green), cut into strips

Cooked jasmine or Short-Grain White Rice (page 271)

Lime wedges, for squeezing

⅓ cup (27 g) toasted coconut flakes (optional), for garnish

Chopped fresh cilantro and/ or Thai basil (optional), for garnish

This satisfying dish is another recipe inspired by Ruby Tandoh's *Cook As You Are*, a cookbook I believe every home cook should own. I was trying, unsuccessfully, to make a sheet pan version of chana masala and concluded that there was no need for that recipe. Then I saw Tandoh's idea for coconut curry. While home-cooked chickpeas are unmatched in their taste and texture, most folks with day jobs might not think ahead to make a batch, which is why canned chickpeas are the unofficial stars of many a pantry. I've made this stewy dish for my family on many winter nights, and it is the warming, nourishing respite we all need.

Olga

Position a rack in the middle of the oven and preheat to 400°F (200°C). Add the coconut oil to a half-sheet pan and let it melt in the oven, about 1 minute.

Remove the sheet pan from the oven, add the tomatoes, shallots, and garlic. Season with the salt and crushed chile, lightly shake the pan to coat, and return to the oven.

Roast for about 25 minutes, or until the tomatoes are bursting and starting to turn jammy and the shallots are beginning to caramelize.

Meanwhile, in a medium bowl, whisk together the coconut milk, curry paste, fish sauce, and lime juice.

Remove the hot sheet from the oven (leave the oven on) and transfer the garlic to a small plate. Squeeze the cloves out of their skins, mash them into a paste, and whisk into the coconut milk mixture. Pour this mixture over the tomatoes, add the chickpeas and bell pepper, and mix well to combine.

Return to the oven for another 20 minutes, or until the coconut mixture thickens and looks stewy. Taste and adjust the seasonings as needed.

Serve with rice and lime wedges for squeezing over. If desired, garnish with coconut flakes and cilantro and/or basil.

Slab "Bee Sting" Pizza

For the dough

2 cups (480 g) lukewarm water

2 teaspoons active dry yeast

3 tablespoons extra-virgin
olive oil, divided

2½ teaspoons kosher salt

4½ cups (563 g) all-purpose
flour

For the sauce

1 cup (270 g) canned crushed
tomatoes

1 teaspoon extra-virgin
olive oil

½ teaspoon crushed red
pepper flakes (optional), or
more to taste

Kosher salt (optional)

For the pizza

3 tablespoon extra-virgin olive
oil, plus more as needed

10 ounces (283 g) low-
moisture mozzarella cheese
(see Hot Tips!), coarsely
shredded

2 ounces (57 g) thinly sliced
spicy soppressata (optional)

½ medium red onion (4 oz/
115 g), thinly sliced

Hot honey (optional), for
drizzling

My favorite pizza was made in the beloved now-shuttered Brooklyn restaurant Franny's (IYKYK) and this pizza is decidedly not it. Instead, after years of trying to re-create it, I've realized that the best version to emerge from my home oven is an unfussy, unfancy sheet pan pizza, aka grandma-style, with a thicker crust reminiscent of focaccia. Here, I channel the toppings of the Bee Sting pizza, made at Brooklyn-based restaurant Roberta's. At Roberta's, the pizza is topped with spicy soppressata and gets finished with honey. (For a meatless pizza, skip the *salumi* and maybe add spicy pepperoncini, Calabrian chiles, or up the amount of crushed red pepper flakes.) The only consideration here is to plan a day (or two) ahead to get more flavorful pizza dough. Alternatively, you can always pick up pizza dough from your local pizzeria. And, if you want to keep things simple, just stick to mozzarella and tomato sauce for that classic grandma slice.

A notable feature of grandma-style pizza is that toppings go on first, followed by the sauce (the reverse of a regular pizza). This allows for the sauce to dry up a little bit, resulting in a more concentrated, tomatoey flavor.

Olga

MAKE THE DOUGH: In a stand mixer fitted with the dough hook, stir together the water and yeast and let sit until the yeast has dissolved, about 5 minutes. Stir in 2 tablespoons of the oil and the salt. With the mixer on low speed, add the flour in two batches, mixing on low until it's incorporated. Increase the speed to medium-low and mix the dough until it's smooth, slightly tacky, and a little elastic, about 3 minutes. (You can also do this by hand, but kneading the dough will take slightly longer, closer to the 8-minute mark.)

Grease a large bowl with the remaining 1 tablespoon oil and use a little bit of that oil to grease a flexible bench scraper. Use this greased scraper to transfer the dough to the prepared bowl. Gently turn the dough to coat in the oil, then cover the bowl with a plate wide enough to sit on top of the bowl without any air coming in; refrigerate for at least 24 hours and up to 48 hours. In this unrushed time, the dough will enjoy a slow, steady rise, which will allow it to develop nuanced, deep flavor.

continued

HOT TIPS! Low-moisture mozzarella is better here than fresh cheese, which is wetter and often delivers a soggy crust with slab pizzas. If you must have fresh mozz at all costs, swap out at most half of the low-moisture kind and be sure to thoroughly dry the fresh cheese. (If you are tearing the cheese or cutting it or slicing it, this means you pat dry individual pieces as thoroughly as possible.)

Other topping ideas? Anchovies, olives, pickled jalapeños, pineapple, sliced meatballs, cooked mushrooms—whatever your heart desires.

MAKE THE SAUCE: In a medium bowl, stir together the tomatoes, oil, and pepper flakes (if using). Taste and season with a pinch of salt, if you like—this will depend on the brand of canned tomatoes as well as your preference.

MAKE THE PIZZA: Position a rack in the middle of the oven and preheat to 450°F (230°C). Grease two quarter-sheet pans with 1½ tablespoons oil each.

Using an oiled bench scraper, divide the dough in half. Each piece should weigh a little over 1 pound (500 g). Plop each piece of dough on a greased sheet pan and coat the dough in the oil, if it's at all sticky. Using your fingers, which should be oiled by now, spread out the dough and dimple it with your fingertips, as you would with focaccia (see page 46). Spread the dough out as far as it'll go, then loosely cover with clean kitchen towels and let sit for about 30 minutes.

Repeat the pressing out of the dough—it should be a lot more pliable and forgiving at this juncture. Let the dough sit for 10 minutes.

Divide the mozzarella, soppressata (if using), and onion between the sheet pans. Divide the sauce between the pizzas—don't worry if it's not an even coating of the sauce, just dollop the sauce here and there and it'll be fine. Lightly brush the crust border with a little oil.

Bake for 25 to 30 minutes, or until the crust is a deep golden brown and the edges look crunchy.

To serve, run a table knife around the perimeter of the pizza and shimmy it out onto a cutting board. Use a large, sharp knife or a pizza cutter to divide the pizza into the desired number of slices. Drizzle with hot honey, if you like, and serve right away. (Leftovers reheat beautifully in a 350°F/180°C oven.)

Sweet Potatoes, Onions, Dates, and Pistachios on Yogurt

SERVES 4

2 medium sweet potatoes (1¼ lb/567 g total), cut into 1-inch (2.5 cm) pieces

1 medium red onion (8 oz/ 227 g), halved and cut into slices ¼ inch (6 mm) thick

¼ cup (60 ml) extra-virgin olive oil, plus more for drizzling

Kosher salt and freshly ground black pepper

3 Medjool dates, pitted and torn into small pieces

½ cup (128 g) whole-milk Greek yogurt

1 lemon

1 teaspoon za'atar

⅓ cup (45 g) pistachios, toasted (see On Toasting Nuts, page 278)

Flaky sea salt, such as Maldon

Warmed pita or naan (optional), for serving

This is one of our favorite recipes to serve as an elegant appetizer, side, or main—in which case, add some oven-toasted flatbread on the side for sopping up the yogurt. It's a stunning combination of soft, creamy, sweet, and salty. The dates, torn into small pieces, provide an additional layer of caramel sweetness. There's very little prep—just chopping sweet potatoes and onion—but the result is impressive with the various colors and textures. If you are allergic to nuts, you can replace the pistachios with ¼ cup toasted pumpkin seeds. Since you're only using lemon zest, save the zested lemon to make a vinaigrette or slice it and add to a carafe of water.

Sanaï + Olga

Position a rack in the middle of the oven and preheat to 375°F (190°C).

On a half-sheet pan, toss together the sweet potatoes, onion, and oil. Season with kosher salt and pepper and arrange in an even layer. Roast for about 40 minutes, stirring halfway through, or until the vegetables are softened and browned.

Remove the hot sheet from the oven and immediately add the dates. Stir together, allowing the residual heat from the pan to warm up the dates.

Spoon the yogurt onto a large plate or platter and with the back of the spoon spread it into an even layer. Using a Microplane rasp grater, finely grate the lemon zest over the yogurt. Top with the sweet potatoes, onions, and dates.

Sprinkle with the za'atar and pistachios and season with pepper and flaky salt. Drizzle with a little more oil and serve immediately, with pita or naan, if desired.

Dilly Feta-Stuffed Zucchini with Mint and Pine Nuts

SERVES 4

3 tablespoons extra-virgin olive oil, divided, plus more as needed

4 zucchini (8 oz/227 g each)

1 medium yellow onion (8 oz/227 g), finely chopped

4 ounces (113 g) feta cheese or chèvre (fresh goat cheese)

Handful of minced fresh dill, plus more for garnish

¼ cup (30 g) toasted pine nuts, plus more for garnish

Freshly ground black pepper

¼ cup (scant 1 oz/25 g) finely grated Parmigiano-Reggiano cheese, plus more for sprinkling

Fresh mint leaves, for garnish

Lemon wedges, for squeezing

Years ago, when I was in college, I used to make this dish for Sunday suppers. Outside of pine nuts, which were a splurge, the rest of the ingredients were pretty scrappy, and it was a good way to use up any odds and ends of feta or goat cheese, which I often had on hand. Feel free to swap out the cheeses based on what you have—though feta or goat cheese should be your starting base. Mix in Gruyère, Grana Padano, Pecorino Romano, or what have you. Don't like dill or mint? Use parsley or tarragon or other preferred herb. Slivered almonds or toasted sunflower seeds or pepitas would be delicious. It's your world, do your thing!

Olga

Position a rack in the middle of the oven and preheat to 350°F (180°C). Lightly brush a half-sheet pan with oil.

Trim off the stem ends of the zucchini, halve them lengthwise, and use a dessert spoon to scoop out the flesh and reserve, leaving a shell ¼ inch (6 mm) thick. Arrange the shells, cut sides up, on one side of the prepared sheet pan. Arrange the onion in a mound on the other side. Drizzle the onion with 1 tablespoon of the oil, gently stirring to coat the onion. Roast for about 15 minutes, or until both the zucchini and onion are softened.

While the shells are roasting, in a food processor, combine the zucchini flesh, feta cheese, dill, pine nuts, the remaining 2 tablespoons oil, and a generous pinch of pepper and process until smooth and creamy.

Remove the sheet pan from the oven, move the rack about 6 inches from the broiling element, and turn on the broiler.

Fold the softened onion into the filling mixture until combined. Divide the filling among the zucchini shells (if you have any leftover filling, refrigerate and use it as a spread or dip). Arrange the filled zucchini shells on the sheet pan you just used. Sprinkle the tops with the Parmigiano-Reggiano.

Broil the stuffed zucchini for 3 to 5 minutes, or until the filling is bubbling and deep golden. Remove from the oven, drizzle with a little oil, and sprinkle with a little more Parmigiano-Reggiano, pine nuts, and mint leaves. Serve warm, with lemon wedges for squeezing over.

Chapter 7

Sweet Treats

Orange-Fennel Shortbread

**MAKES TWENTY-FOUR
2¼ x 1½-INCH (5.7 x
3.8 CM) PIECES**

2 cups (250 g) all-purpose
flour

¾ cup (150 g) granulated
sugar

1 teaspoon kosher salt

1 teaspoon finely grated
orange zest

½ teaspoon ground
cardamom

¼ teaspoon ground fennel or
fennel pollen, or more to taste

2 sticks (8 oz/227 g) cold
unsalted butter, preferably
high-fat European-style, cubed

1 teaspoon orange
blossom water

Everything I know about shortbread I learned from the *New York Times* food columnist and cookbook author Melissa Clark. According to Melissa, the key to successful shortbread is 1 stick of butter to 1 cup of flour—I suggest you commit this to memory. On paper, it seems ludicrous that so few basic ingredients can form something so transcendent: At its most basic, shortbread is just butter, sugar, flour, and salt, but the simple combination—a blank canvas, if you will—lends itself spectacularly to customization. Eager to take on flavorings from extracts to spices, shortbread is not only a great care-package player, it can also easily be scaled up or down, making it ideal for feeding lots of mouths.

Here, I use one of my favorite flavor combinations: fragrant orange blossom water, floral orange zest, aromatic cardamom, and savory fennel, which makes the cookie a little more interesting. If you can splurge on fennel pollen—a pricey but extremely worthwhile spice—it will produce a stunningly fragrant shortbread, but ground fennel is also terrific. Feel free to explore other options such as rose water and cracked pink peppercorns; ground pistachios, mandarin zest, and sumac; or vanilla and coarsely ground black pepper, just to give you a few ideas. This is proportioned to feed a crowd or to give away as edible gifts.

Olga

Position a rack in the middle of the oven and preheat to 325°F (160°C). Line a quarter-sheet pan with parchment paper with generous overhang on the long sides.

In a food processor, pulse together the flour, sugar, salt, orange zest, cardamom, and fennel to combine. Add the butter and orange blossom water and pulse until fine crumbs form and the dough starts to come together. Don't overprocess; the dough should be somewhat crumbly.

Press the dough into an even layer in the prepared sheet pan. To do so more easily and evenly, cut a piece of parchment paper the size of the sheet pan, set it over the dough, and through the paper, press out the dough. Use the bottom of a measuring cup to achieve the most even results. Remove the parchment paper. Using a fork, prick the dough all over and transfer to the oven.

Bake for 30 to 35 minutes, or until golden brown.

continued

Transfer to a wire rack and let cool to the touch, then use the parchment overhang to transfer the shortbread to a cutting board and cut into 24 rectangles (or your preferred shape) while still warm. Let cool completely before serving.

Cacio e Pepe Shortbread

MAKES TWENTY-FOUR 2¼ X 1½-INCH (5.7 x 3.8 CM) PIECES

2 cups (250 g) all-purpose flour

2 teaspoons coarsely ground black pepper

½ teaspoon kosher salt

2 sticks (8 oz/227 g) cold unsalted butter, preferably high-fat European-style, cubed

⅔ cup (65 g) grated Grana Padano cheese

⅓ cup (30 g) grated Pecorino Romano cheese

While this savory shortbread is definitely not dessert fare, I've eaten it in lieu of dessert, and if you're someone who'd rather have a cheese plate than a sweet course after your meal, this will be right up your alley. I often make a batch of this dough and keep it on hand in logs in case people show up at my house last-minute—they make excellent snacks with cocktails. But I also like to make these to bring to parties for a savory nibble with drinks or as a host/hostess gift. Super punchy from the hard, salty cheeses and with an assertive peppery bite from the coarsely ground black pepper, this savory shortbread has never not gone over well.

Position a rack in the middle of the oven and preheat to 325°F (160°C). Line a quarter-sheet pan with parchment paper with generous overhang on the long sides.

In a food processor, pulse together the flour, pepper, and salt to combine. Add the butter, Grana Padano, and Pecorino Romano and pulse until fine crumbs form and start to come together. Don't overprocess; the dough should be somewhat crumbly.

Press the dough into an even layer in the prepared sheet pan. To do so more easily and evenly, cut a piece of parchment paper the size of the sheet pan, set it over the dough, and through the paper, press out the dough. Use the bottom of a measuring cup to achieve the most even results. Remove the parchment paper. Using a fork, prick the dough all over and transfer to the oven.

Bake for 30 to 35 minutes, or until golden brown.

Transfer to a wire rack and let cool to the touch, then use the parchment overhang to transfer the shortbread to a cutting board and cut into 24 rectangles (or your preferred shape) while still warm. Let cool completely before serving.

"Make Someone Happy" Cake

MAKES ONE 13 × 18-INCH
(33 × 46 CM) CAKE /
SERVES 12

For the cake

¼ cup (60 ml) neutral oil, such as canola or grapeseed, plus more for the pan

4 cups (500 g) all-purpose flour, plus more for the pan

2½ teaspoons baking powder

1½ teaspoons kosher salt

¼ teaspoon baking soda

2½ sticks (10 oz/283 g) unsalted butter, softened

2 cups (400 g) granulated sugar

2 large eggs, at room temperature

3 large egg yolks, at room temperature

1½ cups (360 ml) well-shaken buttermilk, at room temperature

1½ teaspoons vanilla extract

For the frosting

1½ cups (9 oz/260 g) semisweet chocolate chips or roughly chopped semisweet chocolate

1½ cups (330 g) crème fraîche or sour cream, at room temperature

ingredients continued

Just about everyone I know loves cake, but few like making it. People feel that cakes are fussy and take too long; they're intimidated by pictures of flawlessly frosted cakes; and when they compare them to their own rustic interpretations, they naturally get discouraged. I'm here to tell you that a) cake is less fussy to make than cookies and b) perfectly frosted cakes, while beautiful to look at, are not the goal. The goal, first and foremost, is to make a cake that is delicious and will make people happy. Here we lean into unfussy with a single-layer cake that's frosted, then cut and served. The crème fraîche frosting, adapted from cookbook author Julia Turshen, has just three ingredients and can be stirred by hand in a bowl. Now that's a cause for celebration!

Olga

MAKE THE CAKE: Position a rack in the middle of the oven and preheat to 350°C (180°C). Lightly grease the bottom of a half-sheet pan with oil and line it with parchment paper. Lightly grease and flour the parchment as well as the sides of the pan.

In a large bowl, whisk together the flour, baking powder, salt, and baking soda until thoroughly combined.

In a stand mixer fitted with the paddle attachment (or in a large bowl with a hand mixer), beat the butter and oil on medium speed until incorporated, about 90 seconds. Add the sugar, increase the mixer speed to medium-high, and continue to beat until the mixture is pale yellow and fluffy, 2 to 3 minutes. Add the whole eggs and egg yolks, one at a time, beating until completely incorporated before the next addition. Stop and scrape the bottom and sides of the bowl and mix briefly to reincorporate.

In a 2-cup (480 ml) measuring cup with a spout, combine the buttermilk and vanilla. Add one-third of the flour mixture to the butter mixture and mix on low speed until just combined. Add half of the buttermilk mixture and mix until just combined. Continue with the remaining flour and buttermilk mixtures, alternating until just combined; do not overmix. The batter will be thick.

continued

1 to 2 tablespoons
maple syrup

1 teaspoon vanilla extract
(optional)

Pinch of kosher salt

For assembly

Rainbow sprinkles (optional,
but highly recommended)

Transfer the batter to the prepared sheet pan and use a small offset spatula to smooth out the batter so it's evenly distributed.

Bake for 23 to 27 minutes, or until the cake is golden brown and starts to pull away from the sides of the pan, and a cake tester inserted in the center of the cake comes out clean. When lightly pressed in the center with a finger, the cake should spring back.

Transfer to a wire rack and let cool completely in the pan.

MAKE THE FROSTING: While the cake is baking, bring a small pot of water to a boil. Put the chocolate chips in a large stainless steel or heatproof glass bowl. Reduce the heat to a simmer and set the bowl over the pot (the water should not touch the bowl—if it does, simply pour some water out). Stir until the chocolate is melted, about 5 minutes. (Alternatively, you can melt the chocolate in a microwave in 15-second bursts, stirring after each.) Remove from the heat and whisk in the crème fraîche, 1 tablespoon of the maple syrup, vanilla (if using), and salt until completely smooth and uniform. Add the remaining 1 tablespoon of maple syrup if you want the frosting a little sweeter. Refrigerate until the cake has cooled completely, about 1 hour; it will thicken as it cools, which is what you want.

ASSEMBLE THE CAKE: Run a table knife around the perimeter of the pan to loosen the cake (but leave in the pan). Add the frosting and use a small offset spatula to evenly spread it out almost to the edge of the cake. If you like, use the spatula to make unfussy, rustic swirls and swoops all over the frosting (I like working with a small spatula for greater control). If you're feeling especially festive, decorate the cake with the sprinkles of your choice (we're a rainbow household). Briefly chill the cake in the refrigerator before serving just to firm up the frosting, about 10 minutes.

Caramelized Bananas with Ice Cream

SERVES 4

2 tablespoons coconut oil
or ghee, melted, divided

4 not-too-ripe bananas,
peeled

2 tablespoons dark
brown sugar

4 scoops vanilla ice cream

Flaky sea salt, such as Maldon,
for sprinkling

This dessert—an ode to Bananas Foster minus the rum—couldn't be simpler and results in the most satisfying combination of warm, caramelized bananas and cold ice cream. As the ice cream melts over the bananas, I'm reminded of a childhood dessert my mother would make on special occasions (since we rarely ate dessert): smashed bananas drizzled with heavy cream.

The bananas fit in a single layer on the sheet pan and don't require any flipping. They're rubbed with a little dark brown sugar and coconut oil to speed up the caramelization. The flaky salt brings this dessert together—please do not skip it!

Make sure to choose bananas that are just ripe but not too ripe, otherwise they won't hold their shape. You could also use bananas that are a tad underripe.

Sanaë

Position a rack in the middle of the oven and preheat to 425°F (220°C). Line a half-sheet pan with parchment paper. Brush the parchment with 1 tablespoon of the oil.

Using a sharp knife, cut the bananas in half crosswise, then split the banana halves lengthwise.

Gently rub the bananas all over with the brown sugar. Place on the prepared sheet pan, cut side down. Brush the tops of the bananas with the remaining 1 tablespoon oil.

Roast for 10 to 15 minutes, rotating the pan front to back halfway through, or until the sugar is bubbling around the edges and a shade darker. (The bananas should still hold their shape and not look collapsed; start checking at 10 minutes.)

Allow to cool for 5 minutes on the sheet. Using a thin metal spatula or a small offset spatula, gently transfer the banana slices to four small plates. (The bananas along the edges of the sheet pan will be more caramelized—make sure everyone gets one of those—though the middle ones are also delicious.) Immediately top each plate of bananas with a scoop of ice cream and sprinkle with a generous pinch of flaky sea salt.

Sour Cherry Slab Pie

MAKES ONE 13 × 9-INCH (33 × 23 CM) SLAB PIE / SERVES 10 TO 12

For the crust

2½ cups (313 g) all-purpose flour

2 tablespoons granulated sugar

¾ teaspoon fine sea salt

2½ sticks (10 oz/283 g) cold unsalted butter, preferably cultured, cut into ½-inch (1.3 cm) pieces

5 to 8 tablespoons ice water, or more as needed

For the filling

1 cup (200 g) granulated sugar

3 tablespoons instant tapioca

¼ teaspoon ground cardamom

¼ teaspoon fine sea salt

2 to 2¼ pounds (907 g to 1.1 kg) sour cherries, rinsed and pitted (about 4½ cups)

1 tablespoon brandy or 1½ teaspoons almond extract

For assembly

Heavy cream, for brushing

Demerara sugar, for sprinkling

The world is divided into pie people and cake people, and they will argue over this until the end of times. For the record, I'm a pie person, and if you ask me for the best pie flavor, I will tell you without missing a beat that it's sour cherry, and yes, please and thank you, I will die on that hill. (I won't tell you your favorite pie isn't as good; I just won't eat as much of it.) Sour cherries, not to be confused with sweet, are smaller, juicier, and have a jewel-like translucence. They're available for exactly three days each year—kidding, but really, their season is fleeting. Of course, it's a cruel twist of fate that this brief season coincides with a time when you might not want to turn on your oven—so every summer, I buy as many sour cherries as I can handle, cook what I can before they spoil, and then pit and freeze the rest to use throughout the year. Which is why you may often see a sour cherry pie at my Thanksgiving table. And while round pies are what we normally expect when we think of pies, slab pies are what feed more people (hey, math is math, and you can't argue with it). So, this is a pie to feed a crowd or a few pie fanatics (me!). Lots of folks like almond extract with cherries, but I far prefer a hint of brandy to contrast the stone fruit, so I've provided both options here. You can easily double the recipe, but for more pieces with crust, I recommend baking in two quarter-sheet pans, rather than one half-sheet pan.

Olga

MAKE THE DOUGH

BY HAND: In a large bowl, whisk together the flour, sugar, and salt until combined. Add the butter and toss the pieces in the flour mixture. Start rubbing the butter into the flour, breaking up the pieces as necessary, until they are the size of kidney or lima beans. This could take a little time, especially if your butter is from the freezer or not the softer, high-fat kind. Don't get discouraged, the butter will eventually yield. Once the butter pieces are the desired size, add 4 tablespoons of the ice water at once, toss the mixture to combine and distribute, then continue to add the water, 1 tablespoon at a time, until the dough is moist enough to hold together (to test, pinch it together and if it holds, it's ready). Transfer the dough to a a piece of plastic wrap—

continued

it should look messy and you should see flecks of the butter. Use a bench scraper or the sides of the wrap—not your hands, which are too warm—to form the dough into a ball, then pat it down into a disk. Wrap the dough disk tightly and refrigerate for at least 3 hours and up to 3 days. (You can also freeze the dough, tightly wrapped in another layer of plastic wrap, for up to 2 months.)

IN A FOOD PROCESSOR: In a food processor, pulse together the flour, sugar, and salt just to combine. Add the butter and pulse until the butter pieces are the size of kidney or lima beans. Once the butter pieces are the desired size, add 4 tablespoons of the ice water at once, and pulse the mixture to combine and distribute. Continue to add the water, 1 tablespoon at a time, and pulsing in short bursts, until the dough is moist enough to hold together (to test, pinch it together and if it holds, it's ready). Transfer the dough to a a piece of plastic wrap—it should look messy and you should see flecks of the butter. Use a bench scraper or the sides of the wrap—not your hands, which are too warm—to form the dough into a ball, then pat it down into a disk. Wrap the dough disk tightly and refrigerate for at least 3 hours and up to 3 days. (You can also freeze the dough, tightly wrapped in another layer of plastic wrap, for up to 2 months.)

ROLL OUT THE CRUST: Remove the dough from the refrigerator and let it warm up slightly, 10 to 15 minutes, depending on the temperature of your kitchen. Divide the dough into two pieces, one about two-thirds (about 460 g) and the other about one-third (about 230 g). Roll out the larger piece to about 11 × 15 inches (28 × 38 cm) and transfer to a quarter-sheet pan, pressing it into the corners and crimping it as desired (or not). Transfer to the refrigerator, then roll out the smaller piece of dough to about 9 × 14 inches (23 × 36 cm), transfer to a lightly floured piece of parchment, and refrigerate.

BLIND-BAKE THE BOTTOM CRUST: Position a rack in the middle of the oven and preheat to 425°F (220°C).

Line the dough on the quarter-sheet pan with foil and weight it down with pie weights (I like to use pennies, but rice, beans, or actual pie weights work well, too). Transfer to the oven and bake for about 30 minutes, or until the crust is light golden brown.

MAKE THE FILLING

While the bottom crust is baking, in a mini food processor, combine the sugar, tapioca, cardamom, and salt and process until the tapioca is ground to a fine powder. Place the cherries in a large bowl, add the sugar mixture and brandy, and gently mix to combine.

ASSEMBLE AND BAKE THE PIE

When the bottom crust is ready, transfer it to a wire rack and let cool slightly. Reduce the oven temperature to 375°F (190°C). Remove the foil with the weights.

Transfer the cherry filling to the pie crust and gently spread it around so it's evenly distributed. Remove the smaller piece of pie dough from the refrigerator and set it on your counter (on the parchment). Using cookie cutters of various sizes (rounds, leaves, what have you), punch out pieces of dough, arranging them over the cherry filling in a pattern of your choosing. Brush the top crust with some cream and generously sprinkle with demerara sugar.

Bake for 50 minutes to 1 hour, or until the crust is dark golden brown and the filling gently bubbles.

Transfer to a wire rack to cool completely, at least 3 hours, before serving.

Salted Honey Apple Tarts

MAKES TWO 14 × 6-INCH
(36 × 15 CM) RECTANGULAR
TARTS / SERVES 6 TO 8

2 firm, crisp apples (1 lb/
454 g), such as Honeycrisp
or Fuji, peeled

3 tablespoons dark brown
sugar, divided

Pinch of kosher salt

One 14-ounce (397 g) sheet
all-butter frozen puff pastry,
such as Dufour, thawed in
the refrigerator

2 tablespoons (1 oz/28 g)
unsalted butter, cut into
small pieces

1 large egg, whisked

2 tablespoons honey

Flaky sea salt, such as Maldon,
for sprinkling

Crème fraîche (optional),
for serving

Because I didn't eat much sugar growing up, my dessert of choice (and one of the few sweet treats allowed into our home for special occasions) was an apple tart, or *tarte aux pommes*, commonly found at French bakeries. My mother would hunt down the one bakery or pâtisserie in our neighborhood that made apple tarts without any glaze, or would preorder the tart, asking that the apple slices be left bare. To this day, it's how I prefer my apple tarts—no sweet coating or jam so the apples and butter crust take center stage—though I've added a drizzle of honey for a bit more sweetness. (Don't tell my mother!)

Apple tart also happens to be my best friend's favorite dessert, so I often make it for her whenever she comes over. The sprinkle of flaky sea salt and dollop of crème fraîche elevate the thin slices of apple in a surprising way that always has my guests asking for seconds, leftovers to take home, *and* the recipe. I love it for the fall or winter, whenever I'm hosting a dinner party. I'll make it a few hours in advance, and once the plates are cleared and we're moving toward dessert, I'll warm up the tarts in a 350°F (180°C) oven for about 10 minutes. As for the Summer Plum Tarts with Cardamom Sugar (page 229), you'll make two long rectangular tarts for the perfect ratio of crust to fruit.

Sanaë

Position a rack in the middle of the oven and preheat to 375°F (190°C).

Cut the apples into quarters and remove the cores. Thinly slice into halfmoons. The slices should be thin enough to be somewhat flexible, but not so thin that they will break. Place the apple slices in a large bowl. Add 2 tablespoons of the brown sugar and the kosher salt. Using your hands, very gently toss the apples until the slices are evenly coated.

Cut a piece of parchment paper the size of a half-sheet pan. Place the sheet of puff pastry on the parchment. Using a sharp knife, cut the puff pastry lengthwise into 2 long rectangles. (Precise dimensions don't matter here, as sheets of puff pastry can vary in size depending on the brand. Most important is that you have 2 long rectangular pieces of puff that fit side by side on a half-sheet pan.) Gently roll out the pastry. (This is to flatten any "wrinkles," but you can skip this step if the pastry looks smooth.) Transfer the puff pastry with the parchment to a half-sheet pan.

Using a sharp paring knife, score a 1-inch (2.5 cm) border around the edges. Arrange the apple slices on the puff pastry within the border, slightly overlapping. Sprinkle the remaining 1 tablespoon brown sugar over the apples (½ tablespoon per tart). Scatter the butter pieces over the top and brush the edges with the whisked egg.

Bake for about 40 minutes, or until the edges of the tarts are deeply golden and the apples are softened.

Remove from the oven and immediately drizzle the apples with the honey and sprinkle with some flaky salt.

Cut the tart into slices and serve warm, with a dollop of crème fraîche, if desired.

HOT TIP! If you find crème fraîche to be too tart on its own, try whipping equal parts crème fraîche and heavy cream with a little sugar and a pinch of salt to make a crème fraîche whipped cream.

Broiled Peaches with Mascarpone, Honey, and Black Pepper

SERVES 4

4 ripe peaches, preferably freestone, halved and pitted

Extra-virgin olive oil, for drizzling

Honey, for drizzling

Coarsely ground black pepper

2 to 4 sprigs fresh basil, leaves picked

One 8-ounce (227 g) container mascarpone cheese, for serving

HOT TIP! No basil? Skip it or use mint or tarragon in its place. In place of black pepper, try pink pepper, which has distinct floral notes. Or forgo pepper altogether and sprinkle the peaches with sumac. You could also make this dish with nectarines or apricots, but we've found plums to slump a bit too much for our liking.

Peak of summer stone fruit such as peaches are best when eaten out of hand, preferably standing over a sink to catch the juices dribbling down your arm. And while we also tuck them into pies, cobblers, jams, or sorbets, sometimes we get overzealous and buy more fruit than we can possibly eat before it starts to spoil. This recipe, if you can even call it such, is an effortless way to dessert (yes, we just used that as a verb) for anyone who's found themselves in this position. It requires just a few minutes of your broiler, a task manageable even on the hottest days. You can prepare the peaches in advance and serve them at room temperature. Just be sure to shower them with basil while the peaches are still hot—the leaves will infuse the fruit with their scent. Even more sublime is when you top these with a dollop of creamy mascarpone.

Olga + Sanaë

Position a rack about 6 inches away from the broiling element and turn on the broiler.

Place the peaches, cut side up, on a half-sheet pan and very lightly drizzle with a little oil. Turn the peach halves over, so they're cut side down, and broil for 3 minutes.

Remove from the oven, gently turn the peaches over, drizzle with a little oil and honey, and sprinkle with some pepper. Broil for 3 to 5 minutes, or until the peaches are gorgeously caramelized.

Sprinkle with the basil leaves; they will wilt onto the peaches and give off an intoxicating perfume. Let cool until still warm, or cool completely.

Divide the peaches among four plates, drizzle with a little more oil and honey, if you like, and add a pinch more of pepper. Top with a scoop of mascarpone and serve.

Summer Plum Tarts with Cardamom Sugar

MAKES TWO 14 × 6-INCH (36 × 15 CM) RECTANGULAR TARTS / SERVES 6 TO 8

One 14-ounce (397 g) sheet all-butter frozen puff pastry, such as Dufour, thawed in the refrigerator

1 large egg, whisked

2 pounds (908 g) plums

3 tablespoons granulated sugar

½ teaspoon kosher salt

¼ teaspoon ground cardamom

2 tablespoons (1 oz/28 g) unsalted butter, cut into small pieces

Whipped cream, crème fraîche, or Greek yogurt, for serving

HOT TIP! If you have a small offset spatula, use it to transfer the sliced plums from the cutting board onto the puff pastry. This will make it easier to transport several slices at once.

I tried many variations of the plum tart and fell in love with this method: Two long rectangular tarts so everyone gets a bite of fruit and crust (no soggy middle pieces) and parbaking the crust so the sections beneath the fruit don't get gummy, since plums release a fair bit of juice as they bake. I recommend saving this recipe for summer, when stone fruit are at their peak sweetness—look for large, ripe but firm plums, as they will be easiest to slice and arrange on the puff pastry. (The ones with a dark purple or reddish flesh yield a particularly gorgeous tart.) A touch of cardamom adds a floral note without overpowering the fruit, but you could omit the spice if you don't have it on hand, and the result will still be delicious. The tarts can be baked a few hours in advance and warmed up in the oven right before serving. They are best eaten the same day.

Sanaë

Position a rack in the middle of the oven and preheat to 375°F (190°C).

Cut a piece of parchment paper the size of a half-sheet pan. Place the sheet of puff pastry on the parchment. Using a sharp knife, cut the puff pastry lengthwise into 2 long rectangles. (Precise dimensions don't matter here, as sheets of puff pastry can vary in size depending on the brand. Most important is that you have 2 long rectangular pieces of puff that fit side by side on a half-sheet pan.) Gently roll out the pastry. (This is to flatten any "wrinkles," but you can skip this step if the pastry looks smooth.) Transfer the puff pastry with the parchment to a half-sheet pan.

Using a sharp paring knife, score a 1-inch (2.5 cm) border around the edges. Prick the inside of the border all over with a fork and brush the edges with the whisked egg. Bake for about 15 minutes, or until pale golden.

Meanwhile, halve the plums and thinly slice into half-moons, discarding the pits. In a small bowl, stir together the sugar, salt, and cardamom.

continued

Remove the parbaked pastry from the oven. If it has puffed up, gently press down inside the border with the back of a large spoon. Reduce the oven temperature to 350°F (180°C).

Arrange the plum slices on the puff pastry (see Hot Tip! on page 229) within the borders, slightly overlapping. Don't worry about perfectly arranging them—they'll soften and meld as they bake. Scatter the butter pieces over the plums, then sprinkle with the cardamom-sugar mixture.

Bake for 35 to 40 minutes, or until the edges of the tarts are deeply golden and the plums are softened.

Serve warm or at room temperature, with whipped cream.

Butterscotch Saltine or Matzo Brittle

MAKES 24 TO 36 PIECES, DEPENDING ON SIZE

48 saltine crackers (about 1 sleeve) or about 5 sheets matzo (see Hot Tips!)

2 sticks (8 oz/226 g) salted butter or vegan butter (such as Miyoko's brand)

½ cup (110 g) packed light brown sugar

½ cup (100 g) granulated sugar

¼ teaspoon kosher salt

1 teaspoon vanilla extract

One 12-ounce (340 g) bag semisweet chocolate chips (see Hot Tips!)

Flaky sea salt, such as Maldon, for sprinkling

I've been extremely fortunate to have had teachers who impacted my life so profoundly that, in some ways, I owe my writing career to them. In sixth grade, I had Georgia Sledge. She was a total badass, and I know she won't mind me saying that. Mrs. Sledge, as we called her then, was a woman of many talents, a mother of four kids, a doting owner of golden retrievers, a Girl Scout troop leader, and a cross-country skier. After retiring to Maine, she took up sailing. Around the holidays, Mrs. Sledge would make butterscotch brittle with saltines, and their taste stayed with me for decades: The magical combination of salted butter and sugar, caramelized in the oven, and topped with chocolate, was irresistible. I didn't get the recipe from Mrs. Sledge then, but when we reconnected in the early aughts, I asked her about it, and she immediately—delighted that I remembered one of her specialties so vividly—emailed me her version. While Mrs. Sledge used all white sugar, I like to use a combination of brown and white for deeper toffee notes and crunch.

If making this for Passover, swap saltines out for matzo and make sure your ingredients are labeled as "kosher for Passover," and if bringing this to an observant household, check if any meat is being served—you may want to use kosher-for-Passover vegan butter or margarine in place of the dairy kind.

Olga

Position a rack in the middle of the oven and preheat to 350°F (180°C). Line a half-sheet pan with a piece of foil large enough to have overhang on the longer sides. Line the foil with a piece of parchment paper.

Arrange the crackers side by side in a single layer in the prepared sheet pan.

In a 2-quart (2-liter) saucepan that's wider than it is deep, combine the butter, both sugars, and salt. Whisking constantly, set over medium-low heat and bring the mixture to a boil. Cook, whisking constantly, until thickened and slightly paler, about 3 minutes. Remove from the heat and stir in the vanilla (the butterscotch will bubble vigorously, so stand back, just to be safe). Pour evenly over the crackers and use an offset spatula to spread it out evenly from end to end.

continued

Bake for about 15 minutes, or until the butterscotch goes from liquid and bubbling to candy-like.

Meanwhile, clean the offset spatula and dry it; you will use it again.

Remove the hot sheet from the oven and turn off the oven. Sprinkle the chocolate chips evenly on top. Return the pan to the turned-off oven and let stand for about 5 minutes to melt the chocolate.

Using the same offset spatula, spread the chocolate evenly over the butterscotch, covering it completely. Sprinkle with some flaky salt and transfer the pan to a wire rack to cool completely, about 45 minutes. Refrigerate for about 1 hour or until needed. Break into desired-size pieces and serve.

The brittle can be refrigerated in an airtight container for up to 1 week.

HOT TIPS! If using matzo, in order to get full coverage on the sheet pan, you will need 2 whole sheets of matzo and then with the remaining 3 sheets, you'll need to break them into pieces to fit. Don't worry so much about making it perfect; you'll cover the matzo with butterscotch, and then chocolate.

You can use dark or bittersweet chocolate, or even milk or white chocolate, if that's your preference.

Don't stop with just flaky salt as your topping—the sky's the limit. Consider toasted coconut flakes; finely chopped nuts, such as peanuts (not kosher for Passover in Ashkenazi Jewish households), walnuts, pecans, pistachios, or almonds; dried fruit, such as raisins or cherries; candied ginger or candied citrus peel; seeds, such as sunflower, pumpkin seeds, sesame, or millet; or crunchy snacks, such as crushed cereal, crushed potato chips, or pretzels (again, check for Passover labeling).

Brownies with Mint Cream

MAKES 12 SQUARES

2 sticks (8 oz/227 g) cultured salted butter, such as Beurre D'Isigny, plus more for the pan

8 ounces (227 g) semisweet chocolate (about 60% cacao), coarsely chopped

¾ cup (94 g) all-purpose flour

1 teaspoon baking powder

1¼ cups (250 g) granulated sugar

3 large eggs

Flaky sea salt, such as Maldon, for sprinkling

Mint Cream (optional; recipe follows)

These brownies are adapted from *The River Cottage Cookbook*, and Sanaë has been making them for a decade. Friends and strangers alike are often asking for the recipe, so we're thrilled to finally share it here. We find these to be the perfect balance of richness and decadence without being too sweet. Because these brownies require so few ingredients, we like to splurge on a high-fat salted European butter and a good-quality chocolate. For a more elegant dessert, we accompany them with a mint-infused cream, but you could also serve them with store-bought mint chip ice cream or your preferred flavor. You can make the brownies a day in advance—if anything their flavor will deepen over time and they'll be easier to cut. Just make sure to wrap them tightly once they've cooled to room temperature. The mint cream can be whipped up to 4 hours in advance and refrigerated until ready to serve.

Sanaë + Olga

Position a rack in the middle of the oven and preheat to 350°F (180°C). Butter a quarter-sheet pan and line it with parchment paper, leaving a 1-inch (2.5 cm) overhang on two sides. Butter the parchment.

In a medium pot, melt the butter over medium heat. Remove from the heat, add the chocolate, and stir until the chocolate is completely melted. Set aside to cool slightly.

In a small bowl, whisk together the flour and baking powder. In a large bowl, whisk the sugar with the eggs until smooth. Add the chocolate-butter mixture (check that it is warm, not hot, to the touch before adding) and whisk to combine. Sift in the flour mixture and whisk until just combined. Pour into the prepared sheet pan, spreading to the edges to smooth the top. Lightly sprinkle with flaky salt.

Bake the brownies for 25 to 30 minutes, or until set and a toothpick comes out with a few crumbs clinging to it.

Cool completely in the sheet. Using the parchment overhang, lift the brownies out of the pan and onto a cutting board, then cut into 12 squares. Serve with the mint cream, if desired.

continued

Mint Cream

2 cups (480 ml) heavy cream

1½ cups (75 g) fresh mint leaves, coarsely chopped

1 tablespoon granulated sugar

Pinch of kosher salt

This recipe comes from Sanaë's dear friend, Tanya Bush, who uses an easy hands-off method of infusing heavy cream overnight with fresh herbs. We love pairing mint with chocolate, but you could play around with the flavors, especially if serving the cream with another recipe—for instance, infusing with basil or lemon zest for pairing with the Rhubarb-Frangipane Galette (page 249).

In a medium bowl, combine the cream and mint. Tightly cover and refrigerate for at least 12 hours and up to 24 hours.

Set a fine-mesh sieve over a large bowl and strain the cream, discarding the mint leaves. Add the sugar and salt to the bowl. Whisk the cream by hand or use a hand mixer on medium-high speed until soft peaks form. The cream can be refrigerated in an airtight container for up to 4 hours.

HOT TIPS! You can replace the cultured salted butter with 2 sticks (8 oz/227 g) unsalted butter and 1 teaspoon flaky sea salt, such as Maldon. Add the salt to the butter when melting it.

Sanaë's friend, the novelist Garth Greenwell, adores these brownies and loves to eat them frozen. Last time Sanaë made a batch, she froze a few squares and discovered how utterly delicious they are straight from the freezer. (Thank you, Garth!) They're cold and a bit chewier, and this way you have a sweet treat at the ready for weeks to come.

Lemon Bars for Winter Blues

MAKES ABOUT 12

For the crust

1½ sticks (6 oz/170 g) cold unsalted butter, cubed, plus softened butter for the pan

1½ cups (188 g) all-purpose flour

½ cup plus 1 tablespoon (113 g) granulated sugar

1 teaspoon finely grated lemon zest

¾ teaspoon kosher salt

For the filling

1¼ cups (250 g) granulated sugar

2 teaspoons cornstarch

2 teaspoons finely grated lemon zest (from 1 lemon)

¼ teaspoon kosher salt

4 large eggs

⅔ cup (160 ml) fresh lemon juice (from 3 to 4 lemons), strained

Powdered sugar (optional), for dusting

There comes a point in every winter when I've just about had it with the late sunrises, early sunsets, frigid temperatures, and all the squashes, tubers, and alliums my local farmers' market has to offer. To counter that, I load up on citrus in as many forms as I can think of: eaten as a snack, sliced into salads, juiced into cocktails, and, of course, refashioned into dessert. These lemon bars may not cure all wintry blues, but they'll certainly brighten up the mood wherever you bring them, because they are meant to be shared. There are many things about these bars that I love—but perhaps my favorite feature is that they might be the easiest ones you'll ever make. The shortbread crust is baked until golden and crisp, and serves as a satisfying foil against the silky lemony filling. The filling, which is a lemon curd, doesn't need to be cooked on the stovetop—just stir the ingredients together, dump over a still-hot crust (no waiting!), and bake away. The bars lend themselves well to adaptation: Throw in a teaspoon of minced lemon thyme leaves while creaming the butter and sugar for the crust, or scent the crust with vanilla or cardamom. The hardest part—for me, at least—is waiting for these bars to cool.

Olga

MAKE THE CRUST: Position a rack in the middle of the oven and preheat to 350°F (180°C). Lightly grease a quarter-sheet pan with the softened butter and line it with a piece of parchment paper with a generous overhang on the long sides. Generously grease the sides of the pan with the softened butter.

In a large bowl, whisk together the flour, sugar, lemon zest, and salt until combined. Add the cubed butter and toss with your hands to coat the butter in the flour mixture. With your fingertips, start to flatten the butter cubes, rubbing the butter into the flour mixture, continuing to toss the butter, flattening it, and rubbing it into the dry ingredients until a shaggy dough starts to come together. The dough should stay together when pinched.

Transfer the dough to the prepared sheet pan, ensuring it's evenly distributed. Place a piece of parchment paper on top and evenly press it out with your palms. Using the bottom of a glass or measuring cup,

continued

pat the dough down to even it out, especially in the corners. Transfer to the freezer for about 15 minutes.

Use a fork to prick the dough in a few places. Bake for 30 to 35 minutes, or until light golden. (For a very crunchy shortbread crust, bake it closer to the 40-minute mark. For a softer base, start checking around the 30-minute mark.)

Transfer to a wire rack. Reduce the oven temperature to 300°F (150°C).

MAKE THE FILLING: In a large bowl, whisk together the sugar, cornstarch, lemon zest, and salt. Gently whisk in the eggs, followed by the lemon juice. Don't whisk too vigorously—you don't want to make the filling mixture frothy, as it will result in a dappled texture when baked. (If that happens, it's not the end of the world—simply dust the bars with the powdered sugar and no one will be the wiser.) If you like, tap the bowl on the counter a few times to knock out some of the larger bubbles.

Pull out the oven rack and return the crust to it. Pour the filling over the crust. Carefully slide the oven rack back in the oven and bake for 20 to 25 minutes, or until the filling is set and doesn't jiggle in the center when the pan is slightly shaken.

Transfer the pan to a wire rack and let cool completely.

Using the parchment overhang, lift the cooled bars out of the pan and transfer to a cutting board. Use a large serrated knife to cut the slab into desired-size pieces, wiping the knife between slices with a damp towel. If you like, dust with powdered sugar just before serving.

The bars can be refrigerated in an airtight container for up to 1 week, but their flavor is brightest the day they are made; the crust may soften over time.

Labneh Cheesecake Bars with Berry Compote

MAKES 12 SQUARES

For the crust

1 stick (4 oz/113 g) unsalted butter, melted, plus softened butter for the pan

7 ounces (200 g) graham crackers (about 13 whole crackers)

¼ cup (28 g) powdered sugar

1 teaspoon kosher salt

For the filling

One 8-ounce (227 g) brick cream cheese, at room temperature

⅔ cup (140 g) granulated sugar

8 ounces (227 g) labneh (see Hot Tips!)

Finely grated zest of 1 mandarin, clementine, orange, lemon, or lime (see Hot Tips!)

3 large eggs, at room temperature

¼ cup (60 ml) heavy cream

For serving

Berry Compote (optional; recipe follows)

I discovered cheesecake when I moved to the United States for college, and while I enjoyed a few bites of the creamy rich filling, I always found myself picking away at the crust and wanting more of it. I never managed to finish the filling on my plate. What I love about these cheesecake bars is that they achieve what I think is an ideal ratio of filling to crust. With every bite you'll get a nice creamy layer with a solid crunchy base of crust. The cheesecake bars are superb on their own, but the berry compote elevates them to a dinner-party dessert, plus it can be made several days in advance.

I've included a gluten-free crust recipe made with Tate's gluten-free coconut cookies, which my friend Joanna makes for her husband, Ben. You can use just about any citrus in this recipe, keeping in mind that the lemon and lime will be sharper than a mandarin or orange.

Sanaë

MAKE THE CRUST: Position a rack in the middle of the oven and preheat to 325°F (160°C). Grease a quarter-sheet pan with the softened butter and line with parchment paper.

In a food processor, pulse the graham crackers until finely ground. (Alternatively, place them in a large resealable bag and crush with a heavy skillet or rolling pin until in fine crumbs.)

In a medium bowl, stir together the graham cracker crumbs, powdered sugar, and salt. Add the melted butter and stir well to combine. Press the crust into the bottom and up the sides of the sheet pan. (Use your fingers and the back of a spoon.) It will be crumbly! Do your best packing it, but don't worry about it looking perfect.

Bake the crust for 15 to 20 minutes, or until the edges are a shade darker.

Remove from the oven but leave the oven on. Use a small spoon to press along the bottom of the sides of the crust to create neater edges and corners. Set aside to slightly cool while you make the filling.

MAKE THE FILLING: In a large bowl, use a flexible spatula to mix together the cream cheese and granulated sugar until fully combined.

continued

Add the labneh and zest and stir to combine. Add the eggs, one at a time, mixing well after each addition. Add the cream and mix until fully combined. Pour the batter into the crust.

Bake for 25 to 30 minutes, or until the filling is just set. It will jiggle slightly at the center but continue to set as it cools. Let the cheesecake bars cool completely, then tightly wrap and refrigerate for at least 2 hours and up to 3 days.

SERVE: Cut the slab into 12 squares. If desired, serve with the berry compote. The crust will be crispest on the first day, but it will still be delicious on days two and three.

Berry Compote

3 heaping cups (450 g) mixed berries, fresh or frozen (no need to thaw)

Juice of 1 mandarin, clementine, orange, lemon, or lime

3 tablespoons granulated sugar

Pinch of kosher salt

In a medium saucepan, combine the berries, mandarin juice, sugar, and salt. Bring to a simmer over medium heat. Reduce the heat to medium-low and cook until the berries are softened and starting to break apart, about 10 minutes. Transfer the compote to a bowl and allow to cool for a few minutes. Serve warm or at room temperature. The berry compote can be refrigerated in an airtight container for up to 1 week.

Gluten-Free Coconut Cookie Crust

21 Tate's Gluten Free Coconut Crisp Cookies (287 g total), from 1½ packs

¼ cup (28 g) powdered sugar

1 teaspoon kosher salt

5 tablespoons (70 g) unsalted butter, melted and cooled

Follow the same directions as in the recipe for the graham cracker crust.

Granola-Topped Apple and Pear Crisp

SERVES 6

For the filling

3 firm apples, such as Pink Lady or Macoun, peeled, cored, and cut into ½-inch (1.3 cm) pieces

2 ripe Bosc pears, peeled, cored, and cut into ½-inch (1.3 cm) pieces

Finely grated zest and juice of 1 lemon

1 tablespoon brown sugar, any kind

1 tablespoon all-purpose flour

¼ teaspoon ground cinnamon

¼ teaspoon ground ginger

¼ teaspoon kosher salt

⅛ teaspoon freshly grated nutmeg

For the topping

2½ cups (250 g) granola, store-bought or homemade (page 33 or 35)

1 tablespoon brown sugar, any kind (optional; see Hot Tip!)

½ teaspoon kosher salt

6 tablespoons (3 oz/85 g) unsalted butter, melted

Heavy cream (optional), for serving

We're both fans of sweet endings to any meal. Sanaë even has "lunch dessert" on most days. What we love as much as dessert, however, is a big payoff with relatively little effort. And it occurred to us while discussing a crisp for this book, that the ideal topping is already in our pantries, just waiting to be used: granola.

We're both avid granola makers: We eat it for breakfast with yogurt, we snack on it in the afternoon, and we gift it to friends and family. And we offer two recipes, side by side. If you don't feel like making your own, as Queen Ina often says, "store-bought is fine." Find a granola you love and use it here, you'll still wind up with delicious (and nearly effortless) results.

Olga + Sanaë

Position a rack in the middle of the oven and preheat to 350°F (180°C).

MAKE THE FILLING: In a large bowl, gently combine the apples, pears, lemon zest, lemon juice, brown sugar, flour, cinnamon, ginger, salt, and nutmeg. Transfer the filling to a quarter-sheet pan.

MAKE THE TOPPING: Wipe the bowl clean (you can quickly rinse it and dry it, but no need to wash it thoroughly) and toss together the granola, brown sugar (if using), and salt until combined. Add the melted butter and toss again to distribute. The granola should look "wet." Sprinkle it evenly over the filling, covering the fruit as completely as possible, but you may have bits of fruit peeking out—that's okay!

Bake for about 50 minutes, or until the top is browned and the fruit underneath is bubbling and is soft when pierced with a knife.

Let cool on a wire rack for 10 minutes before serving. Serve warm in individual bowls with a pour of heavy cream, if desired.

> **HOT TIP!** Most of the sweetness in this crisp comes from the fruit, but, since our granola recipes flirt with slight savoriness, we've added a tablespoon of brown sugar to the topping. If you're using a store-bought granola that's already fairly sweet, omit the sugar in the topping.

Chocolate Layer Cake with Cherry Preserves and Mascarpone Whip

MAKES ONE 2-LAYER CAKE / SERVES 10 TO 12

For the cake

1 stick plus 5 tablespoons (6½ oz/185 g) unsalted butter, cut into 1-inch (2.5 cm) pieces, plus more for the pan

1½ cups (300 g) granulated sugar

3 ounces (85 g) dark chocolate (68% to 70% cacao), roughly chopped

¾ cup (70 g) Dutch process cocoa powder

1¾ cups (220 g) all-purpose flour

2 teaspoons kosher salt

2 teaspoons baking powder

1 teaspoon baking soda

¾ cup (180 ml) whole milk

2 large eggs

1 large egg yolk

For the mascarpone whip

8 ounces (227 g) mascarpone

1 cup (240 ml) heavy cream

2 tablespoons granulated sugar

¼ teaspoon kosher salt

This layer cake is a chocolate-lover's dream. The recipe takes inspiration from my dear friend Tanya Bush, a talented writer and baker who is known for her delectable layer cakes that she bakes entirely in sheet pans. Hers are towering, multilayered creations filled with fresh fruit compotes and flavored whipped creams. I've slightly adapted her recipe for chocolate cake—perfectly moist and rich, and not too sweet—and layered it with barely sweetened mascarpone whip and a thin layer of store-bought cherry preserves. I love this chocolate cake so much that it's become a staple for birthdays, dinner parties, and other celebrations.

Sanaë

MAKE THE CAKE: Position a rack in the middle of the oven and preheat to 325°F (160°C). Butter a half-sheet pan and line with parchment paper, leaving a slight overhang on the two long sides. Butter the parchment, including the sides.

In a medium pot, combine the sugar, butter, and 3 tablespoons water. Cook, stirring, over medium-low heat until the butter is melted. Remove from the heat and add the chocolate and cocoa powder. Mix with a flexible spatula until combined. Set aside to cool for a few minutes. It should be warm, not hot, to the touch.

While the chocolate mixture is cooling, in a medium bowl, whisk together the flour, salt, baking powder, and baking soda. In a large bowl, whisk together the milk, eggs, and egg yolk.

Add the chocolate mixture to the milk-egg mixture and whisk to combine. Add the flour mixture and whisk until just combined. Drizzle the batter into the prepared sheet pan, starting at one end and making your way to the other to evenly distribute it. Use a flexible spatula or a small offset spatula to smooth the top. You want the batter to be evenly distributed in the sheet pan.

continued

For assembly

⅔ cup (213 g) cherry preserves or jam (ideally, sour cherry)

1 ounce (28 g) dark chocolate (68% to 70% cacao)

10 to 12 fresh or alcohol-soaked cherries (optional)

Bake the cake for 18 to 22 minutes, rotating the pan front to back halfway through, or until a toothpick comes out clean. Allow to cool completely in the sheet pan. The cake can be tightly wrapped and kept at room temperature for up to 1 day.

MAKE THE MASCARPONE WHIP: In a large bowl, combine the mascarpone, heavy cream, sugar, and salt. With a hand mixer on medium-low speed, beat until combined, about 1 minute. Increase the speed to high and beat until stiff peaks form, 2 to 3 minutes. (Take care not to overwhisk, or the cream will turn grainy.) The mascarpone whip can be refrigerated in an airtight container for up to 4 hours.

ASSEMBLE THE CAKE: Using the parchment overhang, lift the cake from the sheet pan and place it on a clean work surface. Position the cake with a long side facing you. Using a sharp knife, trim the edges to create straight, even sides. Cut the cake in half crosswise (perpendicular to you) into 2 equal rectangles. Peel off the parchment paper and place one cake rectangle on a large serving plate or turned-over quarter-sheet pan.

Using a small offset spatula or a spoon, spread the cherry preserves over the cake half, distributing it to the edges. Dollop half of the mascarpone whip over the preserves and spread in an even layer to cover. Don't worry if it mixes a bit with the preserves. Carefully place the other cake half on top. (Use a large, thin metal spatula, if you have one. Otherwise gently lift the cake rectangle with your hands.) Dollop the remaining mascarpone whip over the top of the cake and spread it in an even layer to the edges. Using a mandoline or Microplane rasp grater, grate the chocolate directly over the whip.

Cut into 10 to 12 squares. If desired, top each piece with a cherry.

HOT TIP! For easier assembly, leave the cake in one layer and cut it into squares. Using a flexible spatula, fold the jam into the mascarpone whip and dollop each square with it. Grate the chocolate over the mascarpone and serve.

Rhubarb-Frangipane Galette

**MAKES 1 LARGE GALETTE /
SERVES 6 TO 8**

For the crust

1½ cups (188 g) all-purpose flour, plus more for dusting

1 teaspoon kosher salt

1 teaspoon granulated sugar

10 tablespoons (5 oz/140 g) cold unsalted butter, cut into ½-inch (1.3 cm) pieces

4 to 5 tablespoons ice water

For the frangipane

1 large egg

½ cup (60 g) almond flour

4 tablespoons (2 oz/57 g) unsalted butter, at room temperature

¼ cup (50 g) granulated sugar

For assembly

14 ounces (397 g) rhubarb stalks, cut into 2-inch (5 cm) pieces (see Hot Tip!)

2 tablespoons granulated sugar, divided

This is a gorgeous rustic dessert or afternoon treat that we make as soon as we start seeing rhubarb at the farmers' market in the late spring. The crust is the same recipe as for the Potato and Ricotta Galette (page 69) and could be repurposed for just about any fruit or vegetable. We like to keep this galette barely sweet, so the rhubarb's flavor shines through. There's just enough sugar to balance its tartness. For a sweeter dessert, serve each slice with a scoop of vanilla ice cream. The almond frangipane puffs up around the rhubarb to nestle the pieces and meld them together.

This galette is best eaten the day of—ideally still warm from the oven—as the rhubarb tends to release some liquid and get a bit soggy as time goes on. But like most galettes, you can always throw it back into the oven for a few minutes before serving.

When buying rhubarb, try to choose stalks that are about the same size (or halve them lengthwise if they are very thick). We're drawn to the reddish-pink stalks for a colorful presentation, though the greener ones are delicious, too, if that's all you can find.

Sanaë + Olga

MAKE THE CRUST: In a large bowl, whisk together the flour, salt, and sugar. Add the butter pieces and toss to coat in the flour. Incorporate the butter into the flour, pressing the pieces of butter between your fingers and tossing with the flour until the mixture resembles a coarse meal with some visible flat pieces of butter. Drizzle in the ice water, 1 tablespoon at a time, stirring with a fork, until a shaggy dough begins to form—it should just hold together when pressed in between your fingers. Transfer to a large piece of plastic wrap. Using the plastic wrap, press with your knuckles to gather the dough into a disk. Tightly wrap in the plastic and refrigerate for at least 2 hours and up to 3 days. (You can also double-wrap the dough and freeze it for up to 3 months.)

When ready to bake, position a rack in the middle of the oven and preheat to 375°F (190°C).

MAKE THE FRANGIPANE: In a small bowl, whisk the egg until completely blended. Measure out 1 tablespoon of the beaten egg into

continued

another small bowl and whisk in ½ teaspoon water. Set this aside for an egg wash.

Transfer the remaining egg to a medium bowl. Add the almond flour, butter, and sugar. Using a flexible spatula or large spoon, stir until completely combined and smooth. Set aside. Remove the galette dough from the refrigerator and let it sit at room temperature for 5 minutes.

Cut a piece of parchment paper the size of a half-sheet pan. Lightly flour the parchment and roll out the dough on it into a round roughly 15 inches (38 cm) in diameter. Don't worry if it's not perfect; galettes are forgiving and we love how the uneven edges look—part of their beauty is in their rustic appearance. Use the parchment to transfer the dough to a half-sheet pan.

Using a spatula or the back of a spoon, spread the frangipane in an even layer on the dough, leaving a 2-inch (5 cm) border around the edges.

ASSEMBLE THE GALETTE: Arrange the rhubarb over the frangipane, snugly fitting the pieces (the rhubarb will shrink in the oven). Sprinkle 1 tablespoon of the sugar over the rhubarb. Fold and pleat the outer edges of the dough over the rhubarb filling, pressing gently on the pleats to seal. Brush the edges of the crust with the reserved egg wash. Sprinkle the remaining 1 tablespoon sugar over the entire galette, including the crust.

Bake for 50 to 55 minutes, or until the crust is deeply golden brown and the rhubarb looks caramelized and softened.

Serve warm or at room temperature. The galette is best eaten the same day. It can be reheated in a 350°F (180°C) oven for about 10 minutes, or until warm to the touch.

HOT TIP! You can use frozen rhubarb—just make sure to keep it in the freezer until you're assembling the galette, as it'll start to release liquid as it thaws. To freeze rhubarb, cut the stalks into the desired lengths and place in a resealable plastic bag.

Blackberry-Lemon Clafoutis

SERVES 6 TO 8

Softened butter for the pan, preferably salted

4 large eggs

⅔ cup (80 g) all-purpose flour

⅔ cup (160 ml) whole milk

⅔ cup (160 ml) heavy cream

⅓ cup (66 g) granulated sugar

3 tablespoons (1½ oz/43 g) salted or unsalted butter, melted and cooled

Finely grated zest of 1 lemon

½ teaspoon kosher salt

10 ounces (283 g) fresh blackberries

Powdered sugar, for dusting

A fruit clafoutis is one of my favorite French desserts, and the book wouldn't feel complete without including it here. It's my go-to sweet ending for entertaining, as it's easy to throw together and can be made a few hours in advance. Although you can use blueberries, raspberries, or pitted cherries (the most traditional and commonly used fruit), I recommend trying blackberries, as they hold their shape while softening into sweet-tart puddles.

Most clafoutis recipes are too sweet for my taste. I prefer a creamy and lightly sweetened custard that won't compete with the berries. If you happen to have salted butter, use that to grease the sheet pan, as it'll lend a subtle saltiness to each bite. To serve, take a large spoon and scoop out the warm clafoutis into bowls or plates. Or if serving at room temperature, cut it into squares. If you like, reheat the clafoutis in the oven (at 350°F/180°C) for a few minutes, or until warm to the touch.

Sanaë

Position a rack in the middle of the oven and preheat to 375°F (190°C). Generously butter a quarter-sheet pan.

In a blender, combine the eggs, flour, milk, cream, granulated sugar, melted butter, lemon zest, and salt. Blend until smooth, about 1 minute, scraping down the sides as needed.

Evenly scatter the blackberries in the prepared sheet pan. Gently pour the batter around the blackberries.

Bake the clafoutis for 30 to 35 minutes, or until puffed up and golden brown.

Allow to cool for a few minutes. The clafoutis can be served warm or at room temperature. Just before serving, dust with powdered sugar.

Peanut Butter–Chocolate Crispy Rice Treats

MAKES ABOUT TWENTY-FOUR 2-INCH (5 CM) SQUARES

For the crispy rice treats

1 stick (4 oz/113 g) unsalted butter, plus more softened butter for the pan

16 ounces (454 g/1 jar) crunchy peanut butter

⅔ cup (215 g) maple syrup

1½ teaspoons vanilla extract

1 teaspoon kosher salt

4½ cups (190 g) crispy brown rice cereal (see Hot Tip!)

For the chocolate topping

6 ounces (170 g) semisweet chocolate (about 60% cacao), broken or chopped into 1-inch (2.5 cm) pieces

2 tablespoons (1 oz/28 g) unsalted butter

Flaky sea salt, such as Maldon

These crispy rice squares are inspired by a recipe I've been making for many years from the cookbook *The First Forty Days* by Heng Ou, which features nourishing recipes for new mothers. The original recipe, which I make for my breastfeeding mom friends in the days after they've had a baby, has been such a great hit that I wanted to create a less caloric and slightly less rich version for my nonnursing friends. I reduced the butter and sweetener and added a thin layer of dark chocolate to make it feel more like a dessert. Although not very sweet, these treats are still quite decadent, so I recommend cutting them into small squares. The combination of peanut butter and chocolate reminds me of Reese's Peanut Butter Cups, with the satisfying texture of a Nestlé's Crunch bar. You could use creamy peanut butter, but I love the added texture of peanut pieces.

Sanaë

MAKE THE CRISPY RICE TREATS: Butter and line a quarter-sheet pan with parchment paper, leaving a 1-inch (2.5 cm) overhang on the long sides.

In a medium pot, melt the butter over low heat. Add the peanut butter, maple syrup, vanilla, and kosher salt. Stir to combine until the mixture is smooth, then remove from the heat. Transfer to a large bowl.

Add the rice cereal and use a flexible spatula to gently stir the cereal until it is evenly coated in the peanut butter mixture. Transfer the mixture to the prepared sheet pan and press into an even layer. Place in the freezer while you prepare the chocolate topping.

MAKE THE CHOCOLATE TOPPING: Combine the chocolate and butter in a heatproof bowl set over a medium pot of simmering water (make sure the bottom of the bowl isn't touching the water).

Cook, stirring, until the chocolate and butter are completely melted and smooth. Remove the bowl from the pot.

continued

Drizzle the chocolate-butter mixture over the crispy rice mixture. Using a small offset spatula, evenly spread the melted chocolate to cover. Don't worry if the chocolate mixes a bit with the top layer of crispy rice. Sprinkle with flaky salt and refrigerate, uncovered, for about 4 hours or until set.

Using the parchment overhang, transfer the slab to a cutting board, cut into 2-inch (5 cm) squares, and refrigerate in an airtight container for up to 1 week. These treats will be crispiest on the first and second day, but they will still be delicious in the days to come.

Olga's Salted Brown Butter Crispy Rice Treats

MAKES ABOUT TWENTY-FOUR 2-INCH (5 CM) SQUARES

1 stick (4 oz/113 g) salted butter, plus softened butter for the pan and your hands

⅓ cup (105 g) dulce de leche

2 teaspoons vanilla extract

½ teaspoon kosher salt

One 10-ounce (283 g) bag mini marshmallows

6 cups (170 g) crispy rice cereal, such as Rice Krispies

These were inspired by both Deb Perelman's version, as well as queen of easy-peasy desserts, cookbook author Jessie Sheehan, who lovingly tucks sweetened condensed milk into her "secret ingredient" crispy rice squares, making them even more delectable. I use dulce de leche in place of condensed milk to irresistible results.

Olga

Grease a quarter-sheet pan with softened butter and line the bottom with parchment paper.

In a large pot, melt the butter over medium heat and cook until it smells nutty and the solids brown, about 4 minutes.

Stir in the dulce de leche, vanilla, and salt until combined. Stir in the mini marshmallows until melted. Remove from the heat, add the cereal, and stir until thoroughly combined.

Transfer to the prepared sheet pan, rub your hands with a little butter to prevent sticking, and press the mixture to flatten it into an even layer. Set aside for at least 1 hour to set, then slice into 24 roughly 2-inch (5 cm) squares. Serve right away or transfer to an airtight container and store at room temperature for up to 4 days.

Strawberry Snacking Sheet Cake

6 tablespoons (3 oz/85 g) unsalted butter, softened, plus more for the pan

1½ cups (188 g) all-purpose flour

1½ teaspoons baking powder

1 teaspoon kosher salt

1 cup (200 g) granulated sugar

2 teaspoons finely grated lemon zest

1 large egg, at room temperature

½ cup (120 ml) whole milk, at room temperature

1 teaspoon vanilla extract

12 ounces (340 g) strawberries, hulled and halved

2 tablespoons demerara sugar

Unsweetened whipped cream (optional), for serving

This is the kind of cake that works beautifully as a cozy breakfast accompanied by a cup of coffee, an afternoon snack with tea, or a simple but sublime dessert (topped with a swoosh of unsweetened whipped cream). I originally got this recipe from Martha Stewart's website and tucked it away, covered in stains and grease marks, in my recipe binder. This cake received newfound recognition when Deb Perelman wrote about it on her blog, *Smitten Kitchen*. So if you're still on the fence, you can trust Martha and Deb. In my version, I add lemon zest, which highlights the floral notes of strawberries, top the cake with demerara sugar for a pleasant crunch, and adapt it for a sheet pan. If you prefer lightly sweetened whipped cream, do you, I won't be mad.

Olga

Position a rack in the middle of the oven and preheat to 350°F (180°C). Butter a quarter-sheet pan, line the bottom with parchment paper, and butter the paper.

Into a medium bowl, sift together the flour, baking powder, and salt.

In the bowl of a stand mixer fitted with the paddle attachment (or in a medium bowl using a hand mixer), use your hands to rub the granulated sugar with the lemon zest until fragrant, about 1 minute. Add the butter and beat on medium-high speed until pale and fluffy, about 3 minutes. Reduce the speed to medium-low and beat in the egg, milk, and vanilla until fully incorporated. The batter may look curdled; this is fine.

Reduce the speed to low and gradually add the flour mixture until combined. Transfer the batter to the prepared sheet pan—it will be thick—and use a small offset spatula to evenly spread it out to the edges of the pan. Arrange the strawberries on top, cut sides down, and sprinkle with the demerara sugar.

Bake for 10 minutes, then reduce the oven temperature to 325°F (160°C) and continue baking for about 45 minutes, or until the cake is golden brown and firm to the touch.

Transfer to a wire rack and let cool completely in the pan.

Cut into squares and serve, with a dollop of whipped cream on the side, if desired.

XL Galette des Rois

SERVES 8 TO 10

Two 14-ounce (397 g) sheets all-butter frozen puff pastry, such as Dufour, thawed in the refrigerator

10 tablespoons (5 oz/140 g) unsalted butter, at room temperature

⅔ cup plus 1 tablespoon (140 g) granulated sugar

3 large eggs, at room temperature, divided

1 cup plus 3 tablespoons (140 g) almond flour

1 tablespoon cornstarch

1 tablespoon dark rum

1 teaspoon kosher salt

Ceramic fève, almond, or dried bean (optional)

Galette des rois, which in French means "king's cake," is a puff pastry tart filled with frangipane (a sweet almond cream) traditionally served in January on Epiphany Day, but I like to eat it all month long. It's a nostalgic, celebratory treat that reminds me of France, and one I look forward to every year as December comes to an end. But beyond this ritual, I love the flavors: the creamy, not-too-sweet almond filling ensconced in buttery puff that rises and crisps into golden flakes. It's an elegant and delicious pastry that tastes similar to an almond croissant, minus the almond flakes. Every bakery in France makes their own galette des rois starting in early January, but since they're harder to come by in America, I make my own, and I invite a group of friends over for an afternoon of eating.

Because there are so few ingredients, I highly recommend splurging on a high-quality all-butter puff pastry, such as Dufour, which will deliver the best results. To replicate the traditional galette des rois, you can hide a ceramic trinket, called a *fève*, inside the frangipane. If you don't have a fève, you can use a dried bean or an almond. When it's time to serve, the youngest person in the room goes under the table and calls out who gets what slice. Whoever gets the slice with the fève is crowned king or queen, must wear a paper golden crown, and can choose their respective king or queen.

This is a recipe that really benefits from having a digital scale, as you'll want equal amounts of almond flour, sugar, and butter for the frangipane (140 grams!). The galette should be eaten warm, so bake it right before serving or reheat it in the oven if you've made it a few hours in advance.

Sanaë

Gently roll out both puff pastry sheets if they were folded to flatten out any folds. Stack them on a half-sheet pan with parchment paper between the sheets and refrigerate while you prepare the frangipane.

In a large bowl and using a hand mixer on medium speed, beat the butter until fluffy, about 2 minutes. Add the sugar and beat until incorporated and fluffy, about 2 minutes. Add 2 of the eggs, one at a time, beating well after each addition to incorporate. Beat in the almond flour, cornstarch, rum, and salt. (If you don't have a hand mixer, you can do this by hand using a whisk or wooden spoon—just make sure the butter is truly at room temperature so it's easier to work with.) The

continued

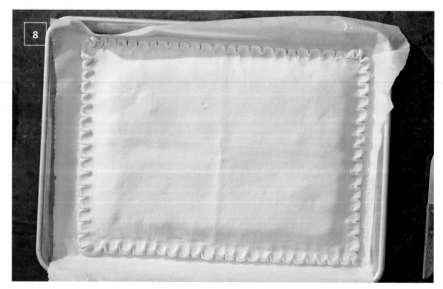

frangipane can be refrigerated in an airtight container for up to 2 days.

In a small bowl, make an egg wash by whisking the remaining egg with 1 teaspoon water. Set aside.

Line a half-sheet pan with parchment paper. Place one sheet of puff pastry dough on the prepared sheet pan. (If you're running out of space, keep the other sheet of puff pastry in the refrigerator.) Using a small offset spatula or the back of a spoon, spread the frangipane on the puff pastry in an even layer, leaving a 1-inch (2.5 cm) border around the edges (1). Press the fève, if using, into the almond mixture. Brush the border with some of the egg wash (2). (Refrigerate the remaining egg wash, covered, as you will use it again.) Place the second sheet of puff pastry dough over the filling (3). Using your fingers, press against the border to seal (4 and 5). It's important to really press the dough together otherwise the filling will leak and burn; you can also lift the edges and pinch with your fingers. Using a sharp knife or a pizza cutter, trim just the very edge of the dough to create straight sides (6). (Don't trim too much dough, otherwise you'll trim the seal!) Crimp the edges by pushing the blunt edge of the knife's blade into the dough between two fingers (7 and 8).

Cover the galette with plastic and refrigerate for at least 2 hours and up to 12 hours.

When ready to bake, position racks in the middle and lower third of the oven and preheat to 400°F (200°C).

Brush the top of the galette with the reserved egg wash, avoiding the sides, otherwise they won't rise. Score the surface with a sharp knife, deep enough to visibly mark the dough but being careful not to cut completely through it. (You can score it however you like, or see the photo on page 259 for a suggested pattern.) Using a chopstick, prick a small hole in the center.

Bake the galette on the lower rack for 25 minutes.

Reduce the oven temperature to 350°F (180°C) and move the galette to the middle rack. Continue to bake for 20 to 30 minutes, or until deeply golden brown. (Lift a corner and check that the bottom of the galette is deeply golden brown.)

Allow to cool for 10 minutes, or until no longer piping hot, then cut into slices. If you make the galette in advance, reheat it in a 350°F (180°C) oven for 10 to 15 minutes, or until fragrant and warm to the touch.

Matcha Swiss Roll with Mascarpone Whip and Strawberries

SERVES 12

Softened butter or baking spray for the pan

For the sponge

1 slightly generous cup (130 g) all-purpose flour

2 tablespoons (12 g) matcha

1 teaspoon baking powder

½ teaspoon fine sea salt

5 large eggs, at room temperature

¾ cup (150 g) granulated sugar

3 tablespoons whole milk, warmed

2 tablespoons neutral oil, such as canola or grapeseed

3 tablespoons powdered sugar, plus more if needed

For the mascarpone whip and assembly

1½ cups (360 ml) heavy cream

⅓ cup (80 g) mascarpone or crème fraîche

3 tablespoons granulated sugar

1 teaspoon vanilla extract (optional)

⅛ teaspoon fine sea salt

6 to 10 strawberries, hulled and thinly sliced

I've long loved Japanese matcha roll cakes with billowy whipped cream filling and thinly sliced strawberries. Each bite is light, moist, and offers just the right amount of sweetness.

Commonly referred to in the States as the jelly roll and elsewhere as Swiss roll, many home bakers avoid making it due to the anxiety of rolling the cake layer without it cracking. I'm here to promise you: It's truly doable for bakers of all skill levels. Just exercise a gentle-but-firm hand when rolling up the still-warm cake and you'll be fine. This version is made even easier, thanks to my friend, cookbook author Jessie Sheehan, who advised me to not separate my yolks from the egg whites, and instead beat the eggs together until thick and ribbony. Jessie also played the role of my hype woman during the development and testing of this recipe, when I was emailing her panicked updates. Should the cake crack in a few places on the outside, you can always make more whipped cream to cover it up, or dust it with powdered sugar, and no one will be the wiser.

Olga

Position a rack in the middle of the oven and preheat to 350°F (180°C). Thoroughly grease the bottom, corners, and sides of a half-sheet pan with butter or baking spray and line with parchment paper cut to precisely fit the bottom of the pan (you don't want any overhang). Press the paper into the bottom, smoothing it out, then grease it as well.

Place a large bowl in the freezer or refrigerator (for the mascarpone whip).

MAKE THE SPONGE: In a medium bowl, thoroughly whisk together the flour, matcha, baking powder, and sea salt until combined.

In a large bowl, with a hand mixer (see Hot Tips!), beat the eggs on medium speed until light and frothy, about 3 minutes. Increase the mixer speed to high and gradually add the granulated sugar, beating until the eggs triple in volume, are pale yellow, and fall off the whisk in a luxurious ribbon. Stop the mixer, add the milk and oil, and mix on medium speed until combined.

Sift the dry ingredients over the egg mixture and mix on low speed for 15 to 20 seconds, until mostly combined. Using a flexible spatula, gently

continued

fold the batter, carefully but thoroughly turning over the sides and bottom of the batter, until just incorporated and no streaks or pockets of dry ingredients remain. (The batter will be somewhat flecked; this is fine.)

Transfer the batter to the prepared sheet pan and use an offset spatula to evenly spread it out. If necessary, use a bench scraper to smooth the top. Firmly tap the sheet pan on the counter a few times to get the air bubbles out.

Bake for 11 to 13 minutes, or until the cake is starting to brown lightly on top and springs back when lightly pressed.

While the cake bakes, spread out a clean kitchen towel with a long side facing you and lightly dust it with half of the powdered sugar.

Remove the cake from the oven and drop the sheet pan on the counter—this will stop the cake from shrinking. Run the tip of a table knife around the perimeter to ensure the cake isn't stuck anywhere. Lightly dust the remaining powdered sugar all over the cake, then invert the pan onto the prepared towel. (Use more powdered sugar if you need to, but skew on the side of restraint.) Carefully, lift the pan from the cake and gently peel away the parchment.

Starting on a short side, gently, and relatively tightly, roll up the cake (along with the kitchen towel)—you want to apply a gentle, steady hand and help shape the cake into a roll with the curve of your palms. Roll up the entire cake and then place it, seam side down, in the kitchen towel, on a wire rack and let cool completely, about 40 minutes.

MAKE THE MASCARPONE WHIP AND ASSEMBLE THE CAKE: Remove the bowl from the freezer or refrigerator, and in it, combine the cream, mascarpone, granulated sugar, vanilla (if using), and salt. With a hand mixer, beat on medium-low speed until blended and smooth, about 1 minute. Increase the speed to high and beat until stiff peaks form, 2 to 3 minutes.

Gently unroll the cake and use a serrated knife to trim the ends at an angle. Use an offset spatula to spread the whipped cream mixture in an even layer over the sponge, leaving about a ¼-inch (6 mm) border. Arrange the strawberries on top of the whipped cream and gently reroll the cake (without the towel this time). Using a large serrated knife, trim the ends of the roll, cleaning the knife with a damp towel between slices, wrap it in plastic wrap or beeswax wrap, and refrigerate for at least 2 hours and up to 2 days.

When ready to serve, use a serrated knife to cut the cake, wiping the knife between slices.

Giant Mille-Feuilles with Walnuts, Pistachios, and Cream

**MAKES 2 GIANT
MILLE-FEUILLES /
SERVES 4 TO 6**

One 14-ounce (397 g) sheet
frozen all-butter puff pastry,
such as Dufour, thawed in the
refrigerator

All-purpose flour, for dusting

For the nut filling

1 cup (100 g) walnuts,
toasted (see On Toasting
Nuts, page 278)

½ cup (75 g) unsalted roasted
pistachios

½ cup (168 g) honey

¼ cup (60 ml) walnut or
hazelnut oil

2 teaspoons orange blossom
water

½ teaspoon kosher salt

For the cream filling

1 cup (240 ml) heavy cream

½ cup (4 oz/120 g)
mascarpone

2 teaspoons granulated sugar

For assembly

Powdered sugar, for dusting

When Sanaë's friend, Rie McClenny, the cookbook author of *Make It Japanese*, suggested we try making mille-feuille on a sheet pan, we were a bit daunted at first, having never made one. But since it's Sanaë's father's favorite recipe, we had to give it a go, and it was surprisingly simple. The store-bought puff pastry first bakes sandwiched between two half-sheet pans—this prevents it from puffing up too much—then finishes uncovered until deeply golden and all the flakes are perfectly cooked through. The filling takes inspiration from baklava with its combination of toasted nuts and orange blossom water. Instead of making a traditional *crème pâtissière*, which would require some stovetop cooking, you'll combine heavy cream with mascarpone for a thick, spreadable whipped cream. This recipe makes two towering mille-feuilles, which we recommend sharing among at least four people, if not six. Serve them with forks and sharp knives, and don't worry if you make a bit of a mess, that's part of the pleasure.

Sanaë + Olga

Position a rack in the middle of the oven and preheat to 400°F (200°C). Line a half-sheet pan with parchment paper.

Place the puff pastry on a second piece of parchment on a clean work surface. Lightly dust with flour and roll out to flatten any folds and to even the thickness.

Using a pizza cutter or sharp knife, cut the puff pastry into 6 rectangles about 7 × 3 inches (18 × 8 cm). The size is approximate here—don't worry if your rectangles are slightly bigger or smaller than the suggested measurements, what matters is that you have 6 rectangles that are roughly the same size, as you will need 3 rectangles (layers) per mille-feuille. Transfer the rectangles to the prepared sheet pan, leaving a sliver of space between them. (They will shrink as they bake.) Place the second piece of parchment (from rolling the puff pastry) on top of the rectangles. Place a second half-sheet pan on top.

Bake for 15 to 20 minutes, rotating the pans front to back halfway through, or until pale golden. (Carefully lift the top sheet pan and parchment to check.)

continued

Remove the top sheet pan and top parchment paper and bake uncovered for 7 to 12 minutes more, or until deeply golden. It's important to go with your eyes here, so the puff is fully cooked through—don't pull it out of the oven until it is deeply golden on the top and bottom.

Remove from the oven and allow the puff pastry rectangles to cool completely on the sheet pan.

MAKE THE NUT FILLING: While the pastry is cooling, place the walnuts and pistachios on a large cutting board and coarsely chop. If you don't have a large cutting board, chop the nuts in batches, so they don't spill over onto the counter. (We like the uneven pieces from chopping by hand, but you can absolutely use a food processor if you prefer.)

In a medium bowl, stir together the nuts, honey, oil, orange blossom water, and salt. The nut filling can be kept in an airtight container at room temperature for up to 1 week.

MAKE THE CREAM FILLING: In a large bowl, combine the cream, mascarpone, and granulated sugar. With a hand mixer on medium-low speed, beat until combined, about 1 minute. Increase the speed to high and beat until stiff peaks form, 2 to 3 minutes. (Take care not to overbeat, or the cream will turn grainy.) Refrigerate in an airtight container for up to 4 hours.

ASSEMBLE THE MILLE-FEUILLES: Once the puff pastry rectangles are completely cool, place them on a cutting board and use a sharp knife to trim them so they are all about the same size. Cutting the edges of the puff will make the flaky layers more visible. Using a small fine-mesh sieve, dust 2 rectangles with powdered sugar and set aside. (These will go on top of each mille-feuille.)

For each mille-feuille, place a puff pastry rectangle (one without the powdered sugar) on a serving plate. Spread with a generous layer of the nut filling, then spread with a generous layer of the cream filling. Repeat with a second puff pastry rectangle and the nut and cream and set it on top of the first rectangle. Top with a reserved puff pastry rectangle dusted with powdered sugar.

Serve immediately with a fork and sharp knife for cutting into, but don't worry if the layers fall apart as you eat.

Chapter 8

Simple
Pantry Recipes

On Rice

Both of us are big rice eaters and can't imagine our kitchens without our beloved rice cookers (Zojirushi for life) and our generous pantry stashes of rice. (Olga buys her rice in twenty-pound bags because her family goes through it so quickly.) Most of the rice we consume is white rice: sushi, basmati, jasmine, Arborio, and so on. We don't enjoy brown rice, so we have no recommendations for it, but, if you prefer brown rice to white, use that. The advice below is for white rice only.

To make rice, we rely on our rice cookers about 90 percent of the time, but we also realize that they're an expensive piece of kitchen equipment many home cooks either can't afford, don't have kitchen real estate for, or both. Keeping that in mind, we provide our failproof stovetop rice recipes here.

Before you cook rice, you need to rinse it to remove excess starches—otherwise you will wind up with a gluey mess. Here's how to do it properly:

Place your preferred measurement of rice in a large bowl, cover with cold water, and use your hand to gently swish the rice until the water becomes milky. Carefully pour off the water (or save it to water plants) and repeat a few more times until the water is almost clear. The water should be clear enough that you can see the rice. Usually, it takes three to five washes, depending on the rice. Then proceed with the recipe.

Last, the quality of your water matters. Rice will absorb the water it is rinsed and cooked with, so we recommend not using tap water if you won't drink it on its own. Olga likes to use filtered water to cook rice, and Sanaë's mother taught her to both rinse and cook with filtered water.

Sanaë + Olga

Short-Grain White Rice

SERVES 4

1 cup (180 g) short-grain rice, such as sushi rice

> **HOT TIP!** I recently discovered microwavable short-grain rice and it's completely changed my life. The cooked rice is shelf-stable and comes in a single-serving size. It just needs to be microwaved for 1½ to 2 minutes, depending on the brand. (You can also simmer it in water for about 15 minutes, or per the package instructions.) This rice is available online or at most Asian grocery stores.

From beginning to end, it'll take you about an hour (including soaking time) to make a pot of perfect short-grain rice, but I promise it's worth the time and effort. If a recipe in this book calls for cooked rice for serving, I recommend starting with the rice, so it soaks and steams while you're cooking the rest. Once you've made short-grain rice a few times, you'll have the recipe memorized and you'll be able to make it in your sleep.

For an electric rice cooker, the rice to water ratio is 1:1 and you probably won't need to soak the rice, as soaking is often included in the machine's cooking time. When I make rice in a pot on the stovetop, I find that there's a bit of evaporation, so I add an extra 2 tablespoons of water. It's important to choose a pot that has a tightfitting lid for a good seal (avoid lids with steam holes). When I make 1 cup of rice, I like to use a pot that is about 5 inches deep and 6 inches wide. If your pot has a thick bottom and you keep the lid on, the rice should remain warm for at least 30 minutes.

Sanaë

Rinse the rice, swishing it in a medium bowl and repeating the process until the water is almost clear (see On Rice opposite for more detailed instructions). Drain the rice in a fine-mesh sieve, then transfer to a small pot and add 1 cup (240 ml) plus 2 tablespoons water. Set aside to soak for 30 minutes.

Cover the pot with a tight-fitting lid and bring to a boil over high heat. Reduce the heat to its lowest setting and cook, covered, for 17 minutes. (Do not open the pot.) Remove from the heat and keep covered for at least 10 minutes and up to 30 minutes. Using a rice paddle, wooden spatula, or large spoon, fluff the rice. Keep covered until ready to serve.

No-Rinse Basmati-Cumin Rice

SERVES 4

1 tablespoons extra-virgin olive oil or a neutral oil

1 teaspoon cumin seeds (see Hot Tip!)

1 cup (180 g) basmati rice

1 teaspoon kosher salt

1 cup (240 ml) boiling water

I learned this method from chef Einat Admony, who posted an Instagram video making no-rinse stovetop rice that she promised would be perfect, with each individual grain of rice separate from the other grains. Her promise delivered rice that was exquisite. It's a great option if you don't have a rice cooker. I make cumin rice often, but it's an absolute must with my Cuban-Style Roast Pork with Mojo (page 103).

Olga

In a 4-quart (4-liter) pot, heat the oil over medium-high heat until shimmering. Add the cumin and cook, stirring often, until aromatic and starting to dance in the oil, about 2 minutes. Add the rice and salt and cook, stirring often, until the rice is coated in the oil and the grains become translucent—the rice should be warm to the touch— 2 to 3 minutes. Carefully add the boiling water—stand back, as it may sputter—and briefly stir to combine. Cover with a tight-fitting lid, reduce the heat to its lowest setting, and cook the rice for exactly 18 minutes. (Do not open the lid.)

Remove from the heat and let stand for 10 minutes. Using a rice paddle or a wooden spoon, gently fluff up the rice. Re-cover and serve warm.

HOT TIP! You can use another spice, such as mustard seeds or coriander, or leave it out altogether. If you don't have basmati rice, another long-grain white rice will work as well.

Quickles

½ cup (120 ml) rice vinegar

1 tablespoon granulated sugar

½ teaspoon kosher salt

1 large carrot (5 oz/142 g),
peeled and cut into
matchsticks

5 ounces (142 g) daikon
radish, peeled and cut into
matchsticks, or 5 to
6 unpeeled red radishes, cut
into matchsticks

I first learned to make quickles—isn't that much more fun to say than "quick pickles"?—when I worked for Melissa Clark, and we tested a banh mi recipe. The magic of gently marinated vegetables, slightly softened but still with plenty of crunch, against the savory sandwich filling, was nothing short of revelatory. Also, near-instant gratification! I started making quickles weekly to spruce up a bowl of plain rice, leftovers, salads, grain bowls, and more. They take minutes to make and are so much more than the sum of their parts.

Olga

In a 3-cup (720 ml) mason jar or glass measuring cup, combine the vinegar, sugar, and salt. Let sit for 2 to 3 minutes, then stir to ensure that the sugar and salt have completely dissolved. Add ½ cup (120 ml) water and stir to combine.

Add the carrot and radishes and use a spoon to incorporate them into the marinade, pressing lightly on them. Set aside for about 20 minutes and serve with whatever meal you are making. (This is an ideal time to get started on your main meal; by the time it's ready, the quickles will be, too.) The quickles can be refrigerated in an airtight container for up to 1 week.

> **HOT TIPS!** Use the leftover marinade to make a quick vinaigrette by combining with the oil of your choice, adding Dijon mustard, and seasoning to taste with additional salt and pepper.
>
> I often make jalapeño-onion quickles for tacos (page 141)—using equal parts water and apple cider vinegar with a little sugar and salt (season to taste until it's pleasing to you), making enough to just cover thinly sliced red onion and jalapeño. Let stand while you prepare the tacos, then serve.

Simplest Arugula Salad

SERVES 2 TO 4

4 cups (80 g) baby arugula
(about half of a 5 oz/
142 g box)

Shaved Parmigiano-Reggiano,
for serving (optional)

Finely grated zest and juice of
½ lemon

Extra-virgin olive oil

Kosher or flaky sea salt

Coarsely ground black pepper

This is the salad we often have with many meals, as it goes with virtually everything and takes about 2 minutes to put together. There's no slicing of vegetables or whisking of the vinaigrette. This is as barebones as it comes, and yet it's always one of the brightest accompaniments to a meal and one that Olga's grade-school child, Avi, eats first. (He happens to love salad, especially made with arugula.) The slightly bitter, peppery arugula makes a good foil to many recipes in this book—and whatever dinner you may have planned. Throwing a pile of greens on a plate also ensures we're getting more green veggies in our diet. And, if we're feeling fancy, we might add thick shavings of Parmigiano-Reggiano and/or toasted pine nuts. If you don't like arugula, this works equally well with other baby greens, such as spinach, kale, or spring mix. In spring and summer months, we love to get greens from our favorite farmers' market stands, as their freshness and flavor can't be rivaled.

If you don't have a lemon, you can replace the lemon zest and juice with a drizzle of your favorite vinegar. Sanaë likes to use sherry vinegar or balsamic for a slightly sweeter dressing, but other vinegars, such as white wine, red wine, champagne, or apple cider, would be lovely, too.

Olga + Sanaë

In a medium bowl, gently toss together the arugula, Parmigiano-Reggiano (if you like), lemon zest, lemon juice, a drizzle of oil (you want just enough to delicately coat the leaves), a pinch of salt, and a few twists of black pepper until combined. Serve immediately.

Fennel and Citrus Salad

3 oranges, ideally one of each: blood, Cara Cara, and navel

1 large fennel bulb (12 oz/ 340 g), trimmed and sliced paper-thin (see Hot Tip!)

⅓ cup (50 g) Castelvetrano olives, pitted and roughly chopped

¼ cup (30 g) chopped toasted pistachios or toasted pine nuts (optional; see On Toasting Nuts, page 278)

A handful of fresh tender herbs, such as mint, basil, or flat-leaf parsley (optional)

Fresh lemon juice, to taste

1 tablespoon extra-virgin olive oil

Flaky sea salt, such as Maldon

Coarsely ground black pepper

HOT TIPS! To get the fennel paper-thin, we use a Benriner brand mandoline.

You could save some fennel fronds to add at the very end for garnish.

Sanaë likes to zest either a lemon or orange into the salad for an extra dose of citrus.

This is more of a framework than a recipe, as the salad is customizable based on what you have on hand and like. That said, there are a few nonnegotiable building blocks, which are shaved fennel, oranges, a briny element, an acidic component, good olive oil, and flaky sea salt. For the oranges, we encourage you to use a variety, if you can find them. Sanaë's favorite combination is Cara Cara and navel, though sometimes she'll also throw in a clementine, mandarin, or tangerine; and Olga loves to sneak in a blood orange, too. Our go-to briny ingredient here is Castelvetrano olives, but Niçoise, Kalamata, oil-cured Moroccan, Spanish olives, and the like will all work well. If you can, avoid already pitted olives, as the brine softens their insides and the olives are often mushy. (On rare occasions when we're out of olives, we throw in drained capers.) If we are awash in fresh herbs, such as parsley, basil, or mint, we add torn or chopped leaves. For texture and crunch, toasted pine nuts or chopped pistachios marry well with the ingredients. The dressing is also adaptable: If you prefer, in place of lemon juice, use whatever vinegar you have on hand—sherry, white, red, or even balsamic.

Olga + Sanaë

Using a sharp paring knife, trim the top and bottom off each orange. Working with one orange at a time, stand it on one flat end and cut downward, following the curve of the fruit, to remove the peel, pith, and membrane (to expose the fruit).

Holding the fruit over a medium bowl, cut each orange segment from its membrane, letting it drop into the bowl. Squeeze any juice from the remaining membrane into a small bowl or jar and drink it or use it to drizzle over the salad. (Alternatively, you can cut the peeled fruit across into slices ¼ inch [6 mm] thick; they might fall apart, and that's okay.)

Arrange the fennel on a large serving platter or bowl. Top with the oranges, alternating colors if your oranges are all different, and scatter the olives all over. If using, sprinkle with the pistachios, followed by the herbs. Drizzle the lemon juice on top, followed by the oil, and finish with a generous pinch of flaky salt and a few grinds of black pepper. Serve right away.

On Toasting Nuts

We are big fans of toasting nuts, as this simple step enhances their inherent flavors without any added ingredients. Taste a toasted and raw almond side by side and note the difference. The trick is to toast the nuts until they are just shy of burning, and this requires some practice and vigilance. If you take them out too soon, their aroma won't be fully developed, but if you take them over the edge, they can quickly go from deeply toasted and aromatic to burnt and bitter. We recommend setting a timer and checking for visual cues. And trust your nose: Start looking inside your oven as soon as you detect that glorious fragrance.

If you are toasting the nuts in advance, preheat the oven to 350°F (180°C). Spread the nuts on a sheet pan, either quarter- or half-sheet pan, depending on the quantity—make sure they have enough room to be in a single layer. Toast for 5 to 10 minutes, rotating the pan front to back halfway through, until a shade darker and deeply fragrant. Start checking at 5 minutes.

However, if your recipe calls for both toasted nuts and a preheated oven, you can do as Sanaë does and toast the nuts on the middle rack while the oven preheats.

We apply this method to all nuts in our arsenal, except one—pine nuts. Because of their high oil content, they can burn extremely fast, and because they're so expensive, we prefer to toast them in a small, preferably light-colored skillet over low heat. Stir frequently and do not take your eyes off the skillet. Once the nuts turn light golden, remove from the heat and immediately transfer to a bowl, so they can cool completely. (If you leave the pine nuts in the skillet they were toasting in, they can burn from the residual heat.)

For all other nuts, remember that toasting times vary with your oven and the type of nut, so pay close attention—and don't walk away.

Sanaë + Olga

Acknowledgments

Olga + Sanaë

This book, as many cookbooks are, is a labor of love. Writing a book takes a certain madness, as it requires sacrificing any and all free time in hopes that the final result can positively impact its readers.

Books also take a village to bring to life. And as such, we're tremendously grateful to the many individuals who touched and helped shape this project.

Alison Fargis, you've been a champion of this book from day one, and we're eternally grateful for your wisdom and counsel as we worked on the proposal and manuscript. You guided us with such warmth and kindness and made every obstacle feel surmountable.

Sarah Kwak, thank you for believing in this project, being our advocate and cheering us on, and your attentive eye and editorial prowess. Thank you, Jacqueline Quirk, for your smart edits and thoughtful queries. Kate Slate, truly the GOAT of copyeditors, we are so lucky to have crossed paths in our Phaidon days. Thank you for everything that you do, and how you leave no stone unturned. And thank you to everyone else at Harvest and HarperCollins, especially, Rachel Meyers, Renata DiBiase, Aryana Hendrawan, Liz Psaltis, Jessica Cozzi, and Theresa Deal.

Mumtaz Mustafa, thank you for a stunning cover and for being cheeky and irreverent, the most necessary qualities in making the outside of this book shine.

Johnny Miller, Rebecca Jurkevich, Cybelle Tondu, Jared Reckamp, and Sarah Smart: You are truly our dream team, and we are still pinching ourselves that you said yes to working on our book. Johnny, your incredible eye, creativity, and use of light are unmatched. Rebecca, Cybelle, and Jared, you made the food look so beautiful—that effortless flick of the wrist, the scoring of the galette des rois, those gorgeous chapter openers. Sarah, you have such a gift for choosing props that look beautiful *and* organic with the food they're paired with. Not only did you all make everything look breathtaking, but it was also a joy to spend time with you. Our lives are richer for knowing you. Thank you to Shio Studio for the loveliest sunlit space, and Luke Stoychoff for making delicious coffees and eating all the leftovers with such gusto.

Thank you to the many food writers and cookbook authors who inspire and nourish us with your recipes, especially Melissa Clark, Hugh Fearnley-Whittingstall, Dorie Greenspan, Eric Kim, Rie McClenny, Deb Perelman, Meera Sodha, Adeena Sussman, Ruby Tandoh, and Julia Turshen.

Lizzie Hart, thank you for giving us your superb design advice.

And lastly, thank you, our readers and home cooks, for taking a leap of faith and trusting us in your kitchen.

Olga

To Sanaë: I'm so grateful for all the events that led up to us meeting and becoming friends. I can't believe my dumb luck that not only did you like this cookbook idea, but also you agreed to come on this insane, intense, and delicious journey. You have such a keen eye for delicious, simple, and unexpected flavors, and I've learned so much from you. Thank you for being my partner in crime.

Literary agents are superheroes behind the scenes, and Alison Fargis, who's been my loudest cheerleader since day one and who took me on as a client without asking what my web traffic was, is one such person. I'm so lucky to know you, work with you, and also call you a friend.

I wouldn't be where I am today without Melissa Clark, who is as generous as she is brilliant, and who took me, a random blogger who desperately wanted a way out of finance, and let me work for her and learn, learn, learn. I often refer to Melissa as my stunningly gorgeous fairy godmother—she truly is.

To Deb Perelman, for not only troubleshooting a pesky recipe, but also for lending an empathetic ear when I sent texts I lovingly refer to as "postcards from the edge," and for her friendship, advice, and the introduction to the inimitable Alison Fargis.

To my husband, Andrew, one of my two favorite people, for giving me the courage to leave a career I didn't love and for seeing something in me I didn't see in myself. I wouldn't be here today were it not for you. To Avi, my other favorite person, who not only ate endless sheet pan meals but also provided invaluable feedback, even on dishes he didn't love.

To my parents: Thank you for not raising an eyebrow when I told you I was leaving finance to become a food writer, of all things. And to my in-laws: Thank you for doing the same, especially since I did this while engaged to your son. To my brothers- and sisters-in-law: Brett and Aviva and Russ and Abby—thank you for the encouragement, for eating recipes in progress without a complaint, and for being there when I needed to vent. I'm so lucky to call you family.

To my WaPo teammates and colleagues on other desks, for listening, eating, and sharing invaluable recipe test feedback, especially to Ann Maloney, for her thoughtful recipe testing notes and moral support! To Joe Yonan, for being the most supportive boss anyone could ask for. To Matt Brooks, Becky Krystal, Aaron Hutcherson, Tim Carman, Emily Heil, Daniela Galarza, Anna Rodriguez, and Tom Sietsema, thank you for being such incredible colleagues. You are all so incredibly talented, and I'm so lucky to learn from you every day.

My friends from near and far: Tina, Stacy, Josey, Jane—for being the most incredible cheerleaders a girl can dream of. Luisa Weiss and Anna Painter, for your expert recipe testing and smart advice (pinching myself to know you both). To Jocelyn Delk-Adams, truly what an honor to call you a friend, and thank you for all your incredible support and advice through this. Laura Mintz, one of the most stylish people I know, for all the wardrobe advice, and for your offbeat, delightful sense of humor. Jessie Sheehan, you're not only one of the smartest bakers, but also one of the kindest and most generous people I know. Adeena Sussman, you are a walking embodiment of the practice of tikkun olam.

To our insatiable Labrador, Latke, who took her payment in vegetable scraps, and Forrest, our senior grumpy cat who still can't figure out why we had to go and get a dog—thank you for the snuggles and unconditional love. And last but not least, thanks to Chad Lowe (IYKYK).

Sanaë

Olga Massov, thank you for inviting me along on this wild journey. I loved your food from the first bite, and my admiration for you as a writer, recipe developer, and friend has only grown in the time we spent writing this book together. Few moments feel like fate, but this one truly does—how lucky that our paths crossed at Phaidon in 2018.

I am indebted to the many individuals who held my hand as I wrote my first cookbook:

Marya Spence, for guiding me with such wisdom and care as I navigate a career writing novels and cookbooks.

Dawn Perry and Jennifer Aaronson, for teaching me so much about food and beyond. Susanne Ruppert, for your advice and encouragement at every stage.

My friends who ate countless sheet pan dishes and asked for seconds and leftovers—your praise means the world, and it's a joy to share a table with you: Forsyth Harmon, Kayla Maiuri, Crystal Hana Kim, Eliza Schrader, Lynn Steger Strong, Linda Pugliese, Nina Xue, Isle McElroy, Daniel Loedel, Beniamino Ambrosi, Emily Cunningham, Garth Greenwell, Raven Leilani, Alana Salguero, and Adam Dalva.

My recipe testers, who provided expert feedback: Theo Kaloudis, Mardi Miskit, Kirsten Saracini, Joanna Ehrenreich, Gabriela Plump, Heidi Jen, Gabriella Burnham, Mina Seçkin, Jean Kyoung Frazier, Elena Megalos, Yurina Yoshikawa, Peter Strong, Kerry Cullen, Amos Posner, and Kira Simon-Kennedy.

Ben Hyman, for coming up with the best cookbook title in the backyard of Washington Commons.

María Fernanda Villegas and William Moore, for being my dream neighbors as I developed recipes and for joyfully eating the same dish over and over again. Thank you for returning my Tupperware in an impeccable state.

Natalie Weinberger, for your gorgeous ceramics. Tanya Bush, for sharing your pastry secrets; your sweets are my favorites.

Matt Fennell, for your unparalleled can-do attitude and belief in my recipes, and for never saying no to a meal with me—thank you a thousand times.

My family, especially my mother and father, for nourishing me with home-cooked meals (i.e., love). Amanda, Sadao, Leo, Nina, Max, and Alejandro, for delicious Sunday brunches and being my home in America. Larisara—every dish you make is magical—how spoiled I am to eat your food. My cousin, Claire, whose extraordinary cooking has inspired my own for decades. Geoffroy, for running to the grocery store at 8 a.m., for washing dishes better than I do, and for your love.

Index

Note: Page references in *italics* indicate photographs.

"There weren't enough Post-it notes in my kitchen to mark the literally dozens of recipes I felt I had to make after reading Olga and Sanaë's smart book. I love their simple yet sophisticated approach to cooking, with sound techniques and beautiful flavor combinations at its heart. With the sheet pan as their anchor, Olga and Sanaë have created a cookbook of stunning range and utility that you'll turn to again and again."

—ADEENA SUSSMAN, *New York Times* **bestselling author of** *Shabbat* **and** *Sababa*